Weber and the Persistence of Religion

At perhaps no other time in history have religion and spirituality played such important social and political roles in our world; and, yet, most people still feel that contemporary society is predominantly secular and that our world is largely disenchanted. Taking Max Weber's interpretations of capitalism and religion as its point of departure, *Weber and the Persistence of Religion* re-examines a wide range of classical and contemporary texts, from Immanuel Kant to Jean Baudrillard, to help explain the peculiar character of religion and spirituality in mature capitalist societies.

Since the mid-19th century, most social scientists have noted an irreversible trend in mature capitalist societies towards ever greater secularization and disenchantment. They have been much slower to pick up on the dramatic transformation in spirituality and religion since the emergence of capitalism in the late 14th century. This book shows how the peculiar disembodied character of contemporary spirituality and religion, along with the disenchanted character of public life, may be formally related to the increasingly disembodied, immaterial character of value in capitalist societies. Joseph W.H. Lough explores how the increasingly antagonistic relationship between contemporary religion and its material forms of appearance displays an unmistakable likeness to what Immanuel Kant described as the *sublime* and Karl Marx described as the sublime value form of the commodity.

More disturbingly, *Weber and the Persistence of Religion* also shows how the growing antagonism between contemporary spiritual subjectivity and practice and its material forms of appearance may explain the unremitting escalation in officially sanctioned mass death since the 14th century. If mass death is a defining feature of contemporary religion, it is vital that we understand why and how it has become so.

This book will be of interest to students and scholars of Social Theory, History, the Sociology of Religion and Philosophy.

Joseph W.H. Lough is a Visiting Scholar in the Department of History at the University of California, Berkeley. He teaches in the social sciences on the San Francisco and Oakland campuses of California College of the Arts, as well as at the DeAnza College, Cupertino, California.

Routledge Advances in Sociology

This series aims to present cutting-edge developments and debates within the field of sociology. It will provide a broad range of case studies and the latest theoretical perspectives, while covering a variety of topics, theories and issues from around the world. It is not confined to any particular school of thought.

Weber and the Persistence of Religion

of Religion

Social Theory, Capitalism and the Sublime

Joseph W.H. Lough

Routledge
Taylor & Francis Group

LONDON AND NEW YORK

First published 2006
by Routledge
2 Park Square, Milton Park,
Abingdon, Oxon, OX14 4RN

Simultaneously published in the USA and Canada
by Routledge
605 Third Avenue, New York, NY 10017

Routledge is an imprint of the Taylor & Francis Group, an informa business

Typeset in Garamond by Keyword Group Ltd.

British Library Cataloguing in Publication Data
A catalogue record for this book is available from the British Library

Library of Congress Cataloging in Publication Data
A catalog record for this book has been requested

ISBN13: 978-0-415-34352-7 (hbk)
ISBN13: 978-0-415-54376-7 (pbk)

For Averil and Yates

Contents

Preface

'It is the fate of our times, with their characteristic rationalization and intellectualization, but above all "disenchantment of the world", that precisely the ultimate and most sublime values have retreated from public life either into the transcendental realm of mystical life or into the brotherliness of direct and personal human relations'.[1] Like most students, I too first came across these words in the Oxford edition of Max Weber's essays in sociology edited by Hans H. Gerth and C. Wright Mills. I read Weber's lamentation with wonder and rapt attention:

> It is not accidental that our greatest art is not monumental, nor is it accidental that today only within the smallest and intimate circles, in personal human situations, in *pianissimo*, that something is pulsating that corresponds to the prophetic *pneuma*, which in former times swept through the great communities like a firebrand, welding them together. If we attempt to force and to "invent" a monumental style in art, such miserable monstrosities are produced as the many monuments of the last twenty years. If one tries intellectually to construe new religions without a new and genuine prophecy, then, in an inner sense, something similar will result, but with still worse effects.[2]

And then came the words that I was certain were directed specifically at me: 'And academic prophecy, finally, will create only fanatical sects but never a genuine community.'[3] Yet, as a recent seminary graduate entering doctoral studies at the University of Chicago, something about Weber's words struck me as odd.

I did not know then that the speech in which they appeared, 'Science as a Vocation', was delivered not in 1918, as the footnote in my 'Gerth and Mills' indicated, but on 7 November 1917. I therefore did not know that they were delivered the day after one of the most costly battles in modern times, the battle for the city of Passchendaele in Flanders. Nevertheless, it struck me as odd that Weber should think that it was the fate of his times much less *our times* that ultimate and sublime values had retreated from the public sphere. From where I sat, the world about me seemed spectacularly religious and spiritual.

Of course, the notion that ultimate and sublime values have retreated from the public sphere is taken for granted by nearly everyone within the social sciences. This is obviously true for Weberians and neo-Weberians who, like me, trace their intellectual pedigree through Jürgen Habermas and Herbert Marcuse back to Georg Lukács, Theodor Adorno, Max Horkheimer, and Weimar Germany's Frankfurt School for Social Research. However updated and revised, we all recognize the family resemblance between Weber's 'iron cage' and Adorno and Horkheimer's 'totally administered world', between the retreat of Weber's ultimate and sublime values and Habermas's decoupling of system and life worlds, or between Weber's 'last men' and Marcuse's 'one-dimensional man'. Yet, we even find traces of this distinctively Weberian trope well outside the circle of Weber's immediate intellectual family, in, for example, Jean-François Lyotard's neo-Kantian differentiation of a 'pragmatics of scientific knowledge' from a 'pragmatics of narrative knowledge', or Jacques Derrida's distinctions between 'structure, sign and play' in social scientific discourse.[4] Yet, at least in the fall of 1990, from the perspective of Chicago's (not London's) Hyde Park, the public sphere seemed anything but disenchanted, social actors seemed anything but one-dimensional, the world seemed anything but totally administered, the pragmatics of narrative knowledge seemed wholly intertwined with its ostensibly scientific counterpart, and the life-world seemed to have won, hands down, over its evil systemic rival.

Would the world have looked different, I wondered, had I been situated in London's Hyde Park? After all, according to a World Values Survey conducted between 1981 and 1993,[5] only eighty per cent of those surveyed in Great Britain said they believed in God, as compared to almost ninety-seven per cent in the United States. But even Great Britain's taste for ultimate and sublime values seemed stout when compared to West Germany's seventy-six per cent or France's sixty-three. Perhaps then ultimate and sublime values had begun their retreat from public life in continental Europe, had only just begun their retreat from the British Isles and had not yet begun their retreat on the other side of the Atlantic. Still, even France's sixty-three per cent struck me as unusually high for a nation whose citizens prided themselves on their worldliness. The deeper I delved into the retreat of ultimate and sublime values, the more doubtful I grew over whether they had retreated nearly so completely or finally from public life as Weber and many, if not most, contemporary social scientists thought they had. To the contrary, it struck me that I was still living in a world that most people took to be quite enchanted.

But then it occurred to me that it was not 'the world' *per se* that people took to be enchanted. It was they themselves, not the world about them, and certainly not their bodies, but their innermost spiritual beings that people took to be enchanted. It was then from this vantage point, the vantage point of Great Britain's eighty per cent, France's sixty-three per cent, and the United States' ninety-six per cent that the external world, the material world, appeared disenchanted. This made anecdotal sense as well. Even in the United States, for example, where by 1990 religion had now assumed a central role in public life, religious practitioners still complained loudly over the 'culture of disbelief',[6] which they believed dominated their nation's courts and legislative bodies. Perhaps then the retreat of ultimate and sublime values had less to do with the personal beliefs of religious practitioners, or the religious convictions of elected officials, or even the religiously sympathetic character of public laws and institutions than it did with the strong suspicion seemingly entertained by nearly everyone that the visible world is governed by laws and principles that are fundamentally hostile to ultimate and sublime values.

This, however, was not a particularly social scientific insight. To the contrary, it was a philosophical insight and I recognized its author immediately: the eighteenth century Königsburg philosopher Immanuel Kant (1724–1804). More than any other philosopher, Kant had been responsible for drawing an analytical distinction between what he had called the 'phenomenal' world (the world available to our senses) and the 'noumenal' world (the world of ultimate meaning). But, what was the philosopher Immanuel Kant doing at the centre of a matter that should have been strictly social scientific? More importantly, why had one of the most influential twentieth century social scientists, Max Weber, relied upon Kant to confirm his suspicion that ultimate and sublime values had retreated from public life? And why had so many of Weber's successors concurred?

These of course are not the kinds of questions normally asked by graduate students in history. Perhaps I might find clues to their solution by rifling through the *Archiv für Sozialwissenschaft und Sozialpolitik*, the journal that Max Weber edited from 1904 until his death in 1920. I hastily compiled an annotated index of all the *Archiv*'s sixty-nine volumes, a feat I discovered that Regis A. Factor had accomplished before me.[7] My graduate advisers took a look at my project and concluded that it was too ambitious. What about producing an intellectual biography of Weber's Heidelberg, I asked. This would allow me to bring in such figures as Karl Jaspers, Otto Gross, Else and Frieda von Richthofen, the accomplished daughters of the famous Red Baron, Frieda's lover D.H. Lawrence, and the seemingly endless stream of personalities who made their way through Max and Marianne Weber's home. Already done.[8] John Boyer asked why I did not limit myself to one figure, Max Weber, for example. Good idea, I thought. But then came the challenge of finding a new angle on one of the most richly documented intellectual lives in history.

Reluctantly, I set to work pouring through Weber's works in translation, followed by his works in German. Then came stacks upon stacks of books and articles about Weber, the Weber circle in Heidelberg, and Weber's sociological method. Most useful, I found, were works that explicitly addressed Weber's neo-Kantian methodology, books such as Guy Oakes' *Weber and Rickert* and the introductory essay to Oakes' translation of Weber's *Roscher and Knies: The Logical Problems of Historical Economics*.[9] Also helpful were Wolfgang Schluchter's *Rationalism, Religion, and Domination* and Dirk Käsler's *Max Weber: an introduction to his Life and Work*, each of which corrected many conceptual and factual errors still circulating among American Weber scholars.[10] Analytically these works were both thoughtful and thought-provoking. Yet, none of these works or their authors addressed what for me were the most pressing questions. What was it about Kant's world or Weber's world or, for that matter, our own world that made it seem particularly well-suited to Kant's interpretive categories? Why, on a purely theoretical level, did I find it so meaningful to think that ultimate and sublime values had retreated from public life, even though empirically they had done nothing of the sort? Why had social actors, if anything, grown even more spiritual and religious since the sixteenth century, while the sensible world around them had grown ever less so? Again, these were questions that graduate students in history seldom raised. And they were certainly not questions graduate advisers in history encouraged their students to pursue in their dissertations.

Nevertheless, I had the good fortune of having dissertation advisers who encouraged precisely these kinds of questions: David Tracy, the well-known theologian from the Chicago Divinity School; Michael Geyer, whose unique combination of military and intellectual history was particularly well-suited to the questions I was raising; and Moishe Postone, whose migration from the Department of Sociology to the Department of History during the course of my dissertation reinforced my own self-imposed liminality in Chicago's Division of the Social Sciences. It was Postone more than anyone else, in fact, who helped me think through the problems arising from an immanent historical critique of Weberian social theory, such as I was proposing.

But Postone, who had himself been a student of Jürgen Habermas, was also of more substantive assistance. Both through his own work and by introducing me to a range of theoretical and historical works whose authors focused on the practical transformation initiated when productive human action was first measured in abstract,[11] equal units of time, Postone gave me my first substantive clue to why Kant's categories appeared to be so well suited to the modern world. Following the fourteenth century revolution in time, value had increasingly assumed an abstract, immaterial form until by the sixteenth century, in many minds it was no longer believed to be substantively related to the objects to which it was ascribed. Abstract value, including religious value, had pulled free from its form of appearance. I recognized almost immediately that this was precisely how Immanuel Kant had described the 'sublime', the very term Weber would use over a century later in his 'Science as a Vocation'. The discovery would eventually become a dissertation, and the dissertation a book.

Beyond my immediate dissertation committee there is an inevitably long list of other people who deserve my sincere thanks. Somewhere towards the top of this list are the members of the Social Theory Workshop at Chicago, which, with considerable assistance from William Sewell and Moishe Postone, I helped found in fall 1991. Among the participants in the Workshop who waded through early drafts of this book special thanks are due to Devin Pendas, now at Boston College, Neil Brenner, now at New York University, and John McCormick, now at the University of Chicago. Special thanks are also due to members of the History Department at the University of California, Berkeley, where since 2003 I have been honoured to serve as a visiting scholar. Martin Jay, in particular, deserves my thanks. Were it not for his support, I could not have gained access to the considerable research resources commanded by the Department and University. So, too, I would like to thank Martin van Buren, Humanities and Science Director at California College of the Arts, whose collegial support and encouragement have been of inestimable value. Thanks are also due to the Board of the California College of the Arts for a travel grant that allowed me to participate in and share my research at the 'Religion and Evil' Conference held in Amsterdam, spring 2005. I also therefore wish to thank Professor Henk Vroom, Free University of Amsterdam, for giving me an opportunity to present an earlier version of Chapter Five, 'The community unto death', at the Conference on Religion and Evil, jointly sponsored by the Vrije Universiteit and the Royal Tropical Institute (KIT) Tropenmuseum, Amsterdam, 17–19 March 2005.

Thanks are also due to my editors at Routledge, Ltd., particularly Terry Clague and Joe Whiting for their patience, assistance, and good humour. Thanks go out to the entire staff at Routledge for making this work possible. Finally, I would like to thank all of my friends and family here in Berkeley, California, and in Madison, Wisconsin, Boston and Paris for giving me the time, space, guidance and resources necessary to complete this book: Mary and Chick, Ed and Emma, Julia, Paul, Carol, Rosie, Ariane, André and Beatrice, Sandra, Gill, David, Keith, Marian, Jane, Mary Kate, Dan, Harold, Matt, Coco, Liz, Tom, Elaine and Alla. Of course, none of this would have been possible without the support and encouragement of Kirsten Snow Spalding and my two sons Averil and Yates, to whom I dedicate this book.

To all of these good friends and colleagues, I offer my deepest gratitude. For the errors in fact and theory, for the oversights and misdirections, inevitable in a study that seeks to break new ground, I take full credit.

Joseph W.H. Lough
Berkeley, California
September 2005

1 Introduction: contemporary religion

By nearly all accounts a book such as this one should not have been possible. By the end of the last century nearly all leading social scientists – from Ferdinand Tönnies to Oswald Spangler, Émil Durkheim to Georg Simmel, on up to Max Weber – were lamenting the complete secularization of the public sphere and thus the emergence of what Theodor Adorno and Max Horkheimer mockingly referred to as the 'fully enlightened earth'.[1] Few if any anticipated that religion and spirituality would come to play so central a role in public life as they have over the past century. Yet, notwithstanding this central role, religion and spirituality and their relationship to public life are still widely contested. Many fear that the liberal democratic and pluralist political arrangements that predominated in the west from the end of World War II at least through the 1970s are giving way to new post-democratic and post-liberal regimes of political, social, economic and cultural regulation.[2] However, even more people seem to feel that the religious 'recolonization' of the secular state has not been nearly as thorough as it needs to be. Our political and legal institutions are still governed by a 'culture of disbelief'.[3] As borne out by recent electoral results on both sides of the Atlantic, both sides of the Channel, and indeed throughout the developed world, mature capitalist society has become increasingly polarized between these two camps.[4] And, yet, if we listen carefully each camp appears to be sounding the same warning signals: we live in a spectacularly religious society whose members nevertheless feel that they are adrift on a sea of unbelief. In some countries this feeling has already reached toxic levels. In others it is still no more than a persistent, if occasionally lethal, annoyance. And yet, when we search the catalogues of our better known research libraries to get a better grasp on how contemporary religion and spirituality may be related to the dominant social formation in which this polarization has appeared, it is easy to get the impression that social scientists have given up on any meaningful attempt to wrap their heads around this complex problem and have punted the problem off to writers whose interests may not be and often have not been those of science.

This work attempts to redress this deficit. Structured around Max Weber's still influential interpretations of religion and capitalism, it seeks to explain how and why Weber's theories respecting secularization and disenchantment have not been borne out by history. As its theoretical point of departure, it examines Weber's interpretations through a lens supplied by critical Marxian and post-Marxian social theory. At the very least, this means that it seeks, in Habermas' words, to 'validate its own critical standards'[5] not transcendentally, but historically and therefore contingently. It aims both to provide a theoretically satisfying and practically meaningful framework within which to understand the complex relationship between religion and capitalism that has emerged over the past five centuries, and to offer some ways that this polarization might be ameliorated. We may be able to get a better grasp of the scope of this problem by looking briefly at the Marxian or post-Marxian lens through which we will be viewing the Weberian and neo-Weberian legacy.

Marx and religion

Of course in its traditional form the Marxian interpretation of religion has tended to be overly economistic on the one hand and overly simplistic on the other. Whatever else college students (and professors) take away from their study of Marx and religion, few forget Marx's famous lines about how 'religion is the opiate of the masses'.[6] But, then what about those among us who are not (or at least not transparently) part of 'the masses'; those of us who experience little physical or economic suffering, and by whom religious practices or spiritual disciplines are valued less for their mortifying than for their enlightening effects? Obviously, in that case we must be among those who consciously (or more often unconsciously) merely 'use' our religion to reinforce our dominant class position over those who do use religion as an opiate. This is certainly a possibility. And, yet, this still suggests that religion and spirituality are things that are independent and isolated from the social formations in which they appear. In other words, at least in this instance, Marx clearly failed to account for the conditions of his own critique. Such a superficial, simplistic and unnuanced grasp of religion clearly will not do, not only because it fails to do justice to how we actually experience, practice and understand religion, but not least because it fails to do justice to Marx's own mature critique of capitalism. Here it appears Marx and his 'orthodox' followers (and not his detractors), may have been guilty of a bit of 'false consciousness'.

   Here also Marx could become his worst enemy. Consider, for example, the build-up to Marx's often-cited reflection on the fetishism of commodities. The value form, he wrote, had lost all its 'sensuous characteristics [*sinnlichen Beschaffenheiten*]'. Marx then observed how the value form lends all the products of abstract, homogeneous labour time 'the same phantom-like objectivity [*gespenstige Gegenständlichkeit*]'. Then when he examined the value of linen out of which a coat had been made, Marx found that even 'the coat represents a supra-natural property [*übernatürliche Eigenschaft*]'. The equivalent form of value, he wrote, possesses a 'mysteriousness' (*Rätselhafte*) and a 'mystical' (*mystischen*) character.[7] All of which laid the groundwork for Marx's discussion of 'The Fetishism of the Commodity and its Secret', wherein he explicitly confirmed that his analysis of the commodity

> brings out that it is a very strange thing, abounding in metaphysical subtleties and theological niceties. So far as it is a use-value, there is nothing mysterious about it. . . . But as soon as it emerges as a commodity, it changes into a thing which transcends sensuousness. . . . The mysterious character of the commodity-form

consists therefore simply in the fact that the commodity reflects the social characteristics of men's own labour as objective characteristics of the products of labour themselves, as the socio-natural properties of these things. Hence it also reflects the social relation of the producers to the sum total of labour as a social relation between objects, a relation which exists apart from and outside the producers. Through this substitution, the products of labour become commodities, sensuous things which are at the same time *supra-sensible* [*übersinnliche*] or social. ... [T]he commodity-form, and the value-relation of the products of labour within which it appears, have absolutely no connection with the physical nature of the commodity and the material relations arising out of this. It is nothing but the definite social relation between men themselves which assumes here, for them, the fantastic [*phantasmagorische*] form of a relation between things.

Marx, therefore, believed that 'in order . . . to find an analogy we must take flight into the misty realm of religion.' How true. Yet, it is here in particular that Marx displayed his poor grasp of religion, for he draws the entirely wrong analogy. 'There [in religion]', he surmised, 'the products of the human brain appear as autonomous figures endowed with a life of their own, which enter into relations both with each other and with the human race'.[8] But, as we will see in greater detail below, what is most peculiar about contemporary religious subjectivity and practice is not its Feuerbach-like *projection* of the sensible world onto the surface of our mental life, but, to the contrary, the complete isolation of religious and spiritual values from their material forms of appearance. Marx's theoretical analysis was impeccable. His grasp of contemporary religious subjectivity and practice was atrocious.

Nevertheless, Marx is indispensable to understanding contemporary religion. Here, Marx's descriptions of the value form of the commodity offer a particularly illuminating window into the sublime character of contemporary religious subjectivity and practice. Consider, for example, Marx's mature analysis of the commodity form in the opening volume of *Capital*. Here Marx aimed to show how the immaterial value form of the commodity could be both a product of productive human activity – of abstract labour – and also the subject or agent of this activity. It was the product of labour in so far as the value of the commodity was the social average of the amount of labour time it had taken to produce it. Since this labour time was the formally free contribution of the labourer, offered in exchange for wages, labour could be said to be the producer of abstract value. In Adam Smith's words, 'labour . . . is the real measure of the exchangeable value of all commodities'.[9] Yet, in so far as investors employed labour to produce commodities only because of the return on their investment it promised, value could also be said to be the subject or agent of this productive process. The promise of abstract value attracts labour. In this sense, Marx argued, when investors contracted with labour, abstract value became the subject of a process – the production process – through which its own value would be enhanced. This expansion of value had, in fact, been both the motivating force and the object of this process all along.

Marx had identified a social form, the value form of the commodity, which reproduced itself by retreating behind and then annihilating its material form of appearance. As we will see below, this will be precisely how Burke and Kant will describe the *sublime*. It is of course ironic that the most 'materialistic' social formation in history should at the same time display the greatest hostility towards its own material form of appearance. Yet, it was precisely the ironic character of capitalism that marked the decisive difference between it and all other social formations. For whereas in other social formations, the creation of material wealth had been the primary object of productive human activity, under capitalism abstract value had taken the place of material wealth, not only as the aim or object of this activity, i.e. the commodity, but also as the subject of this activity. In this process, the abstract social value of the commodity came to be isolated from the materials out of which it was composed. Moreover, the agents of social action too increasingly came to qualitatively differentiate their own abstract immaterial value from their material form of appearance, i.e. from their bodies. This isolation of value from its material form of appearance forms the essence of religion in mature capitalist societies. In such societies, religion owes its persistence to the intimate relationship it bears to the value form of the commodity.

One reason orthodox Marxism has overlooked this connection between religious or spiritual subjectivity and the value form is that it has adopted a largely functionalist interpretation of religion and spirituality, viewing them as tools that serve the economic and political interests of the dominant class. Religious practitioners experience their own religious practices and spiritual disciplines as expressions of their deepest sense of self; what sociologist Robert Bellah has called 'habits of the heart'.[10] It is here, in fact, that Marx's own functionalist treatment of religion should strike us as particularly unsuited to his overall critique. Consider, for example, the quasi-religious qualities that Marx attributed to the value form of the commodity. Should it not strike us as odd that he and his interpreters overlooked the central role this form had come to play in the formation of religious subjectivity and practice under capitalism? Contemporary religion and spirituality are not tools that serve the economic and political interests of one class over another. To the contrary, contemporary religious subjectivity and practice bear too intimate a relationship to the social formation as a whole for us to delegate them to one class or another. Indeed, although we will have to take care to elaborate precisely what we mean, it would not be too strong to say that it is capitalism and not religion that is the surface phenomenon. Religion to the contrary is the spiritual force that bears contemporary social reality, including contemporary social subjectivity, forward under capitalism. Far from being epiphenomenal, contemporary religion and spirituality stand at the heart of capitalist modernity.

Notwithstanding such criticisms, the present study is nevertheless unapologetically Marxist or Marxian or perhaps post-Marxian in form; I am not sure I know the difference. Building upon the work and thinking of Jacques le Goff, E.P. Thompson, Pierre Bourdieu, David Harvey, and particularly Moishe Postone's reinterpretation of Marx's mature social theory, I attempt to show how contemporary religious subjectivity and practice form central constitutive elements of the capitalist social formation. Neglect of these features I believe has led to partial, one-sided and distorted portrayals of both capitalism and religion, and certainly has led to fundamental misunderstandings over how the two are related. Precisely how they are related is the subject of this study.

Our inclination may be to think about this relationship through a lens that selects for domination. And obviously, to the extent that social actors are the agents in a process by which they themselves are dominated, capitalism is a process of self-domination. But, to the extent that social actors and the material wealth they produce are no more than a means through which abstract value enhances its own value, capitalism becomes an incredibly productive abstract system whose aim is the unending creation of ever greater immaterial value. To be sure, in the process of creating ever greater immaterial value, the value form also produces unprecedented quantities of material wealth. But, when we take the aim and object of this process as our point of departure the fact that this process also produces a material by-product, the commodity's material form of appearance, is a largely accidental consequence of the expansion of value.

Marx summarized this process (in characteristically Hegelian style) as follows:

> In the circulation M[oney]-C[ommodity]-M[oney] both the money and the commodity function only as different modes of existence of value itself, the money as its general mode of existence the commodity as its particular or, so to speak, disguised mode. It is constantly changing from one form into the other, without becoming lost in this movement; it thus becomes transformed into an automatic subject. . . . [V]alue is here the subject of a process in which, while constantly assuming the form in turn of money and commodities, it changes its own magnitude, throws off surplus-value from itself considered as original value, and thus valorizes itself independently. For the movement in the course of which it adds surplus-value is its own movement, its valorization is therefore self-valorization. . . . [V]alue suddenly presents itself as a self-moving substance which passes through a process of its own, and for which commodities and money are both mere forms.[11]

As though to again prove his complete miscomprehension of how contemporary religion and capitalism might have been related to one another, Marx then proceeds to compare this process of self-valorization with the Christian doctrine of the Trinity, suggesting that value 'differentiates itself as original value from surplus-value, just as God the Father differentiates himself from himself as God the Son, although both are of the same age and form, in fact one single person'.[12]

There are of course several problems with Marx's reading of religion in general and Christian theology in particular at this point. First, and most obvious, since the doctrine of the Trinity preceded the emergence of capitalism by roughly a thousand years, commodity production and exchange could not have had any influence over the formation of that doctrine. Second, although some social theorists (Max Weber, for example) have argued that Christian theology played a significant role in the birth of capitalism, Marx was not among them. Therefore, the analogy he drew between the Trinity and the commodity form can only have been purely illustrative. Third, and most seriously, however, Marx's clever theological aside actually diverts our attention away from the deeper insight his summary displays. This insight can be appreciated most easily by comparing Marx's summary to the original upon which it was based, Georg F.W. Hegel's description of how the World Spirit or *Weltgeist* realizes itself in the world:

> Further, the living Substance is being which is in truth *Subject*, or, what is the same, is in truth actual only in so far as it is the movement of positing itself, or is the mediation of its self-othering with itself. This Substance is, as Subject, pure, *simple negativity*, and is for this very reason the bifurcation of the simple; it is the doubling which sets up opposition, and then again the negation of this indifferent diversity and of its anti-thesis. . . . It is the process of its own becoming, the circle that presupposes its end as its goal, having its end also as its beginning; and only by being worked out to its end, is it actual.[13]

What Marx was clearly suggesting therefore was not that the movement of the value form was in some mysterious way based on fourth century Nicene Christian orthodoxy, but rather that Hegel's description of the World Spirit's self-realization was in fact a misrecognized account of how the value form of the commodity expanded its own value. In other words, Marx believed that the value form exhibited the same quasi-metaphysical qualities that Hegel had ascribed to the World Spirit. Contemporary religious subjectivity and practice are expressions of the 'Weltgeist' as it unfolds or realizes itself in history; or, in Marx's terms, they are expressions of the movement of the sublime value form of the commodity.

Characterizing religion

This is not to suggest that contemporary 'religion' and 'spirituality' are easy things to get a handle on. Contemporary religion is a peculiar thing. On the one hand almost seventy per cent of people in developed nations – and almost eighty per cent of people living in developing nations – say they are religious.[14] On the other hand, no one seems able to offer a definition of religion that would satisfy all of those who include themselves among them. Even the *Oxford English Dictionary*, usually a reliable source in such matters, gives us several definitions that in all probability would exclude most of those who consider themselves religious. After all, it is fair to assume that the number of us who are 'bound by monastic vows' or who are committed to 'a particular monastic religious order or rule' is statistically insignificant. However, even a more common definition – 'a particular system of faith and worship' (*OED* 1989 2nd edn, definition 4a) – overlooks the increasing number of people, perhaps even the majority of people in developed nations, for whom 'religion' and 'system' are viewed as opposite, not complimentary, terms. For this growing number of people, definition 5a may at first appear more suitable:

> Recognition . . . of some higher unseen power as having control of [our] destiny, and as being entitled to obedience, reverence, and worship; the general mental and moral attitude resulting from this belief, with reference to its effect upon the individual or the community; personal or general acceptance of this feeling as a standard of spiritual and practical life.

Except that here we run into problems with the many adherents to non-theistic religions for whom the very notion of a 'higher unseen power' to whom they might owe obedience or reverence makes little sense. Perhaps it would be best not to define religion at all, but instead to heed Jean-François Lyotard's sage advice: 'All we can do is gaze in wonderment at the diversity of discursive species, just as we do at the diversity of plant or animal species'.[15]

In any case, readers can rest assured that I will offer no definition of religion on the following pages. Nor, however, do I advise that we gaze in wonderment at the diversity of discursive – or rather religious – species. In place of a definition, I propose instead to offer a characterization of contemporary religion; one that I believe will cover most of the cases of religious subjectivity and practice within the developed world and may even cover many cases within the developing world. I propose to characterize contemporary religious subjectivity and practice – which for our purposes includes spiritual subjectivity and practice – as an instance of what Immanuel Kant called *the sublime* (*das Erhabene*).

Religion and the Kantian sublime

In a provisional way, which we will have to supplement and revise as we proceed, we can take one of Kant's many descriptions of the sublime for our point of departure. According to Kant, '*sublime is what even to be able to think proves that the mind has a power surpassing any standard of sense*'.[16] One advantage to Kant's characterization is not only that it captures much of what we mean when we say that we are religious. It also captures what Marx rather clumsily pointed to when he identified the radical isolation of the value form of the commodity from its material form of appearance. Of course, since Marx was referring to a social and historical process and not a transcendental condition of aesthetic judgment he did not believe that this isolation was a condition valid for all times, places and people. Here we side with Marx. The sublime value form of the commodity appeared on the historical scene rather late, in the fourteenth century, and even then only in regions of Western Europe, which then possessed mechanical clocks accurate and loud enough to mark the beginning and end of the work day. Prior to that point, the sublime value form of the commodity did not yet exist, even *in potentia*. Nor did the kinds of religion and spirituality that were to be so fundamentally altered by its appearance.

For reasons that will soon become apparent, this characterization of religion is specifically designed to capture what is most unique about contemporary religious subjectivity and practice while excluding those forms of religion and spirituality whose practices and objects of veneration are more nearly and intimately bound to the world of our senses. This characterization thus excludes not only the endless varieties of animism and ancestor or 'nature' worship that have been practiced everywhere among all known communities for most of human history.[17] It also excludes most so-called 'western' religious formations – principally Christianity, Judaism and Islam – whose practitioners continued to seek and find comfort and guidance in their material surroundings well into the modern epoch. And, yet, curiously it includes many individuals in developed nations missed even by the rather broad net cast by the term 'religious' itself; individuals whose form of spirituality or religion Thomas Luckmann attempted to capture by the term 'invisible religion'.[18]

Lengthy cultural training and habit have taught us to identify 'religion' with historical religious formations that display, among other things, more or less formal or informal hierarchies of teachers and students, more or less well-formed bodies of beliefs, and a more or less well-defined set of rituals or practices such as circumcision, baptism, prayer, meditation, or fasting that distinguish practitioners from non-practitioners. Moreover, we have come to distinguish these 'outward' religious signs from 'inward' spiritual states or processes whose forms, validity or even whose existence is more or less independent from these 'outward' signs. And, yet, it does not take specialized training for us to recognize that what social actors experience and understand as 'religious' or 'spiritual' has changed dramatically over time. Religious practitioners today who view the practices and beliefs of their co-religionists a century, two centuries or a half-millennia ago are likely to feel that they have more in common *spiritually* with their contemporaries, irrespective of their religious convictions, than they do with co-religionists of the distant past. What we are seeking to come to terms with is what Weber's Heidelberg colleague Karl Jaspers called the 'spiritual situation of the age',[19] except that we are defining 'age' somewhat more broadly than Jaspers, as the period beginning in the fourteenth century when social actors first practically isolated value, including spiritual value, from its material form of appearance.

Taking this long view, the 'spiritual situation' of the age is not only what most clearly distinguishes contemporary social actors from social actors in other social formations or at other times, but also what most clearly shows our kinship with one another – irrespective of our religious (or non-religious) upbringing or our current beliefs and practices. Here we might take as an example the almost universal preference that contemporary social actors exhibit for 'spirituality' over 'religion'. In this instance, it matters very little whether this preference is announced by a conservative evangelical Christian, a secular Jew, a liberal Catholic, a Unitarian, an agnostic, a western Buddhist, or a new age follower of Baba Ram Dass. What matters for our purposes is that our reservations over institutional or historical religions – religions embodied in documents and institutions, with established rites and rituals, religions that possess a history with which practitioners are expected to identify – are entertained by religious practitioners or adherents all across the religious spectrum. These reservations identify us as shareholders in the present age. But they also distinguish us from religious practitioners in other times and places for whom spiritual embodiment was not only expected but was, as Pierre Bourdieu has put it, not even taken into account.[20] Today, to the contrary, even where social actors are supposed to have overcome mind-body dualism it is the isolation of sublime value from its material form of appearance that goes without saying.

Finally, however, although it is true that commodity production and exchange are the dominant practices shaping social reality and social subjectivity within the capitalist social formation, *dominant* should not be read as *total domination*. Most of us can still identify pockets of time and space in our lives that we forget to measure in abstract units of time; pockets of time and space that do not therefore lend themselves to the logic of abstract value. Therefore, it should always be borne in mind that like all social formations, capitalism too is full of rifts, gullies, walls, steep cliffs, and fissures that allow the light shed by dissenting practices and thought forms to seep through what can otherwise seem a totally closed system. At the conclusion of our study we will examine some religious practices or spiritual disciplines that could point in directions that fall outside the scope of the present study.

Still, our aim is to offer in as concise a manner as possible a characterization of contemporary religion and spirituality that covers most varieties while at the same time offer clear boundaries that set contemporary religion and spirituality off from their predecessors and counterparts in other social formations. In other words, in so far as forms of religion and spirituality in other social formations would be shaped by – and would in turn shape – different regimes of practice, we have no intention of tackling all of these alternative practical regimes in this study. Thus, while it is clear for example that the body of religion held a dramatically different place and meaning for medieval Catholics or pre-capitalist Muslims than it does for modern Catholics and Muslims, we have no intention of identifying this place and meaning in terms of the practices and structures that shaped medieval Catholic or pre-capitalist Muslim social subjectivity. Our focus is limited to contemporary religious subjectivity and practice.

Our approach

Since our study aims to capture the movement of that 'Weltgeist' or world spirit known as the value form of the commodity, our study follows an outline loosely fit around the contradictory emergence and simultaneous retreat of this form. Therefore, in Chapter 2, which I have titled 'The retreat of ultimate and sublime values', we begin by looking more carefully at Max Weber's lamentation in 'Science as a Vocation'. Our aim is to try to capture both moments mentioned by Weber, both the retreat of ultimate and sublime values from public life and their re-emergence in the bourgeois interior.

Then in Chapter 3, which I have titled 'Disembodiment and the sublime', we jump backwards in time to the historical moment in the fourteenth century when ultimate and sublime values began their retreat from public life. By way of a few well known examples – the late medieval transformation in the body of the Virgin Mary, the disappearance of Jesus' wounds from heaven, and the disappearance of Jesus' Body and Blood from the elements of the Holy Sacrament – we explore both the disenchantment of the body of religion and the disembodiment of the sacred. These transformations are prompted by a dramatic transformation in how value is measured, a transformation that took hold in the mid-fourteenth century when abstract equal units of time were first used to measure social value. We conclude this chapter by exploring how this dramatic transformation in value achieved theoretical clarity in Edmund Burke's, Immanuel Kant's and Georg F.W. Hegel's interpretations of the sublime.

In Chapter 4, which I have titled 'The 'spirit' of capitalism', we leap forward once again to Max Weber's famous study, *The Protestant Ethic and the 'Spirit' of Capitalism* (1904–5), itself a treatment of roughly the same period we explored in Chapter 3. Here, however, our aim is to show how the sublime value form of the commodity came to shape Weber's interpretation of the relationship between capitalism and religion. Just as it already had begun to do in the fourteenth century, here in Weber's *Protestant Ethic* we find immaterial value isolating itself from and violently turning upon its own material form of appearance so that, by the conclusion of his study, Weber was compelled to acknowledge the flight of the spirit of capitalism from the iron cage it had played a large part in constructing. We conclude the chapter by looking at how Weber's early neo-Kantian methodological writings, published between 1902 and 1904, found their way into and decisively shaped Weber's approach to and the conclusions he drew in his *Protestant Ethic*.

At this point, mid-way through our study, the sublime value form of the commodity has achieved its highest level of abstraction. It has now completely isolated itself from its material form appearance. It has flown from the iron cage. Therefore, in Chapter 5, 'The *hiatus irrationalis*', we begin to explore ways in which the sublime value form of the commodity actually strikes out at its outward, public, material form of appearance. The *hiatus irrationalis*, the irrational gulf between concept and reality, expresses the neo-Kantian conviction that whatever meaning we impute to the artificial historical constructions we build, there is still a vast unbridgeable gulf separating our constructions from the actual chaos of reality. This gulf between concept and reality offers us still another way of conceptualizing the way that the sublime is isolated from its material form of appearance. Here, however, we take this isolation one step further by looking at how two of Weber's most influential students, the Hungarian founder of western Marxism Georg Lukács, and the German founder of modern anti-liberalism Carl Schmitt, sought to deal with the isolation of the sublime from its material form of appearance. Both, we will discover, see violence as the only way to bridge the gulf between concept and reality. We conclude the chapter by exploring how through the heirs of the Frankfurt School on the one hand and the followers of Leo Strauss on the other, Lukács' and Schmitt's ideas continue to shape social theory and state policy.

In Chapter 6, 'The prophetic *pneuma*', we take leave of the present and leap way back to the dawn beginnings of human civilization where we find the first evidence of the ancient 'prophetic *pneuma*' which Weber believed to be comparable to the spirit that now occupied the sublime bourgeois interior. Here, we attempt to follow the logic that might have led Weber to draw this comparison between ancient religious warriors and contemporary bourgeois social subjects in his address 'Science as a Vocation'. What we discover is that the religious warrior communities of ancient Greece, Palestine, China and India were in Weber's view entirely unique in so far as they alone in all of history had fashioned a credible public show of force in the face of the rationalistic and bureaucratic forces of traditional religion and society by which they were about to be overcome. To reach this point, however, Weber needed to impute a complex chiastic structure to history wherein initially free, charismatically directed communities of religious warriors were everywhere overcome by their bureaucratic, rationalist successors, the purveyors of traditional religion and society. To complete the chiasm, however, these traditional bureaucrats and administrators need to be annihilated by the brief public reappearance of the sublime in the creatively destructive and destructively creative 'spirit' of capitalism.[21]

Before turning our attention to the form of this chiastic structure as a whole, we look in some detail at Weber's model of traditional society and religion, ancient China. China's bureaucratic form and meaningless rationalism epitomized for Weber the aimlessness of the traditional body. According to Weber, China could only be liberated from its bondage to tradition by externally imposed capitalism. China, we discover, is only a metaphor however for the body that is ripe for destruction. Therefore, after looking closely at Weber's treatment of traditional Chinese society and religion, we seek to show how the overall chiastic structure in which Weber set his economic ethics of the world religions may itself have been strung tightly around the value form of the commodity. What we discover, however, is that since contemporary religious actors are prohibited from bringing their sublime interiors to bear on the disenchanted public sphere by which they are continuously threatened, Weber's chiastic structure was incomplete. To complete the chiasm, Weber would have needed authentic charismatic warrior-leaders bearing a new and genuine prophecy. Weber would have required a true and genuine mortification of the body of modern religion.

In Chapter 7, we therefore look directly at what Weber called 'The community unto death'. The 'community unto death' was how Weber described not only those sent into combat, but also those who, although not themselves on the front lines, nevertheless formed with them a community whose members are knit together in purpose and resolve. Their resolve I suggest is the full annihilation of the body. To support this claim I look carefully at the religious form taken by Weber's analysis of the community unto death. In the end, Weber drew back from the edge of his own analysis, taking comfort in the conviction that authentic religion would see in instances of state sanctioned mass death such as were unfolding all across Europe in 1915, only a mockery of true piety. In our view, however, Weber was simply drawing back from the edge of a more consistent, yet more terrifying, interpretation of how religion and capitalism might be related to one another.

In Chapter 8, our concluding chapter, we briefly examine 'The body of religion', both as we currently find it and as it might be found once social value is dislodged from the intimate relationship it has borne for the past five hundred years to abstract time and value. Drawing upon a wide variety of critical and speculative works, we explore in conclusion what it might take practically to wean religious subjectivity and practice from its dependence upon abstract, immaterial value, and what a future enchanted body or embodied spirit might look like.

Notwithstanding such futurist speculations, the aim of this book is not primarily to stir up hope or invite ridicule by offering simplistic solutions to a problem that is now costing the world nearly five per cent of its occupants every century. Religion and spirituality, which for over two hundred millennia provided social actors a variety of ways to embody the spirits they valued and value the bodies they found sacred, have for the last half millennia turned against the body of religion. This historically recent turn for religious practices and spiritual disciplines coincided with the emergence of capitalism, first in Western Europe and then throughout the rest of the world. But, before we can begin thinking through what it might take to protect or restore the body of religion, we first need to understand the peculiar character of that sublime spirit that aims at its destruction. We need to understand what Weber called 'the retreat of ultimate and sublime values'.

2 The retreat of ultimate and sublime values

On 7 November 1917, the day after the Battle for Passchendaele ground to its gruesome close, 700 kilometres to the southeast in Munich the German sociologist Max Weber mounted a podium and delivered what many count among the most famous academic addresses in modern times, 'Science as a Vocation'. Curiously, Weber made only passing reference to the Great War in his address. Certainly no one reading the address today would suspect that it was delivered at the height of the Great War. Nor should we have expected Weber to call attention to this interminable tragedy. It was after all among Weber's main contentions that academic scholarship was unsuited for providing ultimate answers – be they philosophical, artistic, scientific, religious, or even eudemonistic. It therefore makes sense that here as elsewhere Weber declined to use scholarship as an opportunity to play politics. Nevertheless, it is here at the conclusion of Weber's 'Science as a Vocation', I will suggest, that we should begin our search for a satisfying explanation for the 'sacred grounds' created by capitalist modernity's peculiar variety of religion and spirituality.

We begin our search here at the conclusion of Weber's 'Science as a Vocation' because, like nearly every officially sanctioned act of mass death since the fourteenth century, the Great War too was at heart a religious conflict – i.e. a conflict over which combatants self-consciously sacrificed their material bodies for the sake of immaterial values. And it was this sacrifice to which Weber called attention at the conclusion of his address when he spoke of the 'prophetic *pneuma*, which in former times swept through the great communities like a firebrand, welding them together'.[1] Of course the great communities of which Weber spoke in his address were not in fact those whose soldiers faced one another between 1914 and 1918 across the no man's lands of Western Europe. Nor was the prophetic spirit that in August 1914 swept through these great communities like a firebrand, self-evidently the same spirit that had swept through the communities of the modern world's Great Powers. The communities to which Weber was referring in his address were the communities whose members composed the ancient tribes of Yahweh. And the prophetic *pneuma* he had in mind was the spirit of Yahweh's prophets. So then why begin searching here in ancient Palestine for an explanation for state sanctioned mass death in modern times?

We begin our search here among these ancient communities for the simple reason that Weber at least implicitly invited us to begin our search here. How? His invitation came in the form of a comparison, a comparison between the spirit that he discerned in the bourgeois interior and the prophetic *pneuma* that he believed welded the communities of ancient Palestine together like a firebrand. To be sure, Weber had not intended his listeners to take the additional step and connect the prophetic spirit of the ancient Jewish war god to the spirit prompting the world's leaders to send their youth off to what amounted to near certain death. To the contrary, at least on this occasion, Weber's aim appears to have been to convince his listeners that any public expression of this prophetic spirit and certainly any bellicose outburst in the manner of ancient warriors had been made impossible by what he described as the retreat of 'the ultimate and most sublime values from public life'.

But then why had Weber explicitly invited his readers to draw a comparison between their own private interiors and the prophetic spirit that had once knit ancient Israel's tribes together like a firebrand? Weber had explicitly stated that it was not accidental 'that today only within the smallest and intimate circles, in personal human situations, in *pianissimo*, that something is pulsating that corresponds to the prophetic *pneuma*, which in former times swept through the great communities like a firebrand'. If the contemporary spirit corresponded to the ancient one, then why might it not generate similarly mortifying and similarly *public* results? Yet, whatever else was transpiring on the battlefields of Europe, Weber seemed certain that it had nothing to do either with ultimate and most sublime values or with the spirit he found pulsating within the smallest and intimate circles of social actors throughout the modern world.

Here we need to critically reflect upon Weber's claim that ultimate and sublime values had retreated from public life into what he called 'the transcendental realm of mystic life or . . . the brotherliness of direct and personal human relations'.[2] A compelling case could be made for nearly the opposite claim: that spirituality and religion have gained so firm a foothold in the contemporary public sphere that ultimate and sublime values consistently take precedence over public interest, so much so that social actors will routinely sacrifice their physical well-being, often to the point of death, for the sake of their spiritual values.

Nevertheless, on at least one point Weber should have found broad agreement among his colleagues: the validity religious and spiritual practitioners have claimed for their values during the modern epoch has tended not to rest as it once did upon the suitability or adequacy of these values to public life. To the contrary, more often than not, the validity of these values has rested upon their proposed superiority or even their hostility to the norms, conventions and values that otherwise prevail (or were believed to prevail) in the public sphere. The oppositional form assumed by ultimate and sublime values may therefore have lent plausibility to Weber's claim that these values were best suited to 'the transcendental realm of mystic life' or 'the brotherliness of direct and personal human relations'. But did the retreat of ultimate and sublime values constitute a wholesale evacuation of the public sphere? Or, might this retreat not have confirmed Hegel's insight into the 'Weltgeist', whose retreat was but a precursor to its returning and annihilating its own material form of appearance?

The retreat of ultimate and sublime values from public life

It is important that we appreciate at the outset how for Weber the retreat of ultimate and sublime values did not entail anything so dramatic or far-reaching as the end of public spirituality or religion. It of course meant that one should no longer anticipate receiving divine guidance, grace, or comfort from entities found in the world of the senses. And it meant that one should no longer anticipate finding ultimate and sublime values lurking behind the practices, structures, processes or dispositions that shaped or mediated action in the public sphere (*Öffentlichkeit*). But it did not mean that people in large numbers would cease to be religious. To illustrate his point, Weber offered a comparison with which he rightly believed his audience would be intimately familiar, the comparison between monumental and intimate art. 'It is not accidental', he reminded his listeners, 'that our greatest art is intimate and not monumental'.[3] Clearly, Weber could not have meant that monumental art (much less art *as such*) had suddenly disappeared from Europe's landscape. Rather, it seems clear that Weber was referring instead to the increasing preference Germany's educated bourgeoisie displayed for the kind of art produced by painters such as Franz Marc, a leader of Munich's *Blaue Reiter* movement. Weber himself displayed such a preference as did his close friend and colleague the economist Edgar Jaffé, who purchased and prominently displayed a Marc print in his home in Heidelberg. If monumental art had ever been appropriate – a matter open to dispute – such art in Weber's view clearly no longer fit in a society where public decisions were the outcome of lengthy, statutorily circumscribed and bureaucratically administered procedures. Such rationalized procedures seemed to Weber to obviate the need for monumental works of art. Such works now functioned as mere propaganda.

The sublime bourgeois interior

If appreciation for the intimate art of Franz Marc and the pulsating spirit of the prophets captured Weber's understanding of the sublime bourgeois interior, the archnemesis of this spirit was clearly the modern constitutional state, the so-called *Rechtsstaat*. Later, we will examine the rage Weber felt at its impersonal form. Here, however, it is worth bearing in mind that the bourgeois interior was not simply a reverse image of the *Rechtsstaat*. Weber scholars and neo-Weberians have tended to focus their attention on the disenchanted, instrumentally rational and bureaucratic character of the contemporary public sphere and have paid relatively little attention to the rich interior into which Weber felt ultimate and sublime values had retreated. And, yet, clearly the two belong together. For, while it is certainly true that few individuals, however wealthy, could warm-up to the monuments that littered public squares, avenues and museums throughout Europe, one can easily imagine the personal attachments individuals might forge with a Kandinsky, Marc, Pechstein or Klee. Thus, while today we may be preoccupied with the 'fate of times such as those characterized by rationalization and intellectualization and, above all, by the 'disenchantment of the world', there is nothing to suggest that Weber's audience might not have been equally or even more drawn to the enrichment of bourgeois private life suggested by his argument.[4] And, in fact, alongside the disenchanted public sphere vacated by ultimate and sublime values, Weber invited his audience to contemplate an interior whose richness and complexity had been significantly enhanced by the fact that it was into interiors such as these that ultimate and sublime values had retreated.

This suggests that prior to the retreat of ultimate and sublime values from public life not only was it unlikely that social actors would develop personal attachments to pieces of monumental art – pieces which after all were designed to command obedience and respect, not love – but that intimate art itself would have been unthinkable. It is as though Weber was suggesting that prior to the retreat of these values from public life, the bourgeois interior itself was somehow deficient and as yet incapable of comprehending or receiving what Marc or Klee or the ancient prophetic *pneuma* had to offer.

Now, however, it was the public sphere that was no longer capable of comprehending these values because they no longer corresponded to and therefore were no longer reinforced by the constellation of actions, structures and processes out of which the public sphere was now composed. Now the validity of these values rested not on external force, but upon their correspondence to our innermost being. Indeed, it was presumably this heightening and intensification of their inner life that made it possible for members of the educated bourgeoisie to appreciate the intimate qualities visible in the new artistic style. But, it was also this heightening and intensification that made it possible for Weber now to characterize the bourgeois interior not as 'this nullity' (*dies Nichts*),[5] the phrase he had used in his 1904–5 *Protestant Ethic*, but rather as a 'transcendental realm' (*hinterweltliche Reich*) whose spirit he now believed comparable to the ancient prophetic *pneuma*.[6]

It is therefore worth recalling at this point how twelve years earlier, in his 1905 *Protestant Ethic*, Weber had described something similar to the retreat of ultimate and sublime values from public life. There, however, it was not ultimate and sublime values to which he called his readers' attention but the 'spirit of Christian asceticism' (*Geist der christlichen Askese*). According to Weber, after wholly transforming the world, this spirit ultimately proved inadequate to the world it had created and, much like ultimate and sublime values, it too had been forced to retreat or escape from that world.

> As asceticism began to change the world and endeavoured to exercise its influence over it, the outward goods of this world gained increasing and finally inescapable power over men, as never before in history. Today its spirit has fled from this shell [i.e., iron cage (*stahlhartes Gehäuse*)] – whether for all time, who knows?[7]

Yet, in contrast to 1905, where Weber had felt that the flight of the spirit of asceticism was on the verge of transforming bourgeois social subjects into 'specialists without spirit' (*Fachmenschen ohne Geist*), now in 1917 he believed that the retreat of ultimate and sublime values had transformed the bourgeois interior into the last secure dwelling place for the 'prophetic *pneuma*'. Here, Weber now discerned 'something pulsating' (*Etwas pulsiert*) that he found comparable to the prophetic spirit (*prophetisches Pneuma*) that once 'welded the great communities together in a stormy fire' [*was früher … in stürmischem Feuer durch die großen Gemeinden … sie zusammenschweißte*]'.[8]

What appears to have changed between 1905 and 1917 was not Weber's evaluation of the public sphere, but rather his evaluation of the bourgeois interior. The capitalist public sphere was still a moral wasteland governed by means–ends rationality on the one hand and the coercive powers of the state on the other. In between the two Weber saw nothing but intellectualization, rationalization and, of course, a world now wholly disenchanted. This had not changed. But, in contrast to 'specialists without spirit' and 'hedonists without a heart', Weber now discerned at least 'in the smallest and most intimate circles, in *pianissimo* [*innerhalb der kleinsten Gemeinschaftskreise, von Mensch zu Mensch, im* pianissimo]',[9] something he had not found and perhaps had not even searched for in 1905. He found the interior in which ultimate and sublime values had taken refuge following their retreat from the public sphere. He found the sublime bourgeois interior.

Of course the bourgeois interior was not an unknown territory to Weber. Most Sundays, Max and his wife Marianne convened their own intimate circle, their own *Gemeinschaftskreise* – affectionately known as their '*Sonntagskreise*' or Sunday Circle – at their home on the Ziegelhäuserlandstrasse in Heidelberg. Here on any given Sunday in this smallest of circles, one might find the Webers entertaining the likes of the philosopher Karl Jaspers and his wife Gertrud, or Otto Gross, the wayward disciple of Freud who advocated free love and who was among the Webers' principle *entrées* into Schwabing Munich's intellectual, artistic and literary circles. Or one might meet the opera star Mina Tobler, in whom Max experienced a 'magnificent pool of beauty and love' and whom he called his 'Tobelchen'.[10] Then there were Weber's colleagues such as the aforementioned Edgar Jaffé, the economist and frequent contributor to Weber's journal, and his wife Else von Richthofen, a leading feminist scholar whom Max had had a fling with in the 1890s.[11] And then there was Else's sister Frieda, D.H. Lawrence's lover, the other daughter of Germany's Baron von Richthofen, the famous *Roter* or Red Baron. Or one might find other colleagues such as the eminent economist Emil Lask, whose analysis of the *hiatus irrationalis* (the gulf between concept and reality) was to play such a crucial role in the thinking of so many European intellectuals. There was the theologian Ernst Troeltsch,[12] upon whose insights into religious history Weber depended, and the philosopher Heinrich Rickert to whose neo-Kantian philosophy of science Weber was indebted and Heinrich's wife Sophie. And, of course, there were the students, only the most promising or interesting of whom Max and Marianne invited to share in their intimate gatherings. And so one might find the likes of the Italian socialist and future fascist Robert Michels, the Hungarian literary scholar and future communist leader Georg von Lukács or Lukács' friend, the mystic philosopher Ernst Bloch.[13] Is there any wonder why Weber might have felt that something was pulsating (*jenes Etwas pulsiert*) in his and Marianne's *Sonntagskreise* that corresponded to the prophetic *pneuma* or spirit 'which in former times swept through the great communities like a firebrand, welding them together?'

But, of course, in former times the purpose behind the 'stormy fire' (*stürmischem Feuer*)[14] set ablaze by the prophetic spirit was not to draw educated and cultural elites together in one another's homes, *in pianissimo* or otherwise. Elsewhere, Weber himself reserved these terms almost exclusively for situations of war and combat, as for example when he described the 'fierce bravery [*stürmische Tapferkeit*] of the Calvary'[15] sent to battle Cromwell's disciplined, rational and sober troops; or again in his study of ancient Judaism when he wrote about the '"spirit", the *ruach* of Yahwe . . . the god of war' as 'an acute demonic–superhuman power of varying, most frequently frightful, character'.[16] It is therefore curious not only that Weber used these terms to describe the bourgeois interior, but also that he was so insistent that his audience not let this stormy fire escape into the public sphere. What danger could there possibly be in deploying this spirit once again for its intended purpose?

Whether justified or not, what Weber clearly feared was that this spirit was so out of conformity with the intellectualization, and rationalization and disenchantment that predominated under capitalist modernity that it would either tear the public sphere apart or perhaps even destroy itself.

> If we attempt to force and to 'invent' a monumental style in art, such miserable monstrosities are produced as the many monuments of the last twenty years. If one tries intellectually to construe new religions without a new and genuine prophecy, then, in an inner sense, something similar will result, but with still worse effects. And academic prophecy, finally, will create only fanatical sects but never a genuine community.[17]

And, yet, clearly, just as Weber acknowledged that the lack of conformity to the intimate bourgeois interior had not prevented 'miserable monstrosities' (*jämmerliches Mißgebilde*) from littering the avenues, public squares and public buildings of cities all across Europe, so he must have seen that, however inadvisable, the sublime bourgeois interior *had already* spilled over into the public sphere producing precisely the 'still worse effects' that he most feared. But then in what sense did it hold true that 'ultimate and sublime values' had in fact retreated from the public sphere into the bourgeois interior?

How one determines the extent to which any given form of social subjectivity – in this case, ultimate and sublime values – is 'adequate' to the social and historical landscape in which it appears is obviously fraught with difficulties, practical and theoretical. For, on the one hand, no one is suggesting that social conflict in and of itself is a sure sign of social or historical inadequacy. Nor is any one suggesting that the social or historical inadequacy of a social form – let us say, the struggle for women's rights in early modern Europe – necessarily means it is improper for social actors to work to change the norms and values to which it is inadequate. Since they are invariably composed of disparate elements, many of which resist logical reduction to one another, we should not expect social formations to perform like logical syllogisms. One person's 'miserable monstrosity' might be another person's sublime memorial, just as one professor's 'academic prophecy' might be another's inappropriate propaganda.

To say therefore that a social formation might display a kind of logical coherence could mean simply that we can distinguish one social formation from another and that the distinctions we find between them are subject to rational explanation. Clearly, in this instance, Weber felt that any attempt to subject cosmopolitan social actors to religious or spiritual laws, which only a small minority might believe to be valid, could create social disorder of a magnitude few would be willing to accept. At the same time, had most social actors been content to restrict their ultimate and sublime values to 'the transcendental realm of mystic life or . . . the brotherliness of direct and personal human relations', we would have found little disagreement in Germany over Weber's description of capitalist modernity. At the beginning of the twentieth century, however, over ninety per cent of Germans still felt quite deeply about the practical significance of their faith. Germans as a whole did not experience a 'crisis of faith' until war, revolution and political turmoil challenged the most basic premises of their religion. And, even then, judging from how elderly West German's have responded to recent surveys, most of those who reached adulthood shortly before or during the Third Reich actually recall that their faith grew stronger during this decade and a half. Certainly in November 1917, Weber must therefore have known that most Germans, though perhaps not as many of those who attended his address in Munich, were deeply and publicly committed to their faith.[18]

Yet, rather than take this commitment at face value, Weber instead took the very popularity of all things religious and spiritual in turn of the century Germany as *prima facie* evidence of their superficiality. For it stood to reason that since ultimate and sublime values had retreated from public life, any widespread public display of religious or spiritual sentiment had by definition to be a mere surface phenomenon. This at least was Weber's interpretation of the spectacular popularity of books on spirituality and religion.

> The need of literary, academic, or café-society intellectuals to include "religious" feelings in the inventory of their sources of impressions and sensations, and among their topics for discussion, has never yet given rise to a new religion. Nor can a religious renaissance be generated by the need of authors to compose books on such interesting topics or by the far more effective need of clever publishers to sell such books. No matter how much the appearance of a widespread religious interest may be stimulated, no new religion has ever resulted from such needs of intellectuals or from their chatter. The pendulum of fashion will presently remove this subject of conversation and journalism.[19]

But, of course, the pendulum did not remove this subject, at least not in the way that Weber may have hoped. True, following the Great War many Germans may have drifted away from traditional religious disciplines and spiritual practices towards Luckmann's 'invisible religions'. Many may thus have adopted religious practices or spiritual disciplines so privatized and individualized that they fit 'without conflict with the functionally rational norms of the primary institutions'.[20] In 1917, however, religion in Germany and the rest of Europe was nothing if not visible. All evidence suggests that it became ever more-so up through the middle of the twentieth century. How then if not by counting heads and surveying beliefs did Weber mark the retreat of ultimate and sublime values from public life?

The constitutional state and the spirit of Yahweh

One of the ways he marked this retreat I would suggest is in the transition from what he termed the pre-capitalist world's 'personalistic status order' (*der personalistischen ständischen Ordnung*) to the impersonal modern status order.

> In a personalistic status order it is quite clear that one must act differently toward persons of different status. . . . Today, however, the *homo politicus*, as well

as the *homo oeconomicus*, performs his duty best when he acts without regard to the person in question, *sine ira et studio*, without hate and without love, without personal predilection and therefore without grace, but sheerly in accordance with the impersonal duty imposed by his calling, and not as a result of any concrete personal relationship.

Weber's insight in itself was not particularly original. What was original was the dramatic, seemingly unbridgeable, infinite gulf Weber fixed between the old and new status orders. Of course, this gulf is made to appear all the more dramatic by the abrupt transition from the age of Thomas Aquinas to 'today'.

Yet, it was less this narrative device than it was a specifically religious insight that allowed Weber to infinitely extend and permanently fix the gulf between the impersonality of the contemporary state and the personalism that once prevailed. This is because Weber found he could accurately convey the infinite distance between the near and far sides of this gulf only by drawing upon an image – the image of the war god Yahweh – that for him epitomized everything that the modern constitutional state or *Rechtsstaat* was not.

> This is comparable to the impersonal retribution of *karma*, in contrast to Yahweh's fervent quest for vengeance. The use of force within the political community increasingly assumes the form of the *Rechtsstaat*. But from the point of view of religion, this is merely the most effective mimicry of brutality. All politics is oriented to *raison d'état*, to realism, and to the autonomous end of maintaining the external and internal distribution of power. These goals, again, must necessarily seem completely senseless from the religious point of view.[21]

Here once again, in the form of the personal status order, we encounter Yahweh's stormy fire, the same fire that burned in the intimate, personal situations, *in pianissimo*, in Weber's account of the bourgeois interior. What this suggests is not only that it is from the 'religious point of view' (*religiös angesehen*), from Yahweh's vantage-point, that capitalist modernity appears so completely brutal and senseless, but also that the reason this vantage-point might be readily accessible to most of Weber's readers was because it was this vantage-point that was fanned to life by the retreat of ultimate and sublime values into the bourgeois interior. In other words, the religious point of view, the view that exposes capitalist modernity for the moral wasteland it truly is, can be known, recognized and embraced because social actors possess a spirit comparable to Yahweh's ancient prophetic *pneuma*.

Yet clearly there is a potentially lethal problem here. Since presumably Weber was not referring to two separate individuals or groups of individuals here, but rather to one and the same individual or group of individuals, his contrast between the sublime bourgeois interior and the bureaucratic automata suggested an inner conflict of gigantic proportions. The men or women who perform their duty best were not different men and women from those who recognized the senselessness and the brutality both of their performance and of the constitutional state for which they performed. In other words, Weber was clearly not contemplating one group of individuals on one side who performed their duties well and another group of individuals across from them who, inspired by the prophetic spirit, felt nothing but the deepest hostility and need to exact vengeance against those who performed their duty best. Instead, Weber clearly had in mind someone not altogether unlike himself, a civil servant, bound by an oath of loyalty to act without regard to the person in question, *sine ira et studio*, but a man who inwardly and privately knew that from the religious point of view the fulfilment of his oath and the performance of his duties were completely senseless.

Part of the problem we face conceptually when we attempt to wrap our heads around the character of contemporary spirituality or religion is that almost invariably we begin to think of distinct groups of individuals, some on one side, some on the other, when in fact what we need to bear in mind is that the spiritual tension seething deep within the bourgeois soul is a tension that each person bears within his or her own empirical body. We are both civil servants or technicians or nurses or professors or administrators who perform our duties best when we perform them according to standard operating procedures; *and* we are lovers, mothers, fathers, Christians, Muslims, Jews, or even *pagana* who find the inhumanity and impersonality of these operating procedures so brutal as to demand their immediate, total annihilation. The excessive hostility raging today against the so-called liberal, secular humanist state – a rage that we find both inside and beyond the western, nominally Christian, polity of nations – has its origin in this simple fact. The sublime value form of the commodity, the 'spirit' of modern religion, has brought us to despise its blunt and brutal material form of appearance. It is this very 'spirit' that has brought us to contemplate the annihilation of its own body, the body of religion.

3 Disembodiment and the sublime: the birth of modern religion

Modern religion emerged at the moment in history when religious practitioners in large numbers first discovered and were embarrassed by the profanity entailed by the body of religion; or, in the alternative, modern religion emerged when in large numbers religious practitioners first discovered that 'true' religion had no body. Not surprisingly, this was also the moment in history when, again in large numbers, social actors first concluded that sacrificing their bodies in acts of state sanctioned death might actually possess emancipatory value. Thus, in Europe, between 900 and 1450, less than a half million soldiers sacrificed their lives in acts of war. Nevertheless, as an omen of things to come, the fifteenth century alone accounts for nearly half (roughly 194,500) of these deaths.[1] And from there the figures climb to the heavens. The relationship between modernity and war has, of course, occupied some of our best minds. Among the best is Modris Eksteins. In his masterful work on the relationship between war and modernity, *Rites of Spring*, Eksteins called attention to the curious relationship between the 'avant-garde' and storm troops. Eksteins suggested 'there may be a sibling relationship between these two terms that extends beyond their military origins. Introspection, primitivism, abstraction, and myth making in the arts, and introspection, primitivism, abstraction, and myth making in politics, may be related manifestations'.[2] Yet, if our figures are correct, the connection between war and modernity may actually have taken root much earlier, perhaps as early as the fourteenth century itself.

Although it is difficult to pinpoint the precise moment when religious practitioners in large numbers first began to isolate an immaterial or spiritual dimension of their religious devotion from the material forms in which it appeared, two studies published over the last decade give us reason to begin our search for clues in or around fourteenth century western Europe. For it was here according to Donna Spivey Ellington's research that practitioners of the Roman Catholic cult of the Virgin Mary first began to perceive subtle changes in the object of their devotion. Ellington's study looks at the sermons of fifteenth and sixteenth century preachers – Bernardino of Siena, Bernardino of Busti, Johannes of Verden, Michel Menot, Olivier Maillard, Gabriel Bartletta, Jean Gerson, Lawrence of Brindisi, Christopher Cheffontaines, Francis Panigarola, Peter Canisius Robert Bellarmine and François de Sales – for signs of a shift in practitioners' experience of Mary that reflected broader social, cultural and economic changes taking place throughout Western Europe as a whole. In the fifteenth century, according to Ellington, it seemed the 'Blessed Virgin was able to do more for God than God could do for himself'.[3] But what Ellington found was that over time 'the Church's portrait of the Virgin gradually changed during the sixteenth century and became less focused on her body and more on her soul as religious life in Western Europe was increasingly dominated by a piety that stressed the inner life at the expense of the concrete and the material'. By the dawn of the early modern period, Ellington concludes, Mary 'was a changed individual, no longer quite the same woman who had participated in so dramatic a way in fifteenth-century sermons, artworks, and treatises. She is more distanced from the action, more spiritualized, more passive, and more silent.'

Of course these changes may tell us more about what was going on in the thoughts and lives of Roman Catholic preachers than they do about changes in how participants in the Cult of Mary were actually experiencing the Blessed Virgin. Ellington, for example, points to the sudden invasion of print media over the course of the fifteenth and sixteenth centuries, an invasion that presumably would have had a greater impact on the literate preachers who published their sermons than on illiterate participants in the cult itself. After all, the sermons continued to be delivered in the same manner as they had before, i.e. orally. Yet, Ellington's point is that this invasion of print literature prompted 'increased reliance on sight and visual awareness' among Western Europe's literate preachers, leading to subtle shifts in the content of their speech about the Virgin Mary. So while it is certainly true that literate Western Europeans saw profound changes in their experience of God, Ellington acknowledges that speech and not the written word would have remained the 'primary and most natural form of human communication; therefore, bodily presence represented by relics or even images would continue to be an important source of assurance [that Mary] was truly present and able to hear supplications'.[4]

According to Peter Widdicombe, the physical character of divine representation before God in heaven also played a critical role in how late medieval religious practitioners experienced and explained the persistence of Jesus' wounds in his resurrected and glorified body.[5] According to Widdicombe, 'prior to the Reformation, those who wrote about the wounds and the gloried body assumed that the glorified body does retain the marks'.[6] However, this is not to say that, particularly towards the close of the Middle Ages, theologians did not find themselves devoting considerable more energy explaining their retention than they had earlier on. Justin Martyr, the second century Christian Apologist, took recognition of the persistence of Jesus' wounds as a point of orthodoxy. According to Justin, it was not the earthly faithful who were at risk of missing the significance of Jesus' wounds but rather the heavenly hosts, that is those who were to welcome Jesus into glory.

> When our Christ rose from the dead and ascended into heaven, the rulers in heaven, under appointment of God, are commanded to open the gates of heaven, that he who is king of glory may enter in, and, having ascended, may sit on the right hand of the Father until he make the enemies his footstool, as has been made manifest by another Psalm. For when the rulers of heaven saw him of "uncomely and dishonoured appearance" (Is. 53:2 and 3), and inglorious, not

recognizing him, they inquired "Who is this king of glory?" And the Holy Spirit [...] answers them, "the Lord of hosts, he is the king of glory."[7]

Widdicombe notes that the propensity for the heavenly host to fail 'to recognize Christ because of the incongruity between the condition of his ascended boy and what they seemingly had expected to see is a theme we shall see in later writings',[8] for instance in the fourth century church father Gregory of Nazianzus' *Second Oration on Easter*. Here, however, according to Widdicombe, Gregory 'goes on to say more than Justin had'.

> To those who marvel at such an appearance and say words like those of Is. 63:1–2, [...] "Who is this that comes from Edom and the things of earth? Or how are the garments of him red who is without blood or body, as one that treads in the full wine press?", he advised that one should "Set forth the beauty of the array of that body that suffered, adorned by the passion, and made splendid by the godhead, than which nothing can be more lovely or more beautiful."[9]

Also during the fourth century, Saint Augustine offered a less aesthetic, more rationalistic explanation: 'That form which stood before the judge will be judge: that form will judge which was judged; for it was judged unjustly, it will judge justly'.[10] Correctly I believe, Widdicombe takes this to mean that for Augustine 'it is not only that Christ retains his body eternally, but that integral to it are the wounds. It is the wounds, and the suffering and judgment on him to which they testify, that are the basis for our confidence that Christ will judge justly'.[11] Similarly for Bede, the seventh century historian and Doctor of the Church upon whom Thomas Aquinas principally relied, the persistence of Jesus' wounds are both practically and theologically necessary. According to Bede,

> [Jesus] retained the marks in order that the one who intercedes for us with the Father, "might demonstrate to him forever, by showing the scars of his wounds, how much he [Christ] laboured for human salvation," and that he might tell the Father, who is "always prepared to show mercy, how just it would be for him to show mercy toward human beings," of whose "sorrow and suffering the Son of God became a sharer" and "overthrew the sovereignty of death."[12]

Interestingly Thomas Aquinas, who otherwise relied so heavily upon Bede, at this juncture returned to the pure beauty of Jesus' wounds. 'He argues', writes Widdicombe, 'that the wounds should not be thought of as indications of corruption or imperfection, because they are "signs of virtue" intended "to manifest a greater degree of glory."' Indeed, there 'even appeared in the place where the wounds were a special type of beauty'.[13]

So why did theological reflection on Jesus' wounds grow increasingly strained after the thirteenth century until by the sixteenth century it was a matter of course that neither Martin Luther nor John Calvin felt compelled to defend this doctrine? Widdicombe speculates that it may have been 'the fascination of medieval and early

modern writers and artists with the physicality of the wounds and the blood, that ...
in part account for why Luther and Calvin shy away from the topic of the wounds'.[14]
More tellingly, Widdicombe suggests that our own reluctance to attach significance
to the persistence of Jesus' wounds in heaven may follow from our living in what he
calls 'a modern post-Kantian world, a world in which theology adheres closely to the
historical narrative of the biblical texts'.[15] Whatever the reason,

> for earlier theologians, the reign of Christ in all its fullness is signified by
> the retention of the marks. Suffering and sinful humanity indeed funds itself in
> the Son at the right hand of the Father and it can see there the evidence that the
> divine heart has and continues to beat with compassion for humanity in its con-
> tinuing brokenness.[16]

It could not have been mere coincidence, however, that just as the Mother of God
was changing from a sacred body into an angelic soul, the glorified body of the divine
Son whom she bore was undergoing a similar transformation. In each case, both in the
case of the Mother and in the case of her Son, religion was losing its body, shedding
what Ellington identified as 'the material, concrete devotional forms so popular in the
Middle Ages' and replacing these forms with a 'more inward piety'.[17] Nevertheless, as
both Ellington and Widdicombe appear ready to acknowledge, it would take several
decades and in some cases several centuries for popular piety to fully catch up with the
changes taking place among academic theologians. Just as many Protestants continued to venerate Mary, so many also continued to receive comfort from the thought that
Jesus retained and displayed his wounds before God the Father in heaven. What
Ellington and Widdicombe are describing is not a shift so dramatic that we can
pinpoint it on a timeline. They are describing a transition that began to set in some
time during the fourteenth or fifteenth centuries, a transition that took several decades
and in some cases several centuries before it would come to dominate religious piety
generally.

The disappearing body and blood of the Holy Eucharist

Evidently, such was not the case with the Holy Eucharist. So central was the sacrament of Holy Communion to the practices and beliefs of Christians during the late
Middle Ages and early modern period that it would have been virtually impossible
for the finer points of this doctrine to be missed even by the most common of practitioners. Today of course most Roman Catholics are happy to follow Saint Thomas'
advice and take the real presence of Christ's Body and Blood in the elements of the
Holy Eucharist on Christ's faith and authority:

> The presence of Christ's true body and blood in this sacrament cannot be
> detected by sense, nor understanding, but by faith alone, which rests upon
> Divine authority. Hence, on Lk. 22:19: 'This is My body which shall be deliv-
> ered up for you,' Cyril says: 'Doubt not whether this be true; but take rather the
> Saviour's words with faith; for since He is the Truth, He lieth not.'[18]

However, we should not forget that for most Catholics up through the early modern epoch, it would have been impossible to isolate the spiritual and material change brought about by the words of consecration *hoc enim est corpus meum* – this bread is my flesh – from their general awareness that the material world about them was chock full of beings, divine and otherwise. So that the broader question might have been not whether Jesus' flesh and blood were physically present in the bread and wine, but how this specific presence differed from other instances of real divine presence. The clear, unmistakable answer was of course that, although divine and demonic beings certainly took up residence in and communicated through other kinds of bodies, it was only these seven 'sensible things', the seven Sacraments, that God designated as unique means to convey divine grace.[19]

However inconsistent they may have been with his Aristotelian leanings, Saint Thomas' answers were in broad agreement with eleven centuries of settled Catholic dogma. Moreover, they were consistent with men and women's common, every day sense of how their world was put together. And, yet, already in the thirteenth century and certainly by the fourteenth the settled dogma of the Holy Eucharist – dogma that made the value of the elements dependent upon the real presence of Christ's Body and Blood in them – was beginning to come under attack from the same ideas that were to challenge Saint Thomas' interpretation of value in general.

Here, parenthetically, we should note that neither John duns Scotus (1266–1308) nor William of Occam (1285–1349), the two divine doctors most often held responsible for the ensuing catastrophe, believed themselves to be doing anything untoward when, against St Thomas' appropriation of Aristotle's natural law, they insisted that God's power superseded all claims Nature could itself make either in support of or in opposition to the inscrutable purposes and will of God. It is, in fact, ironic to think that when nineteenth century Catholic theologians commandeered Aquinas' natural theology to oppose political liberalism and democracy, they may in fact have been wielding a weapon originally fashioned by an 'atheist' (Aristotle) delivered to them by an 'infidel' (Islam). Perhaps even more ironic or tragic, however, when this opposition to liberalism was resurrected in the 1920s by Weber's student Carl Schmitt, the decisionism in which it was cloaked bore a resemblance nearer to that of Scotus and Occam than to Aquinas.

Briefly, the problem for Aquinas was how to distinguish between the precious metals out of which money was composed and the money itself. The value of the former, St. Thomas believed, was settled by nature, i.e. by the substance out of which the metal was composed. On the other hand, St. Thomas held that the value of money was a matter of political will.[20] This interpretation struck John Buridan as plausible, but dishonest. According to Buridan, the prince had an obligation to fix the value of money as near as possible to the value of the precious metal.[21] Nicholas Oresme went even further, arguing that it was not only metal and money values that needed coordination, but the value of goods as well.[22]

It is perhaps significant here that both Buridan and Oresme were nominalists, which, at the very least, meant that they were ready to draw a qualitative distinction between the value ascribed to any thing and the substances out of which it was composed. Yet, at least where money was concerned, St. Thomas too was ready to draw a similar distinction. The value of money was determined not by the material composition of specie, but by the declaration of the prince. Nevertheless, to the extent that Buridan and Oresme were prepared to decentre this authority, either by attempting to rationally calculate the relationship between specie and money or by placing such determinations in the hands of the community, this already signalled a further step in the isolation of value from its material form of appearance.

The point to be noted here, however, is that not unlike bread and wine, precious metals (in this case largely gold, silver and copper) were felt to hold the values they did strictly owing to the material elements out of which they were composed. However, since coins were not only precious metal, but also money for exchange, it is easy to see how the relationship the prince holds to money – declaring its value – could be likened to the relationship the priest holds to the elements of the Holy Eucharist – declaring their transubstantiation. Even more confusing, in each case the real 'value' of the item – Body and Blood, on the one hand and metal on the other – need not in fact 'appear' in the things representing them – bread and wine, or money. Might it then be only the declaration of the prince or priest that gave each its value, the elements of the Holy Eucharist on the one hand, the money value of precious metals on the other? It is worth noting, of course, that none of these theologians felt compelled to bring their lines of reasoning to bear on the matter of the Holy Eucharist. Nevertheless, the very fact that these doctors of theology were probing into questions surrounding the value of material things at all certainly helped ease the way for the fourteenth century revolution in value, a revolution that would eventually tear the western church asunder.

Time, value and the emergence of the sublime

According to Moishe Postone, this revolution in value was closely related to the transition from a system of 'variable' or 'temporal' hours 'to a system of commensurable, interchangeable, and invariable hours', a transition which was itself 'closely related to the development of the mechanical clock in Western Europe in the very late thirteenth century or the early fourteenth century'.[23] Most other scholars who study the fourteenth century revolution in value also stress the important role played by the introduction of invariable hours into the rhythms of daily life. And, yet, as Postone points out, most do not offer a plausible social explanation for why invariable hours were adopted when and where they eventually were, among the textile manufacturers of medieval Western Europe.[24] Following Jacques Le Goff's lead, Postone shows how the 'proliferation of various sorts of bells in medieval European towns, especially the work bells', may offer precisely the kind of rigorous social explanation we are looking for. Ironically, the original function of these bells was to mark ecclesiastical, not merchants' hours.[25] Yet, it is certainly possible, perhaps even likely, that the constant ringing of these bells at all hours of the day and night attuned medieval ears to the constant units of time that would eventually come to wholly dominate their lives. Postone suggests, however, that one of the reasons why clock time may first have been adopted in the medieval cloth industry was not only the proliferation of clocks, but the organization of the cloth making industry itself.

The craftsmen of most other industries sold what they produced, but in the textile industry there was a strict separation between the cloth merchants, who distributed the wool to the workers, collected the finished cloth from them and sold it, and the workers, many of whom were "pure" wage earners, possessing only their labour power. The work generally was done in small workrooms that belonged to masters, fullers, dyers, and shearmen, who owned or rented the equipment, such as the looms, received the raw materials as well as the wages from the cloth merchants, and supervised the hired workers. The organizing principle of the medieval cloth industry, in other words, was an early form of the capital–wage labour relationship.[26]

Since their enterprises aimed of course at making a profit, enhancing the productivity of 'their workers' was an ongoing struggle for merchants in cloth manufacturing.[27] And here is where the annoying clocks came into play.

The clocks, as we know, chimed hours noticeably at odds with the variable time marked out by the rising and setting of the sun. This meant that the work day was longer in the summer and shorter in the winter. Workers in the cloth making industry, inured to the incessant ringing of church bells, were well aware that they were working longer in the summer than in the winter. It therefore makes sense that they would have demanded shorter hours in the summer and that they would have demanded that church bells, not the sun, announce the beginning and end of their work day. This, however, is not quite what appears to have taken place.

> It seems that it was the workers who, at the beginning of the fourteenth century, demanded initially that the work day be lengthened in order to increase their wages, which had declined in real value as a result of the [economic] crisis [at the end of the thirteenth century].[28]

However, it was the merchants who eventually turned the incessant chiming of church bells into means for increasing productivity. They did so by tying the human action of cloth making and the value of the cloth produced to the abstract time marked out by these bells.[29] Obviously, this had scarcely been the intention of the cloth makers whose only aim presumably was to make up for the shortfall created by economic crisis. Nevertheless, as Postone points out, 'the workers' demands for a longer work day (that is, longer than the daylight period), already implied a loosening of the tie to "natural" time and the emergence of a different measure of duration'.[30]

It is important for us to grasp how this loosening of social actors' relationship to the 'natural' rhythms traced in the heavens by the rising and setting of the sun marked a fundamental break not only with how social actors experienced time, but also with how they experienced their relationship to the rhythms of work. E.P. Thompson has shown, for example, how the metaphors with which workers described these rhythms changed dramatically between 1300 and 1650, from metaphors that related time to specific tasks to those that related time to abstract units. Thompson, for example, calls attention to how 'a petition from Sunderland in 1800 includes the words "considering that this is a seaport in which many people are obliged to be up at all hours of the night to attend the tides and their affairs upon the river"'.[31] The point, according to Thompson is that the rhythms in this seaport 'follow upon the rhythms of the sea; and this appears to be natural and comprehensible to fishermen or seamen: the compulsion is nature's own'.[32] In addition to the sea's 'natural' rhythms, Thompson notes several others:

> sheep must be attended at lambing time and guarded from predators; cows must be milked; the charcoal fire must be attended and not burn away through the turfs (and the charcoal burners must sleep beside it); once iron is in the making, the furnaces must not be allowed to fail. The notation of time which arises in such contexts has been described as task-oriented.[33]

Obviously in the fourteenth century cloth making industry it was not the bodily rhythms and needs of farm animals, the ebb and flow of the tides, or the burning time of charcoal, but the rising and setting of the sun upon which workers' set their internal clocks. Once these internal clocks came to be calibrated according to the ringing of church bells, the actions whose value would be measured by these bells were now linked not to nature but to a human social institution: to abstract time.

Postone points out that what is critical here, however, is not that church time is any less constructed than merchants' time, but that whereas in church time the devout were reminded 'when various activities were to be done', once these same bells were used to announce the beginning and end of the work day, they marked the *duration* of an activity itself.[34] Moreover, whereas social actors knew full well that church time was dictated by a specific institution, albeit a divine institution, which aimed to bring human activity in line with the dictates of their God, when church time was transferred to economic activity and used to measure the duration of the work day, it lost its explicit divine sanction and therefore required a new ground for its legitimacy. For, as Postone points out, 'unlike the concrete time of the Church, a form of temporality controlled overtly by a social institution, abstract time, like other aspects of domination in capitalist society, is "objective"'.[35] That is to say, the equal, abstract units of time with which productive human activity eventually comes to be measured appear to be imposed by no one in particular and to apply to everyone in general. This appearance of 'objectivity', however, begins to fade as soon as we ask about the kinds of activities and experiences of time and value to which it does not seem to be particularly well-suited; for example, the kinds of activities and experiences of time and value – milking cows, attending to the tides, minding the hearth – to which E.P. Thompson called attention in his study.

At the same time, we should also bear in mind that the invention of abstract time and its application to productive human activity was, at least initially, not intended as a form of social domination. No one person or group or institution *intended* the drive to fix exact times of prayer (i.e. in independence from the variable rising and setting of the sun) to lead to the use of the ancient Chinese clock works for this purpose; no one *intended* the ringing of bells that announced times of prayer to inure social subjects to a new sense of time; and no one *intended* this new sense of time to be applied outside of the church to measure the duration of productive human activity. As Postone notes:

> It would . . . be mistaken to regard this "objectivity" as no more than a veil that disguises the concrete particularist interests of the bourgeoisie. . . . [A]bstract time is a form that emerged historically with the development of the domination of the bourgeoisie and has served the interests of that class; but it has also helped to constitute those interests historically (indeed, the very category of "interests"), and it expresses a form of domination beyond that of the dominating class.[36]

As social actors increasingly came to isolate their productive activity from the specific tasks they were performing, as they increasingly experienced the value of their actions in terms of abstract, equal units of time, and as they increasingly isolated the value of the products of their labour from the materials out of which these products were composed, they appear to have been entirely unaware that it was these transformed practices as such – *their own practices* – and their own transformed experiences of time and value that were themselves in large measure responsible for the new forms of domination to which they were being subjected. Thus, by the late seventeenth century, when workers in large numbers began to complain about the time-disciplines to which they were being subjected[37] they also appear to have been entirely unaware that these disciplines had already been two centuries in the making and that they now constituted the social fabric into which all social actors – the owners of capital as well as the owners of labour – were now tightly interwoven.

And what is the evidence that this new experience of time and value had already been two centuries in the making? The evidence I would suggest is precisely in the changed attitudes admirers of the Virgin Mary displayed towards her body, the changing dispositions religious practitioners displayed towards the persistence of Jesus' wounds in heaven, the doubts doctors of philosophy and theology were beginning to entertain over the real value of precious metals, but therefore the doubts they were also beginning to entertain over God's real presence in the Holy Eucharist. In each instance, we can see an increasing readiness to isolate value – the spiritual value of Mary's body, the religious value of Jesus' wounds, the real value of precious metals, and the salutary value of God's real presence in the Eucharistic feast – from its material form of appearance. This is because ever since abstract units of time marked off by mechanical clocks first came to be used to measure the value of productive activity, social actors had grown increasingly aware of the difference between the abstract value of the articles they were producing and the materials out of which these articles were composed.

It is noteworthy in this regard that the reversal of sentiment that Peter Widdicombe found in religious attitudes towards Jesus' wounds seems to occur without cause or notice and that the transformation of Mary from a sacred body into an angelic soul appears entirely out of proportion to the cause from which it is said to spring: the increasing role played by print literature among the clergy. Once, however, we recognize the ubiquity of the chimes of church bells beginning in the fourteenth century for all Western Europeans – irrespective of their literacy, their religious convictions or theological training – and once we recognize the practical character of the transformation in time and value that was then catching hold and spreading throughout all of Europe, it becomes somewhat easier to understand how religious practitioners might over the course of two centuries be brought to experience the objects of their devotion or the instruments of their salvation in the new ways identified here. In each case, the expression of this transformation was the same. In each instance, religious practitioners were finding it easier to isolate spiritual values from their material forms of appearance; or, in the alternative, they were finding it easier to disembed and disembody the objects of their devotion, to think of these objects or processes as wholly or primarily immaterial and 'spiritual'.

The overall effect and outcome was a split in western Christendom that has shown signs of healing only within the last half century. For, notwithstanding all of the other specific causes for the rupture in western Christendom, it was this fundamental difference over the relationship between value and its material forms of appearance that ultimately brought Protestant Reformers to separate themselves from the Catholic church. More importantly, two centuries of transformed practice and experience help to explain why when Christian men and women all across Europe were told that the visible, institutional church no longer held divine sanction or authority, that the elements of the Holy Eucharist did not in fact contain Christ's Body and Blood, or that their own salvation rested not on observable practices but on unseen faith, these Christian men and women did not simply reject such claims outright as the heterodox musings of crazed heretics.

It was not the rarefied nominalist ruminations of John duns Scotus, William of Occam or Nicolas Oresme that caused this split. For the hundreds of thousands of Catholics who embraced the new Protestant teachings, most did so because the intimate relationship between spiritual value and the material things through which this value was conveyed no longer made *practical* sense to them. They did so because they knew from experience that immaterial value differed qualitatively from its material form of appearance. And they knew this because two centuries of practice had already taught them that the value of their own practices as well as the value of the products of their labour arose not from the substances out of which these products were composed, but out of the abstract labour time it had taken to compose these products generally.

Obviously, on some level and for most people, very little had changed in Western Europe between 1300 and 1600. As E.P. Thompson has shown, most social actors continued to keep two reckonings of time: one marking the new equal units of abstract time, the other displaying the concrete, variable units marked by changes in tides, seasons, meteorological patterns, lunar and solar cycles and the like. Indeed, for most social actors, whether Protestant or Catholic, it was the latter, variable time, that continued to dominate well into the nineteenth century. So, too, we know that many if not most religious practitioners, particularly in rural areas, continued to anticipate direction from God not only through the Word and Sacrament, but through Creation itself, which, or so it was argued, could legitimately serve as a vehicle for divine direction and instruction. This was explicitly so for Catholics, but it also held true for many Protestants who continued to derive moral instruction from the events (and primarily from the catastrophes) God visited upon the earth.[38]

The sublime value form of the commodity

At the same time, it must be clear that where the value of labour and the products of labour were no longer governed either by custom or by decree, and where laws respecting just price and wages were becoming increasingly de-politicized and left to rise and fall according to market forces, the relationship of immaterial value to its material forms of appearance were no longer quite as straightforward as it had been before. Prior to the fourteenth century, this relationship was subject either to natural law or to politico-religious authority. Thus, as we have seen, precious metals were believed to hold their value by nature, whereas money – the means of exchange composed out of precious metals – was believed to hold its value by political and religious authority. (Remember, Aquinas and Oresme were in fundamental agreement over the natural character of the value of *precious metals* and disagreed only over who and how the political and religious authorities should establish the value of money.) Gradually, however, the relationship of value to its material forms of appearance had also been freed from its political and religious obligations and, in a sense, returned to 'nature'. However, the nature to which value was now returned was no longer Nature as Aristotle had understood it – no longer a fixed, determinate nature whose end or goal could be scientifically discovered and rationally understood. The value of money was now subject primarily or wholly to a 'nature' composed of the collective, yet independent decisions and actions of the market place. It was subject to a nature composed of the conscious decisions of all social subjects taken as a whole as expressed in the market place. In other words, it was subject to what would subsequently be called the 'invisible hand'.

Abstract labour time had in this sense already become what Adam Smith and, on another level, what Karl Marx would describe more than two centuries later as the 'real measure of the exchange value of all commodities' (Smith)[39] or, more simply, the 'value form of the commodity' (Marx).[40] Nevertheless, we need to take care not to allow the economic form of either Smith's or Marx's descriptions overshadow the fundamentally religious and spiritual character of the transformation that had taken place. For it must be clear that from the very moment productive human activity came to be measured in equal units of abstract time, a practical transformation was already afoot that would fundamentally alter how religious practitioners also experienced and understood religious value. Whether we think here of the value of Mary's body, the value of Jesus' wounds, or the value of the Body and Blood in the Eucharist, in each instance we see the isolation of immaterial value from its material form of appearance.

Our point, however, cannot be that these religious transformations veil or conceal what were essentially economic transformations. To the contrary, our point must be that these economic transformations, grounded as they were in fundamental changes in social practices, were also at the same time religious transformations, grounded in changes that were richly displayed in and captured by religious subjectivity and practice. That is to say, this fundamental transformation in religious subjectivity and practice was also at the same time a fundamental transformation in how religious actors carried themselves in and engaged with the physical world about them. Precisely in Pierre Bourdieu's sense, therefore, we need to describe this relationship between religious subjectivity and practice as mutually constitutive.[41] The transformed practices initiated by the harnessing of productive human activity to abstract time and value reshaped how religious practitioners experienced and explained the sacred world about them; and this sacred world, thus transformed, in turn reshaped how these same religious practitioners experienced a world that from this religious vantage point was coming to appear to them increasingly profane.

The problem is, however, that recognition of the mutually constitutive character of religious subjectivity and practice, the intimate relationship between social subjectivity, including religious subjectivity, and social practice, including religious practice, was itself subverted and undermined by the new experience and understanding of value itself. This new experience and understanding suggested that, far from being contained within, subject to, or dominated by its material forms of appearance, value bore an independent and superior relationship to them. And it is here perhaps that we can speak practically and therefore intelligibly for the first time about the social and historical content of 'disenchantment'.

Disenchantment, which is often confused with secularization, does not after all entail the disappearance of religion or spirituality. Indeed, at least within the western context, it evidently meant nearly the opposite – not the disappearance, but rather the heightening, elevation, or concentration of spirituality. Not unlike the fate that awaited Rabelaisian laughter,[42] spirituality, which until the fourteenth century had not yet known embarrassment over Jesus' wounds or the sensuality of Mary's body, suddenly became aware of how different it was or, rather, how different this spirituality had become when set over against its own body. It had become aware of what Bakhtin called the 'peculiar crisis of splitting' painfully displayed in the 'double existence' which Cervantes' images of the body were forced to lead.[43] And, as a consequence, spirituality from the sixteenth century forward is even more spiritual and religion even more religious than either had been at the end of the Middle Ages. But, of course, this heightened, elevated and concentrated spirituality came at a price.

The price was not, as some have argued, the persistence of nominalist philosophy or theology. To be sure, nascent capitalism found in nominalism a ready-made theoretical system upon which to hang its new metaphysics. And, of course, it is not by accident that Protestantism, the prototypical capitalist religious formation, displayed a special fondness for nominalism. Nevertheless, without the emergence of capitalism itself in the fourteenth century, it is doubtful that duns Scotus' contest with Aquinas would have gained much traction.

The price western Christendom had to pay was the price of its own body, the body of religion, which was increasingly denied any meaningful role in the new spiritual formation. We know what this meant in practice. It meant a Holy Eucharist that was predominantly or wholly symbolic. It meant that the whole array of sacraments – seven in the Roman Catholic Church – were reduced to two vessels only (the Word and Holy Communion or Preaching and the Lord's Supper) that were believed to be divinely authorized to effectively convey or merely symbolize the conveyance of God's grace. In some ways, however, the theoretical price was even more severe than the practical. For it meant that religious value, which was no longer believed to express itself in the physical world, was for this reason no longer permitted to confirm or corroborate its own validity in the body of religion. Therein the mutually constitute character of faith and practice, of spirit and body, was practically and theoretically effaced. But, precisely because this effacement was practical, because it in fact accurately reflected a practical rupture that severed immaterial value from its material form of appearance, every subsequent merely theoretical attempt to heal this rupture has necessarily seemed forced, unnatural and implausible.

Edmund Burke, Immanuel Kant, G.F.W. Hegel and the sublime

The practical character of this rupture also helps to explain why the isolation of immaterial value from its material form of appearance, which prior to the fourteenth century seemed so patently absurd and implausible, now seems inescapable. The ultimate and most sublime values have not simply retreated from public life. Their very authenticity or validity would appear to hinge upon their isolation or independence from and hence their superiority to the merely material forces that surround but never interpenetrate or otherwise influence their sublime movement. This, in fact, was already how Immanuel Kant and Edmund Burke understood the sublime, not as something unnaturally torn from the body of religion, but as something whose very validity consisted precisely in this independence, isolation and superiority. Thus, both Kant and Burke explicitly set the sublime over against our senses. Burke in 1754 already indicated the direction the argument would take. The world of the sublime was a manifestation of terror, obscurity, power, privation, vastness, and infinity. 'Infinity', he wrote, 'has a tendency to fill the mind with that sort of delightful horror, which is the most genuine effect, and truest test of the sublime'.[44] Indeed, Burke claimed to know of nothing sublime that was not 'some modification of power. And this branch rises as naturally as the other two branches, from terror, the common stock of every thing that is sublime'.[45] Similarly, he felt that 'whatever is fitted in any sort to excite the ideas of pain, and danger, that is to say, whatever is in any sort terrible, or is conversant about terrible objects, or operates in a manner analogous to terror, is a source of the *sublime*'.[46]

Much has been made about the inherent violence of the sublime.[47] However, if the sublime appears particularly violent under Burke's hand, this may be because he was not yet ready to fully relinquish the relationship between the sublime and its material body. For Burke, the sublime still 'appears' *in* 'terrible objects', *in* 'nature', *in* 'things which *directly* suggest the idea of danger', *in* '*Vacuity, Darkness, Solitude* and *Silence*'.[48] Indeed, it is precisely Burke's inappropriate search for the sublime *in* 'things' that brought Immanuel Kant to fault Burke's treatment of the sublime and to refine and perfect Burke's *Enquiry* in his own 'Analytic of the Sublime'. In Burke's defence, as a Roman Catholic, it made a great difference whether the sublime expressed itself only beyond reason and above nature or whether, as in the Holy Eucharist or the Divine Right of a Catholic Monarch, it expressed itself in and through divinely authorized vessels. Nevertheless, as an indication of how deeply troubled Catholic thinking had grown with the new practical realities introduced by abstract value, it is worth noting that even for Burke, the sublime could no longer articulate with the physical world in a consoling, gentle, or 'natural' manner. When it penetrates the material world, the sublime terrifies and horrifies. It induces astonishment, it brings pain and 'effectually robs the mind of all its powers of acting and reasoning'.[49] For Burke, this ability to induce terror proved to him that God still held the capacity to turn material objects to divine ends, for he realized that since, by itself, nature was entirely reasonable, the horror it induced in us must of necessity arise from some other region. Our experience of power, vastness and infinity through material objects was, in this sense, proof of the validity of the Catholic understanding of the sacraments. Our experience of the sublime in nature proved that God could use material objects to direct our attention to those things that by their very nature were not subject to our senses. The violence and terror of the sublime were evidence of the divine presence. Kant, Burke's Protestant contemporary, drew a slightly different conclusion.

'*Sublime*', wrote Kant in 1790, '*is what even to be able to think proves that the mind has a power surpassing any standard of sense*'.[50] If Kant's interpretation of the sublime is less violent and terrifying, at least on its surface, this may have been not only because Königsberg was a less violent and terrifying place in the 1790s than Burke's England in the 1750s, but also because unlike Burke, Kant was free from the dogmatic constraint imposed by the divine presence. He was therefore free to reject the violent collision Burke imagined between the sublime and its material form of appearance and replace it with the, for us more familiar, complete isolation of the sublime from the world of the senses. 'Hence, considered on this basis', Kant concluded against Burke, 'nothing that can be an object of the senses is to be called sublime'.[51] This is not to say that Kant rejected Burke's association of the sublime with violence in its entirety. For Kant, however, Burke's association was overly physical and material[52] and for this reason it directed our attention in the entirely wrong direction, not towards our divine vocation, but towards our earthly bondage.

> [W]e must point to the sublime not in products of art (e.g., buildings, columns, etc.), where both the form and the magnitude are determined by a human purpose, nor in natural things *whose very concept carries with it a determinate purpose* (e.g., animals with a known determination in nature), but rather in crude nature (and even in it only insofar as it carries with it no charm, nor any emotion aroused by actual danger), that is, merely insofar as crude nature contains magnitude.[53]

Magnitude or 'vastness' also figured in Burke's *Enquiry*. But, in Kant's opinion, it pointed in the wrong direction. Where Burke pointed to the objects or things that horrified or terrified those who beheld them, Kant invited his readers to bracket and dismiss the material forms of their appearance. 'A pure judgment about the sublime', he believed, 'must have no purpose whatsoever of the object as the basis determining it, if it is to be aesthetic and not mingled with some judgment of understanding or of reason'.[54] And this is certainly a large part of the reason why Kant focused less on the violence, horror, pain and terror of the sublime than on its pure magnitude.

'We call *sublime* what is *absolutely* [*schlechthin*] *large*'.[55] And for this reason, the violence that Kant contemplates is not limited to the body. Kant contemplates a violence inflicted by the sublime upon the mind, which simultaneously perceives the sublime, but recognizes its incapacity to grasp what it perceives.

What we perceive is something that Kant had already argued as superior to our senses, which of course are only suited to perceiving things that are relatively and not absolutely large.

> Now the greatest effort of the imagination in exhibiting the unity the imagina-tion needs to estimate magnitude is itself a reference to something *large absolutely*, and hence also a reference to reason's law to adopt only this something as the supreme measure of magnitude. Hence our inner perception that every standard of sensibility is inadequate for an estimation of magnitude by reason is itself a harmony with laws of reason, as well as a displeasure that arouses in us the feeling of our supersensible vocation, according to which finding that every standard of sensibility is inadequate to the ideas of reason is purposive and hence pleasurable.[56]

What we perceive, in other words, is something beyond our senses. But, unlike our perception of the beautiful, which reinforces our senses, our perception of the sublime conflicts with our senses. It conflicts with our senses because we are sensibly incapable of perceiving that which is absolutely large. Our incapacity, it should be noted, does not arise however solely from our inability to physically take in absolute magnitude, but primarily because we do not command the time necessary to comprehend that which is absolutely large in a single instant. As Lukács rightly perceived, space and time had thus become indistinguishable.[57] We are therefore compelled to divide the absolutely large, as though it were some *thing* that could be made more manageable through division; which, of course, is absurd.

> Measuring (as [a way of] apprehending) a space is at the same time describing it, and hence it is an objective movement in the imagination and a progression. On the other hand, comprehending a multiplicity in a unity (of intuition rather than of thought), and hence of comprehending in one instant what is appre-hended successively, is a regression that in turn cancels the condition of time in the imagination's progression and makes simultaneity intuitable. Hence, (since temporal succession is a condition of the inner sense and of an intuition) it is a subjective movement of the imagination by which it does violence to the inner sense [*inner Sinne Gewalt antut*], and this violence must be the more significant the larger the quantum is that the imagination comprehends in one intuition. . . . And yet this same violence [*Gewalt*] that the imagination inflicts on the subject is still judged purposive *for the whole vocation* of the mind.[58]

And this violence is purposive precisely because it shows that 'the mind has a power surpassing any standard of sense'.[59] Thus, albeit in language seemingly more tame and humane than Burke's, Kant was nonetheless able to affirm with him that 'the object is apprehended as sublime with a pleasure that is possible only by means of displeasure'.[60] Or, as he pointed out in another context, while the 'beautiful prepares us for loving something, even nature, without interest; the sublime [prepares us] for esteeming it even against the interest of our senses'.[61]

Obviously it is of some importance to determine whether Kant understood this opposition of the sublime to the interest of our senses, as Burke did, in more than a purely theoretical sense. Hegel did not think so.[62]

> Kant's view is that "the sublime, in the strict sense of the word, cannot be contained in any sensuous form but concerns only Ideas of Reason which, although no adequate representation of them is possible, may be aroused and called to our mind precisely by this inadequacy which does admit of sensuous representation" (Critique of Judgment, 1799, p. 77 [§ 23]). The sublime in general is the attempt to express the infinite, without finding in the sphere of phenomena an object which proves adequate for this representation. Precisely because the infinite is set apart from the entire complex of objectivity as explicitly an invisible meaning devoid of shape and is made inner, it remains, in accordance with its infinity, unutterable and sublime above any expression through the finite.[63]

Thus, unlike Burke's sublime, in Hegel's view, Kant's sublime, however violent in theory, remained remarkably tame in practice. Indeed, in opposition to this remote Kantian sublime, Hegel urged that we rediscover the sublime ground of the material world.

> This outward shaping which is itself annihilated in turn by what it reveals, so that the revelation of the content is at the same time a supersession of the revelation, is the sublime. This, therefore, differing from Kant, we need not place in the pure subjectivity of the mind and its Ideas of Reason; on the contrary, we must grasp it as grounded in the one absolute substance [*eine absolute Substanz*] *qua* the content which is to be represented.[64]

What in Kant still bore a purely formal character, here in Hegel breaks out into the open. Did Hegel then endorse Burke's physiological sublime? Clearly not, but neither did he endorse Kant's overly formal sublime. Instead, he invited his readers to embrace the living, powerful and actively creative and destructive absolute substance.

It is clear then that Hegel did not intend that we return to the thirteenth century. He did not intend that we abandon or forget the isolation of abstract value from its material body. Nor did he intend that we rediscover Jesus' wounds in heaven, or the comforts of Mary's body, or the divine taste of Jesus' Body and Blood. To the contrary, the isolation of the sublime from its material form of appearance, which in Kant still bore traces of its relative, contingent and historical origins, Hegel now perceived as a single unified absolute substance, *das Erhabene*, the Sublime, underlying and bearing the material world forward.

And it is here that we again meet the object of Weber's 7 November 1917 lamentation, the sublime, except that Weber, in contrast to Hegel, explicitly prohibits the sublime from bearing the world forward. To the contrary, since Weber was a Kantian, the sublime must retreat inward. That is to say, it must behave much more nearly as Kant suggested it would and should. It cannot display itself in natural or public objects. For, as we have seen, were it to do so, it would invalidate its very authenticity. Instead, the sublime must retreat from public life into what Hegel derisively called 'the pure subjectivity of the mind and its Ideas of Reason'.[65] It must retreat into 'the smallest and intimate circles', into 'personal human situations'; it must restrict itself to 'the brotherliness of direct and personal human relations . . . in *pianissimo*'.[66] And, so, at least in Weber's opinion and in the opinion of traditional sociology, ultimate and sublime values have retreated or been forced to retreat from public life, from *Öffentlichkeit*, into the bourgeois interior.

Did Weber's contemporaries share his views? It seems not, or not entirely. The standard household dictionary in Weber's Germany, *Der Grosse Brockhaus*, defined the sublime as follows:

> **Sublime:** an object or process whose inner excellence abnormally heightens or threatens to shatter its material form of appearance. The force it exerts must be greater than normal. Examples: the stormy sea is sublime in contrast to other powerful expressions of nature, the expanse of the heavens is sublime in contrast to other experiences of space; the art of an Aeschylus, Dante, Michelangelo is sublime because in it humans are drawn up into the superhuman. As subspecies of the sublime, we often include "dignity," the "solemn" and the "pathetic." If we explore the subjective meaning of the sublime, we find many terrors, even fear, but always inner ennoblement, a certain compulsion to transgress the boundaries of normal everyday experience.[67]

Was Weber then the only German in 1917 who did not appreciate the profoundly public and therefore profoundly dangerous character of the sublime? My best guess is that he appreciated it far better than most of his contemporaries. Thus his lamentation.

4   The 'spirit' of capitalism

First published just over a century ago in the spring 1904 and 1905 issues of *Archiv für Sozialwissenschaft und Sozialpolitik*, Weber's *Protestant Ethic and the 'Spirit' of Capitalism* brilliantly captures the complex mutually constitutive relationships that play out between a scholar's interpretive framework, the object of that scholar's research and the socio-historical context within which the research is conducted. In this case, Weber's *Protestant Ethic* illustrated how an object of social scientific research, the 'spirit' of capitalism, could help constitute the very social and historical conditions that made that research, including the selection of this object, possible in the first place. As we will see, what this meant practically was that Weber saw the social and historical conditions created by the 'spirit' of capitalism and by capitalism itself as preconditions for his own methodological isolation of this 'spirit' from the endless variety of other 'historical individuals' that also presented themselves as possible objects of social scientific research. In other words, Weber came to view capitalism not only as the object of his research, but, since capitalism was responsible for isolating religious asceticism from the material forms in which religious practitioners had formerly placed their trust, Weber also came to view capitalism as the precondition for his own research.

Here it is worth noting that Weber's earlier attempt in 1902 to develop a purely formal articulation of his unique approach to social scientific research, since it failed to adequately confront the social and historical conditions that had made this approach possible, had not proven entirely satisfying. On a purely formal level, Weber could already see in 1902 that settling upon one socio-historical feature that caught his attention, such as the 'spirit' of capitalism, when he might just as easily have settled upon another, lent a certain arbitrariness to the whole enterprise of social scientific research.[1] But, was his interest in the 'spirit' of capitalism really as arbitrary as it might have appeared?

The problem

I would argue that it was not arbitrary, and not simply because, as he put the matter in the lead article for the inaugural issue of the *Archiv* also published in 1904, the 'spirit' of capitalism was 'meaningful to us'.[2] For this begs the questions, why, in what ways and for what reasons was the 'spirit' of capitalism 'meaningful' (*bedeutsam*)? As Weber himself remarked in the same article:

All the analysis of infinite reality which the finite human mind can conduct rests on the tacit assumption that only a finite portion of this reality constitutes the object of scientific investigation, and that only it is "important" in the sense of being "worthy of being known." But what are the criteria by which this segment is selected?[3]

Why the 'spirit' of capitalism, or why the protestant ethic? The most compelling answer, though by no means the only one, that strikes me appears in a seemingly peripheral remark towards the end of Weber's article. There Weber acknowledged that while the presupposition of all knowledge, whether social or natural scientific, is 'the *value* of those *truths* which empirical knowledge alone is able to give us, ... belief in the value of scientific truth is the product of certain cultures and is not a product of man's original nature'.[4] In this sense, the meaning Weber found in the 'spirit' of capitalism and the protestant ethic can be ascribed to his interest in understanding why, as he put it in the 1920 'Introduction' to his *Collected Works on the Sociology of Religion*, it was 'only in Western civilization that cultural phenomenon appeared (or so we like to think) that lie in a line of development having universal significance and value'.[5] But even this query of the ostensible universal significance and value of scientific truth elides the pathos this question generated for Weber.

This pathos is potently conveyed only on the final page of Weber's 1904 essay on 'Objectivity', where he cast his gaze forward to a time when value-relevance itself might lose its significance.

> All research in the cultural sciences in an age of specialization, once it is oriented towards a given subject matter through particular settings of problems and has established its methodological principles, will consider the analysis of the data as an end in itself. It will discontinue assessing the value of the individual facts in terms of their relations to ultimate value-ideas. Indeed, it will lose its awareness of its ultimate rootedness in the value-ideas in general.[6]

Obviously this cold, analytical, disinterested handling of the facts pointed to a serious diminution in the meaning and value that social actors might attribute to or find in them. Still, at least at this point, Weber could give what appears to be unequivocal approval to this lost awareness of the value-relevance of research. 'It is well that it should be so.' And, yet, his approval is immediately cast in doubt. 'But there comes a moment when the atmosphere changes', noted Weber. 'The significance of the unreflectively utilized viewpoints becomes uncertain and the road is lost in the twilight.' And, now, standing face to face with the 'last men' (*letzten Menschen*) who would figure so large at the conclusion of his *Protestant Ethic* – those 'specialists without spirit, hedonists without a heart' – Weber could not help but qualify his approval. 'Then science too prepares to change its standpoint and its analytical apparatus and to view the streams of events from the heights of thought. It follows those stars which alone are able to give meaning and direction to its labours.' And then came Weber's much-remarked upon conclusion drawn from Act I, Scene II, of Goethe's *Faust*, where Faust cries: 'The newborn impulse fires my mind; I hasten on, his beams eternal drinking; The Day before me and the Night behind; Above me Heaven unfurled, the floor of waves beneath me'.[7]

And, yet, within this context, Weber's reference to Faust was wholly understandable and fully in agreement with his remarks thirteen years later to his distinguished listeners in Munich. There as well, for those who wished to pursue social scientific research believing that it would illuminate the path to true being, true art, true nature or true God, Weber could only redirect their attention to the 'streams of events from the heights of thought', which, for Weber, naturally recalled Goethe and Goethe's Faust. However, for those who were in search of some meaningful explanation for why the world about them no longer offered a path to true being, art, nature or God, who were instead eager to learn of the 'combination of circumstances' that had simultaneously elevated empirical science and degraded ultimate and final values, Weber offered his study of the *Protestant Ethic*.

But if this was what Weber believed to have been of cultural interest in the 'spirit' of capitalism and the protestant ethic, then why did he introduce his study with an entirely different problem; not with problems surrounding the social and historical constitution of modern science, but instead with the problem of why social actors from predominantly Protestant regions of Germany and Europe proved themselves better workers and businessmen than social actors from predominantly Catholic regions? Weber set out from this question, it is clear, because in his view the formation of the modern scientific outlook was not fundamentally a matter of philosophical or theoretical reflection, but rather a matter of cultural, economic and social practices. To demonstrate that this was so, Weber invited his readers to reflect upon the cultural dimensions of a phenomenon of which most Germans believed they had a firm grasp: the relative economic backwardness of Catholics in Germany. The question for Weber was, how can we account for this backwardness?

Capitalism and religion

Weber believed he had found the answer to this question in '*distinct mental characteristics [anerzogene geistige Eigenart]* which have been instilled into [Catholics]' and in 'the influence on them of the religious atmosphere of their locality and home background'.[8] To the suggestion that Catholic economic backwardness had been the result of political persecution, Weber pointed out that elsewhere, among Poles in Russia, Huguenots in France, Nonconformists and Quakers in England, and Jews throughout Europe, political persecution had had the very opposite effect.

> When excluded from politically influential positions by the dominant group (or when choosing to exclude themselves), these minority groups generally come under *particular* pressure to pursue a business career; in this way their most talented members seek to achieve the ambition that can find no fulfilment within the service of the state.[9]

'It follows', thought Weber, 'that the reason for these differences in attitude must be sought principally in their distinct internal characteristics [*dauernden inneren Eigenart*] and *not* in the external historical and political situation of different denominations'.[10] This may have suggested that Weber bought into the belief, widely entertained by German Protestants, that 'the greater "*unworldliness*" of Catholicism'[11] was to blame for their economic backwardness. He did not. Nor did he buy into the belief, widely entertained by German Catholics, that Protestant economic success was a reflection of their 'materialism', which Catholics believed to have been the 'consequence of the way Protestantism has secularized every aspect of life'. Both explanations were in Weber's view 'too general to explain anything'.

At issue, thought Weber, was neither unworldliness nor materialism, but rather the specific kind of unworldliness or materialism that predisposed the first Protestants to display what at the time must have seemed from an economic point of view entirely irrational conduct. After all, Weber pointed out, what was striking among those groups that pioneered the new economic rationality was not their materialism, but 'the combination of religious control of life and an extremely well developed business sense which existed within a number of those sects renowned equally for their detachment from the world and their prosperity.' Here, Weber felt that Montesquieu's insight respecting the success of the English was particularly *a propos*: 'This is the people in the world who have best known how to take advantage of each of these three great things at the same time: religion, commerce and liberty.' 'Could it be', asked Weber, 'that their superiority in the field of commerce and ... their aptitude for free political institutions perhaps have some connection with that unrivalled degree of piety that Montesquieu attributed to them?'[12]

The problem, for Weber, was thus how to grasp a social form or constellation of social forms sufficient to account for these two seemingly contradictory dispositions: the disposition on the one hand to success in business and on the other hand the disposition for religious piety. To capture this constellation of seemingly contradictory forms Weber settled upon a figure, the 'spirit' of capitalism, which seemed on its very face to embody these contradictory qualities. How, after all, could capitalism, renowned for its materialism, possess anything remotely connected to a 'spirit'? Still, as Weber had already pointed out and would seek to demonstrate in great detail throughout the remainder of his study, the fact was that the first pioneers of capitalism were deeply religious individuals who, if anything, displayed an exaggerated distrust for attachment to material possessions. In this light, Weber saw his task as attempting to '*formulate* as clearly as possible what we are vaguely aware of, given the inexhaustible complexity of all historical phenomena'.[13]

Here, however, the impression Weber left is that his interest in exploring this 'spirit', the reason it proved meaningful to him and to others, was its capacity to explain the relative economic success of Protestants when compared to Catholics, which, without question, was an interesting topic. However, as his study unfolds, it quickly becomes clear that the '*cultural significance*'[14] that Weber attributed to this social form had less to do with differences between Catholics and Protestants than it did with a fateful contradiction he discerned within the 'spirit' of capitalism itself. The 'spirit' of capitalism was meant to capture the unity of this internally contradictory social form. Its significance or meaning consisted in its ability to conceptually pull together these two historical configurations. The 'spirit' of capitalism, in other words, fulfilled the conditions that Weber established for any object of social scientific research. As Weber explained at the beginning of his *Protestant Ethic*:

> If any object can be found for which the use of this term [i.e., "Spirit of Capitalism"] can have any meaning, then it can only be a *"historical individual,"* that is, a complex of configurations [*Zusammenhängen*] in historical reality which we group together conceptually from the point of view of their *cultural significance* to form a single whole [*zu einem Ganzen zusammenschließen*].[15]

To illustrate the significance of this 'historical individual' Weber next quoted at some length from two pamphlets, the first written by Benjamin Franklin, *Advice to a Young Tradesman*, in 1748. Contrasting Franklin's advice to the crassly chrematistic disposition of the businessman Jakob Fugger (who 'intended to go on making money as long as he could'), Weber went on to note how 'what in the case of Fugger expresses commercial daring and a personal inclination, ethically neutral, has for Franklin the character of an ethically slanted maxim for the conduct of life.' It was, wrote Weber, in *'this specific sense that we propose to use the concept of the "spirit of capitalism"'*.[16]

But how did social actors come to embrace hard work and parsimony as an ethically slanted maxim for the conduct of their lives? The answer, believed Weber, had to do with the peculiar way that Protestants had come to view their *religious* duty in terms of their pursuit of a 'calling' (*Berufspflicht*), and not simply any calling, but, more specifically, a calling to a *secular* or *worldly* occupation (*weltlichen Berufslebens*).[17] This view differed dramatically from *traditional* perspectives not only on work, but also on what could and could not rightly be considered a religious duty. Here as we have already noted, the principle difference however was not that social actors in traditional societies failed to see the religious significance of everyday practices and common artifacts in their lives. To the contrary, social actors in traditional societies were liable to find a religious significance in everything they encountered. What was peculiar about the new attitude was precisely that the religious duty social actors sought to fulfil in their secular callings had nothing to do with the *substance* of this calling. As distinguished from traditional social actors, Protestants, in other words, did not anticipate their everyday practices to offer divine guidance or convey grace to them in any substantial form. As Weber would reiterate throughout his study, what was therefore peculiar about the new discipline of labour was that social actors performed their work 'as though it were an absolute *end in itself* [*absoluter Selbstzweck*] – a "calling"'.[18] Indeed, from a traditionalist vantage point, thought Weber, this pursuit of a calling for its own sake was completely senseless. 'It is precisely this however that seems so incomprehensible and puzzling, so sordid and contemptible, to precapitalist man'.[19]

Therefore, to explain the emergence of this new understanding of one's professional calling and, more importantly, to explain why anyone would have embraced it, Weber set out to review in some detail the various conceptions of work held and defended by the spokesmen of the leading protestant sects. Here there were no surprises. Luther, or so Weber thought, was even more traditionalist when it came to his views on the religious duty Christians fulfilled in their callings. According to Weber, 'Luther was suspicious of the element of *ascetic self-discipline*' displayed in too serious a devotion to one's vocation; it 'smacked of sanctification by works and as such was increasingly discouraged by his Church'.[20] The emergence of this new understanding of vocation therefore had to come not from Luther or from Lutheranism, but from elsewhere. It appeared, not surprisingly, in Calvinism and the Protestant sects that traced themselves to the Protestant reformed tradition.

The key for Weber was Calvinism's peculiar doctrine of divine election to salvation, the doctrine according to which God was held to have predestined from all eternity those who would be saved from eternal damnation; and, at least in its most developed and consistent form, the doctrine that God had also decreed from all eternity those who would not be saved.[21] Why this doctrine should have given Christians the liberty to view their secular vocations as a religious duty, however, is far from self-evident. As has frequently been noted, since their destiny has already been determined from all eternity, it seems more natural to assume that individuals would come to view their actions as entirely immaterial to their eternal destiny. And, yet, as Weber pointed out, such indifference grossly underestimated the seriousness with which sixteenth century individuals viewed the matter of their eternal destiny.

> In what was for the people of the Reformation age the most crucial concern of life, their eternal salvation, man was obliged to tread his path alone, toward a destiny which had been decreed from all eternity. No one and nothing could help him. Not the preacher – for only the elect could spiritually understand the word of God. Not the sacraments – for although the sacraments were decreed by God for his greater glory and were therefore to be steadfastly observed, they were not a means of attaining the grace of God but were only subjective "externa subsidia" of faith. Not the Church – for although the principle "extra ecclesiam nulla salus" still applied, in the sense that anyone who remained apart from the true Church could never be among the elect of God, the reprobate also belonged to the (outward) Church, indeed they *must* belong to it and be subject to its discipline, not in order to attain salvation through it – that was impossible – but because they too must be compelled to abide by God's commandments for his glory. Finally – not even God, for Christ had died for the elect alone; God had determined from all eternity that Christ's sacrificial death should be for their benefit alone.[22]

Far from providing means through which God could provide grace to believers, which was still true in some sense for Lutherans, the world of the Calvinist was a means through which Christians glorified God in all their conduct. Yet, according to Weber, even obedient conduct was completely emptied of its substantive religious significance. 'Linked with the harsh doctrine of the absolute worthlessness and remoteness from God of all mere creatures', Weber argued, 'this inner isolation of man contained, on the one hand, the basis for the absolutely negative attitude of Puritanism toward all sensual and *emotional* elements in culture and subjective religiosity.' 'It thus formed the basis,' he thought, 'for a fundamental rejection of every kind of culture of the senses.' This, of course, is fully consistent not only with Kant's account of the sublime, but also with Marx's account of abstract value. However, this inner isolation also 'formed one of the roots of that *disillusioned* and *pessimistically* tinted *individualism* which is still discernible in the "national character" and the institutions of peoples with a Puritan past'.[23] Given this rejection of the senses and this pessimism, one might well wonder why Calvinists would feel any compulsion whatever to view their secular profession as in any sense a divine service to God.

Yet, according to Weber, there was one small caveat to this whole dreary scheme. Granted that individuals could never be completely certain of their eternal destiny; and granted that nothing individuals could do could alter God's eternal decree. Still, since divine election produced in those whom God *would* save the obedience that brought glory to God's name, it stood to reason that those whom God had elected would display signs of God's grace in the ways that they conducted their lives. 'The Reformed Christian, too, wants to be saved "sola fide"', noted Weber, 'but since in Calvin's view all one's feelings and moods, however sublime they may appear, are deceptive, faith must prove itself in its objective *effects*, if it is to serve as a reliable guarantee of *certitude salutis*: it must be a "fides efficax"'.[24] So, while they could never be completely certain of their eternal destiny, individuals could be certain that if they were among the elect, their conduct, including their conduct in a secular vocation, would complement this election, always to God's greater glory. Obviously, this meant a considerable amount of self-examination or testing (*Bewährung*) and a good deal of examination of others as well to ensure that all conduct was performed in full conformity to the full counsel of God and, as always, to God's greater glory. But what was crucial, according to Weber, 'was always the view (which recurs in all denominations) of the religious "state of grace" as a status that separates man from the depravity of the creaturely and from the "world"'.

> Possession of this status, however – no matter how the dogmas of the different denominations might teach their followers to acquire it – could only be guaranteed by *proving oneself* [*Bewährung*] in a specific form of conduct unambiguously distinct from the style of life of the "natural" man. The consequence for the individual was the drive to *keep a methodical check* on his state of grace as shown in how he conducted his life and thus to ensure that his life was imbued with *asceticism*.

But, according to Weber, this could only mean 'a *rational* shaping of one's whole existence in obedience to God's will'. And, for Weber, it was this '*rationalization* of the conduct of life in the world with a view to the beyond' that was itself 'the *idea of the calling* characteristic of ascetic Protestantism'.[25]

Of course – and this was Weber's point – this *rationalization* was itself part and parcel of the 'spirit' of capitalism. For, once it had acquired this uniquely practical character, this form of rationalism proved itself infinitely superior to every other form of economic rationality it encountered.

> Now it would enter the market place of life, slamming the doors of the monastery behind it, and set about permeating precisely this secular everyday life with its methodical approach, turning it toward a rational life *in* the world, but neither *of* this world nor *for* it.[26]

Was then Weber's initial interest in the difference between Catholic and Protestant economic conduct a misstep or, worse, a sham? Not at all, Weber's aim was to show that this difference was grounded not in one or another superficial chance trait that Catholics or Protestants might display, but rather in 'a complex of configurations' which 'from the point of view of their *cultural significance* ... form a single whole'.[27]

Having identified and described this whole in some detail, it now remained for Weber to show how this historical individual, the 'spirit' of capitalism, had in fact come to completely dominate the totality of social life. His proof was simple, yet profoundly influential. As he had already shown, the Protestant ethic compelled individuals to prove their election by rationally and methodically applying themselves in a secular vocation. This proving of oneself was *ascetic*, however, not because it consisted of tireless labour, but because those who performed this labour were explicitly prohibited from attaching religious significance to the specific practices in which they were engaged. 'A religious value was placed on ceaseless, constant, systematic labour in a secular calling,' Weber noted, 'as the very highest ascetic path and at the same time the surest and most visible proof of regeneration and the genuineness of faith.' Yet, individuals were also prohibited from engaging in activities that could be judged wasteful, unproductive, covetous, greedy or otherwise indicative of a depraved soul. 'While favouring the *production* of private economic wealth,' noted Weber, 'asceticism was opposed to injustice and purely *instinctive* greed'.[28] More importantly, 'if that restraint on consumption is *combined with* the freedom to strive for profit, the result produced will inevitably be the *creation of capital* through the *ascetic compulsion to save*'. For this reason, Weber believed that the Puritan philosophy of life 'always benefited the tendency toward a middle-class economically *rational* conduct of life'. 'It stood,' he felt, 'at the cradle of modern "economic man"'.[29]

It only remained for Weber to draw this complex of configurations, the 'spirit' of capitalism, forward to the present. He did so by calling attention to the confidence that Puritans felt over their ability to withstand the temptations presented by the unprecedented wealth they had produced and by contrasting this confidence to the complete domination victorious capitalism had in fact achieved over all aspects of life, public and private. Thus, whereas the Puritan writer Richard Baxter had felt that 'concern for outward possessions should sit lightly on the shoulders of his saints "like a thin cloak which can be thrown off at any time,"' Weber believed that 'fate decreed that the cloak should become a shell as hard as steel' – *ein stahlhartes Gehäuse* – or 'iron cage'. Again, it was not as though social actors had ceased believing or showing interest in things religious or spiritual. But, because of the contradictory character of this *historical individual*, because this variety of religious asceticism practically predisposed religious actors to deprive the material world of all religious value or significance, it actively helped constitute a world that in the end proved hostile to its interests. For, Weber noted, 'as asceticism began to change the world and endeavoured to exercise its influence over it, the outward goods of this world gained increasing and finally inescapable power over men, as never before in history'.[30]

The mechanistic *Triebwerk* of capitalism and its sublime spirit

Weber's imagery here is instructive, recalling a kind of materialistic determinism towards which he otherwise displayed only contempt. And, yet, within this context,

Weber had little trouble describing 'victorious capitalism' as 'that mighty cosmos of the modern economic order (which is bound to the technical and economic conditions of mechanical and machine production)'.[31]

> Today this mighty cosmos determines, with overwhelming coercion [*mit über-wältigendem Zwange bestimmt*], the style of life *not only* of those directly involved in business but of every individual who is born into this mechanism, and may well continue to do so until the day that the last ton of fossil fuel has been consumed.[32]

But, then, in language similar to the language we found in his Munich address, Weber described how the spirit of asceticism, this *historical individual* that had proven so powerful in helping him to explain the formation of modern capitalism, had retreated from the world it had thus helped create. 'Today its spirit has fled from this shell – whether for all time, who knows? Certainly, victorious capitalism has no further need for this support now that it rests on the foundation of the machine.'

However, in contrast to the tenderness with which Weber would describe the occupants of the bourgeois interior only twelve years later, here in 1905 Weber adopted an openly mocking tone. 'Even the optimistic mood of its laughing heir, the Enlightenment, seems destined to fade away, and the idea of the "duty in a calling" haunts our lives like the ghost of once-held religious beliefs.' And, so, consistently Weber called attention not to the direct and personal human relations these social actors forged or how the prophetic spirit that lit up their intimate circles was comparable to the spirit that long ago welded the tribes of Yahweh together. Instead he called attention to how these social actors resembled Friedrich Nietzsche's 'last men': 'specialists without spirit, hedonists without heart, these nonentities imagine they have attained a stage of humankind never before reached'.[33]

Even here, however, Weber's description of contemporary social actors obviously referred to how they conducted themselves in public life – as civil servants, accountants, bureaucrats, administrators and professors – which, as we know, is far different from how they might have conducted themselves in their own homes surrounded by family and friends. For although Weber did not specifically call attention to the spirit that fills the bourgeois interior, we cannot automatically conclude that his account entirely precluded this possibility. Indeed, if we pause to consider the vantage point from which Weber composed his account, a vantage point which after all allowed him to appreciate the emptiness and meaninglessness of the 'last men' he described, it makes sense to presume that this vantage point was itself lodged in a place not unlike the bourgeois interior Weber described at the conclusion to his address in Munich – a vantage point that he would elsewhere describe as 'religious'.

Below we will seek to come to terms with this vantage point in a somewhat more rigorous manner. Here, however, it should be noted that without this vantage point it would have been impossible for Weber to develop the kind of narrative he did. It would have been impossible because it was this vantage point that first allowed social actors to 'step outside' the built world in which they were seated and to set themselves over against this world. After all, this world could no longer have any sacramental value for them. In this sense as well, then, when the 'spirit' of capitalism formed the basis for what Weber called 'a fundamental rejection of every kind of culture of the senses',[34] or when it taught believers 'to lead a life which is dead to the influences of the world and based on the will of God in every detail',[35] this could only reinforce the conviction that the sensible world held no mystery. The mystery was therefore wholly in the supersensible world which Kant and, much later, Weber himself would call the 'sublime'. Here then was the vantage point from which the wasteland of victorious capitalism came into focus for Weber. But it may never have done so were it not for Weber's encounter during the spring of 1902 with Heinrich Rickert's *Die Grenzen der naturwissenschaftlichen Begriffsbildung* (*The limits of concept formation in the natural sciences*).[36]

Immanuel Kant, Heinrich Rickert and Max Weber

Guy Oakes has correctly noted that Weber's career as a social theorist did not begin in 1904 with his work on '"Objectivity" in the social sciences and social policy', but in 1902 with his critical essay on Wilhelm Roscher and Karl Knies.[37] Perhaps more tellingly it began after Weber read Heinrich Rickert's book on the limits of concept formation in the natural sciences. As Marianne Weber recounts, it was during the summer of 1902, while Weber was away convalescing in Florence, that she received his letter. 'I have finished Rickert. He is very good; in large part I find in him the thoughts that I have had myself, though not in logically finished form'.[38] And while Weber admitted in his letter to having 'reservations about his terminology', it is noteworthy how many of the concepts that appeared in Weber's works between 1902 and 1905 – historical individual, causal nexus, complex of configurations or constellation, imputation – first appeared in Rickert's 1902 study. Indeed, it could be argued that Weber's *Protestant Ethic* was a cleverly devised intellectual experiment with which he sought to test the validity of Rickert's conceptual framework on an actual complex of configurations which together composed the historical individual, the 'spirit' of capitalism.

But perhaps Weber's study turned out the way it did, not because this spirit actually had flown from the iron cage, but rather because, by definition, things as law-bound and mechanical as social life had become within the iron cage could not contain historical individuals. Indeed, both Rickert and Weber repeatedly returned to the same fundamental point: in their view historical individuals were foreign to the laws of natural science. As Rickert had pointed out in his *Grenzen*, historical individuals differed from natural scientific objects not in regards to the selection and simplification that every researcher was obligated to perform. 'As regards simplification, therefore, the product of this sort of concept formation is analogous to that of natural science'.[39] Where they differed was in the substantive results to which each was driven by the logic of their concept formation. For, as Rickert observed,

As regards the substantive result of concept formation, however, they are logically antithetical. The concept of natural science comprises what is common to several individual configurations. What belongs to single individuals alone is excluded from the content of the concept itself. When the concept is formed *on the basis* of a single individual reality, however, the historical concept includes precisely what distinguishes the different individuals from one another.[40]

The logical antithesis that Rickert and Weber discerned between objects of natural scientific research and the historical individuals of social scientific research need not have implied a hostility between the two. Neither Rickert nor Weber ever gave any indication that they bore animosity toward the natural sciences. Their disagreement, it is clear, was with their colleagues, in both the social and natural sciences, who violated the logical antithesis separating these two areas of scientific research, either by grounding natural scientific research upon historical individuals or by treating historical individuals as though they were subject to generalizable, abstract, social or historical laws.

Was this then the antagonism that Weber was actually trying to articulate, an antagonism between what was irreducibly itself and therefore could not be generalized into a universal law, on the one hand, and a social formation that was growing increasingly law-bound and mechanical on the other? This is clearly how Jürgen Habermas has interpreted Weber's approach.[41] But, read how Weber summarized the matter in his 1904 essay on '"Objectivity" in the Social Sciences'. Following Rickert almost word for word, Weber agrees that

> the focus of attention on reality under the guidance of values which lend it significance and the selection and ordering of the phenomena which are thus affected in the light of their cultural significance is entirely different from the analysis of reality in terms of laws and general concepts.[42]

Or, again, Weber was all too ready to admit to the 'one-sidedness' of his approach to the social sciences because, in his view, the reasons for this one-sidedness lay 'in the character of the cognitive goal of all research in social science which seeks to transcend the purely *formal* treatment of the legal or conventional norms regulating social life'.[43] And, against those social scientists who claimed that the '"laws" which we are able to perceive in the infinitely manifold stream of events must … contain the scientifically "essential" aspect of reality',[44] Weber shot back that, like the social sciences, many of the natural sciences (Weber thought of astronomy) also concerned themselves with *individual* phenomena, although not historical individuals.

> But [astronomy] too concerns itself with the question of the *individual* consequence which the working of these laws in an unique *configuration* produces, since it is these individual configurations which are *significant* for us. … As far back as we may go into the grey mist of the far-off past, the reality to which the laws apply always remains equally *individual*, equally *undeducible* from laws.[45]

And, so, for Weber, the deeper, more fundamental and authentic *meaning* of 'laws', whether natural or social scientific, concerned their '*significance* for us'. If, for purely historical reasons, the natural sciences were compelled to abstract from individual phenomena to the general laws 'under' which these phenomena were placed, as instances of the law, this did not mean that 'reality' was composed in such a way that the 'laws' under which empirical reality 'fell' in any sense held greater validity or reality than the individuals themselves. In any case, Weber felt certain that 'it is not a question of the subsumption of the event under some general rubric as a representative case but of its imputation as a consequence of some constellation'.[46]

Because it would assume such terrible significance for Weber's admirer, the young Georg Lukács, we will take up Weber's notion of imputation later in our study. Here, we need simply to bear in mind that Weber's neo-Kantian theory of imputation allowed Lukács to ascribe to historical individuals qualities and characteristics that empirically they might not actually possess. We will take up this problem directly later on. Here, we are interested in explaining how Weber's reliance upon Rickert may have shaped his approach to religion and capitalism. We need to ask what light Weber's embrace of Rickert's neo-Kantian philosophy of science might shed upon the conclusions he was to draw in his *Protestant Ethic*.

At the very least, recognition of Weber's relationship to Rickert helps us to make sense of Weber's commitment to the 'historical individual' as a basic interpretive category. For Weber, isolation of this individual from the general phenomenal conditions in which it was embedded was a precondition of social scientific research. Similarly, Weber's relationship to the Heidelberg neo-Kantian tradition, represented by Rickert, helps us appreciate the important role that 'value' played in Weber's interpretive framework. Value was significant not only because of the central role that 'values' played in the individual social scientists' selection of what they found meaningful or significant, but also because only certain events and constellations in history could be traced to actions that had 'value-relevance'. 'Value-relevance' concerned events or constellations in which social actors conducted themselves in 'value-laden' ways. But the central role played by 'value' in social scientific research also clearly had an impact on the tragic cast Weber gave to the overall trajectory of the story he was telling.

This story could, after all, have been cast in such a manner as to exaggerate the sublime character of the bourgeois interior, or to cast in a more positive light the increasingly critical, rational and instrumental character of public life. It could have been told in such a manner as to celebrate both the increasingly sublime interior and the increasingly critical exterior of the mature capitalist social formation. This, in fact, is the direction that Habermas was to take Weber's neo-Kantian grasp of the sublime. But, for Weber, the increasingly instrumental, intellectualized, rationalized and disenchanted character of the public sphere was not at all something to celebrate. To the contrary, as we have seen, the disenchanted public sphere was something to lament. At the same time, was it not precisely its law-like, 'nomothetic' character that made society a possible object of social scientific research in the first place?

We need to ask this question because not all societies did lend themselves to social scientific research. For example, since their actions were charismatically inspired,

Weber could tell us very little about the rationality that shaped ancient religious warrior communities. For similar reasons, Weber also found it impossible to fathom actions that arose from within the sublime bourgeois interior. Such actions, it stood to reason, would not conform to the means–ends rationality that governed activity in the public sphere. Here we need carefully note that while Weber's definition of sociology as 'a science concerned with the interpretive understanding of social action and thereby with a causal explanation of its course and consequences'[47] made his particular approach unsuited to sublime action orientations, his definition was specially well-suited to exploring a social formation in which 'historical individuals' in Rickert's sense were over-determined by social forms that behaved in a law-like or mechanistic manner. Mechanistic capitalism was in this respect ideally suited to Weber's approach to the social sciences.

At the same time, the special affinity Weber's method displayed for victorious capitalism could be felt to contradict Rickert's and even Weber's own qualitative differentiation of social scientific concept formation from natural scientific concept formation. If Weber was searching for a 'causal explanation' (*deutend verstehen*) for the 'course and consequences' (*Ablauf und Wirkungen*) of social action, how did this differ from the natural scientist who sought causal explanations for the course and consequences of physical activities?

A large part of Weber's answer to this question would appear to lie in the role he gave to what he called 'imputation' (*Zurechnung*). Because the natural sciences aimed at identifying general laws that have universal significance, causal *imputation* within the natural sciences aimed at imputing general laws to all instances that fell under this law. In the social sciences, by contrast, causal *imputation* aimed to impute specific qualities or forces to specific *individual* phenomena.

> Where the *individuality* of a phenomenon is concerned, the question of causality is not a question of *laws* but of concrete causal *relationships*; it is not a question of the subsumption of the event under some general rubric as a representative case but of the individual constellation to which it is imputed as a consequence [*welcher individuellen Konstellation sie als Ergebnis zuzurechnen ist*]. It is in brief a *question of imputation* [*Zurechnungsfrage*]. . . . It facilitates and renders possible the causal imputation [*kausale Zurechnung*] to their concrete causes of those components of a phenomenon the individuality of which is culturally significant. So far and only so far as it achieves this, is it valuable for our knowledge of concrete relationships.[48]

However, what if these 'causal relationships' begin to take on law-like characteristics? What if they take on the appearance of a 'general rubric' (*Erscheinung als Exemplar*)? According to Weber, 'the more 'general', i.e. the more abstract the laws, the less they can contribute to the causal imputation [*der kausalen Zurechnung*] of *individual* phenomena and, more indirectly, to the understanding of the significance of cultural events'.[49]

But is this not precisely the problem faced by social scientists who take 'victorious capitalism' as their object of research, on the one hand, but who adopt Rickert's or Weber's neo-Kantian methodology on the other? For, as we have seen, Weber believed that the capitalist social formation was (or had become) 'a mighty cosmos . . . bound [*gebundenen*] to the technical and economic conditions of mechanical machine production'. Moreover, he believed that this mighty cosmos 'determines [*bestimmt*] with overwhelming force [*überwältigendem Zwange*] the style of life *not only* of those directly involved in business but of every individual who is born into this mechanism [*dies Triebwerk*]'. On the other hand, Weber also believed that the spirit of capitalism had fled from this social formation's iron cage, that 'victorious capitalism has no further need for this support now that it rests on mechanical foundations [*auf mechanischer Grundlage ruht*]'.[50] Weber in other words had been brought to impute a general law-like character to the causal constellations out of which the capitalist public sphere was composed. But, as Weber himself had concluded, the more 'general' and thus 'abstract' the laws disclosed by one's research, 'the less they can contribute to the causal imputation of *individual* phenomena and, more indirectly, to the understanding of the significance of cultural events'.[51] Weber, in other words, had developed a history of capitalism, which because of the mechanistic and indeed deterministic laws it imputed to this formation, proved less successful in accounting for individual phenomena or for the significance of cultural events.

But let us suppose for the moment that Weber had developed a history of capitalism wherein, instead of fleeing from the iron cage, the spirit of capitalism was itself conceptualized as a quasi-rational, immaterial social form; a 'spirit' that, while continuing to shape social action and social subjectivity, nevertheless did so in such a manner that it never became identical with or lost in the practices, structures or processes to which it was intimately related. This was precisely how Marx had described this process. My guess is that this conclusion would have proven entirely unacceptable to Weber, not because he could not make room for such 'spirits' within his methodology. Indeed, at least initially, the 'spirit' of capitalism had been precisely this kind of spirit. That is to say, the 'spirit' of capitalism had initially stood outside traditional, instrumentally rational and value rational action orientations and, therefore, had from these perspectives been deemed highly 'irrational'.[52] Rather, this conclusion would have proven unacceptable to Weber because the persistence of the 'spirit' of capitalism *within the capitalist social formation* would have deprived this 'spirit' of the sublime quality without which scientific objectivity itself would have been placed at risk. Moreover, it would have deprived the sublime bourgeois interior of that quasi-objective vantage point outside the iron cage of capitalist modernity. The flight of the 'spirit' of capitalism – understood as protestant asceticism – was necessary not only because it rendered the phenomenal world fully transparent to scientific inquiry. This is important, but it is not conclusive. The flight of the 'spirit' of capitalism is logically necessary because it preserves a vantage point outside the 'mechanism' (*Triebwerk*) from which the value of the mechanism itself can be accurately and objectively esteemed and condemned.

Talcott Parsons, Weber's first English translator, seems to have appreciated this fact better than many of Weber's later, otherwise better-informed interpreters. Desiring an adequate introduction for the English translation of Weber's *Protestant Ethic*, Parsons settled upon the Introduction to Weber's 1920 *Collected Works on Sociology of Religion*. It is here in 1920 – and not in his 1904 or 1905 articles – that

Weber noted how western scholars could not avoid wondering 'to what combination of circumstances the fact should be attributed that in Western civilization, and in Western civilization only, cultural phenomena have appeared which (as we like to think) lie in a line of development having *universal* significance and value'.[53] Yet, it had been Weber's, not Parsons', decision to place this '*Vorbemerkung*' at the front of his collection of essays, a collection featuring Weber's *Protestant Ethic* at its head. It therefore made some sense for Parsons to feature the two pieces in precisely the order they had appeared in the 1920 volume.

However, it also made sense on another level of which Parsons himself may not have been fully aware. If it is appropriate to interpret Weber's *Protestant Ethic* in light of the methodological essays he composed between 1902 and 1904, then it seems clear that among Weber's most pressing intellectual problems was establishing the socio-historical validity of the extraordinarily powerful neo-Kantian methodology he shared with his colleague Heinrich Rickert. For while logical validity may have satisfied Rickert – who was not a sociologist like Weber, but successor in Philosophy to Heidelberg's highly regarded Wilhelm Windelband – Weber needed to reinforce this logical validity with a compelling socio-historical narrative.

Still, the question he asked in 1904 and 1905 was not quite the same question he asked in 1920. In 1920, Weber asked why western history held universal significance. In 1904 and 1905, by contrast, Weber asked more modestly how, on the one hand, it was that a historical landscape first appeared that lent itself to social scientific research, and how, on the other hand, social actors had been adequately prepared to interpret this disenchanted landscape. Why, in other words, was there an adequacy between the intellectual tools Weber and his colleagues commanded and the socio-historical landscape they were seeking to explore? Weber's *Protestant Ethic* explained this adequacy of interpretive categories to the object of their inquiry, on the one hand, by means of a narrative in which social and historical reality were deprived of magical content thereby lending this landscape a rationality it did not previously possess. On the other hand, Weber's narrative also explained how social subjectivity had been both brought into conformity with this disenchanted landscape while at the same time enjoying sufficient distance from it to disdain it. Here, Weber may have been drawing upon his brother Alfred Weber's notion of a 'free-floating intelligentsia'.[54] There was another alternative. At the conclusion of his narrative, Weber appeared ready to face the fact that he himself might be one of Nietzsche's 'last men', a 'specialist without spirit' and a 'hedonist without heart', a 'nonentity' who imagined that he had attained a stage of humanity never before reached.[55] And such he would have been compelled to face were it not for the flight of the 'spirit' from whose vantage point Weber had portrayed this now desolate landscape all along.

Weber was not only the object of his scathing critique of capitalist modernity. He was not only the 'specialist without spirit'. He was also a human being whose sublime interior was irreducible to the machine-like qualities that now dominated every individual born into this mechanism. Capitalist modernity is like a shell as hard as steel. It is an iron cage, *ein stahlhartes Gehäuse*. But Weber also felt certain that from this cage a spirit – the spirit of capitalism – had escaped.

And what may have been the significance of the flight of this spirit for Weber? Just this: that without the flight of this spirit, we are left without any *historical individuals* in any sense of the term. We are left without any social actors who are not in every way bound to the mechanism of capitalist modernity. And we are left without any social subjects whose interpretive frameworks are not wholly determined by this mechanism. We are left, in short, with complete identity, a deadening singularity from which no one and no thing can escape.

This brings us back to 7 November 1917 and to Weber's address before the Union of Free Students at Munich. In 1904 and 1905, the 'spirit' that Weber made escape from the iron cage was, of course, this 'spirit' of capitalism; or, more specifically, the 'spirit' of Protestant asceticism. This spirit, according to Weber, was responsible both for constituting an objective world in which naked, disenchanted, desacrilized reality reigned supreme, and it was responsible for qualitatively isolating social actors from this disenchanted world in such a manner that things in this world had no bearing upon their eternal destiny. But, whereas in 1904 and 1905, Weber seemed entirely uncertain over the fate and destiny of this spirit – 'its spirit has fled, . . . whether for all time, who knows?' – in November 1917 Weber no longer seemed in doubt. The spirit of religious asceticism, which by 1917 had come to be embodied for Weber more generally in what he called 'ultimate and sublime values',[56] had settled 'into the transcendental realm of mystic life' and in the 'brotherliness of direct and personal human relations'.[57]

We know this, however, not only because of the many formal similarities between Weber's 'spirit' of capitalism and the 'ultimate and sublime values' of 1917. Weber himself already established the relationship between the two in 1904 at the end of his essay on 'objectivity' in the social sciences. There Weber invited his readers to reflect upon the 'belief which we all have in some form or other, in the meta-empirical validity of *ultimate and final values* [*letzter und höchster Wertideen*], in which the meaning of our existence is rooted'.[58] In Weber's view, this reality, though irreducible to the empirical world, was not incompatible with it. The 'incessant changefulness of concrete viewpoints, from which empirical reality gets its significance'[59] was intimately related to and compatible with these ultimate values in which according to Weber our existence was rooted. But, of course, since these values were in his view 'meta-empirical' (*überempirische*) they intersected at no observable point with the world he was called upon to study in his own research. Here in a place beyond empirical observation, a place beyond science, Weber believed the meaning of our existence was rooted.

In this sense as well, Weber's *Protestant Ethic* showed not only how these two worlds – the meta-empirical root of our existence and our physical or empirical world – may have become isolated from one another. It also showed how the vantage point from which this isolation became visible may have been preserved in the very process of its expulsion from the world. The flight of the spirit from the world was thus necessary not only from a methodological perspective, but also from a meta-empirical perspective. For from what vantage point could the barrenness of the empirical world be recognized if not from this vantage point? Herein as well, ultimate and final values – sublime values – clearly displayed their difference from values that we might have found merely pleasing or pleasurable.

If we are correct in interpreting the *Protestant Ethic* as Weber's attempt to show that Rickert's and his neo-Kantian methodology possessed socio-historical as well as logical validity, then the radical contrast Weber drew at the end of his study between the iron cage of capitalist modernity and the 'spirit' that flees from this cage may itself be instructive. From it Weber's readers could have concluded that the bitter antagonism they felt between the barrenness of their world and the meta-empirical spirit within them was itself evidence that they were not as dominated by the mechanism of victorious capitalism as their status as 'last men' might indicate. Indeed, their hostility to the iron cage could thus be taken as a sign of hope.

War and hope

Should we expect any less from Weber? After all, it was Immanuel Kant himself who described the sublime as '*what even to be able to think proves that the mind has a power surpassing any standard of sense*'.[60] But, here we need to remind ourselves that the Kantian sublime not only surpassed any standard of sense. It was also hostile to any standard of sense. Here, Kant noted, the sublime differed dramatically from the beautiful. For, unlike the beautiful, which 'we like when we merely judge it', the sublime is what, 'by its resistance to the senses, we like directly'.[61] 'The beautiful prepares us for loving something, even nature, without interest; the sublime for esteeming it even against the interest (of our senses)'.[62] As described by Weber, life within the iron cage is anything but attractive or beautiful. We do not like it. It prepares us for loving nothing. Nevertheless, in Kant's sense, because it reveals something about ourselves, namely that we have a power that surpasses any standard of sense, the iron cage of capitalist modernity is something that we may esteem even against our senses.

Much as Kant believed that the sublime elevated humanity above the material world by showing human beings that they were superior to the violence, pain, terror and suffering meted out by the world upon humanity, so it seems Weber also believed that it was 'only within the smallest and intimate circles, in personal human situations, in *pianissimo*, that something was pulsating that corresponds to the prophetic *pneuma*'.[63] Whatever violence, pain, terror and suffering soldiers and civilians were being subjected to all across Europe and the world in 1917, this experience only proved that human beings possessed a sublime power superior to any standard of sense. Indeed, as Kant himself had observed in 1790, nearly a century and a quarter before Europe's Great War, when considering our natural attraction to soldiers:

> Even in a fully civilized society there remains this superior esteem for the warrior, except that we demand more of him: that he also demonstrate all the virtues of peace – gentleness, sympathy, and even appropriate care for his own person – precisely because they reveal to us that his mind cannot be subdued by danger. Hence, no matter how much people may dispute, when they compare

the statesman with the general, as to which one deserves the superior respect, an aesthetic judgment decides in favor of the general. Even war has something sublime about it if it is carried on in an orderly way and with respect for the sanctity of the citizens' rights. At the same time it makes the way of thinking of people that carries it on in this way all the more sublime in proportion to the number of dangers in the face of which it courageously stood its ground. A prolonged peace, on the other hand, tends to make prevalent a merely commercial spirit, and along with it base selfishness, cowardice, and softness, and to debase the way of thinking of that people.[64]

Here then in 1790, in Kant's 'Analytic of the Sublime', we already see the faint outlines of Weber's 1917 address. Without the retreat of ultimate and sublime values from public life, the world of the senses cannot take on its harsh and unforgiving – objective – form of appearance. Nevertheless, we prove our superiority to its power by our sublime resistance to it. And we display our resistance to it not by conforming to its form of appearance – not by attempting to 'force and to "invent" a monumental style in art' – but by embodying that 'prophetic *pneuma*, which in former times swept through the great communities like a firebrand, welding them together'.[65]

Of course Weber did not explicitly say that this was the spirit of the tribes of Yahweh. Nor did he explicitly raise the issue of war or the inner demeanour appropriate to war. Nevertheless, throughout Weber's address there is an unmistakably violent undertone – a *sublime* undertone in precisely Burke's or Kant's sense. For, if the sublime is something we like *because* it resists our senses, if it is something in which we take pleasure precisely *because* it brings us pain, then can there be any more accurate summary of Weber's description of science as a profession? How else might we describe this consistent and persistent doubting of all sense data, this resistance to all of the forces that bid that we consider them divine, but in the face of which we are professionally bound to hold ourselves aloof? Is this not a kind of violence, a kind of terror, a kind of masochism? Of course, in Weber's view, it was most definitely a very distinct kind of violence, masochism and terror. As we have already seen, for Weber, the 'spirit' of capitalism provided 'the basis for the absolutely negative attitude of Puritanism toward all sensual and *emotional* elements in culture and subjective religiosity. . . . It thus formed the basis for a fundamental rejection of every kind of culture of the senses'.[66] However, since the social actors who bore this absolutely negative attitude were themselves sensual and emotional beings, and since those who rejected every kind of culture of the senses could not help but construct a culture that could be experienced only through their senses, their hostility could not help but translate into self-hatred and masochism.

Peter Gay has written eloquently of how nineteenth century Europeans cultivated a way of life that proved conducive to hatred.[67] Weber's point – and Kant's – appears to differ from Gay's only slightly. Where Gay restricts his discussion to Europeans between Victoria and Freud, Kant wanted his readers to embrace the sublime (and the violence it implied) as a condition that applied to all individuals in enlightened societies. Similarly, Weber appears to have believed that the kind of self-hatred and violence he described would apply to social actors in all mature capitalist social formations. Moreover, only Kant and Weber explicitly appear to have recognized that the violence, hostility and terror directed towards the body was an essential feature of contemporary religious subjectivity and practice. It was an indispensable feature of the sublime. In this sense, Weber's *Protestant Ethic* may also be taken as a preliminary discussion or prolegomena on the prodigious hostility towards the body to which we have grown accustomed under capitalism.

5   The *hiatus irrationalis*

The spirit of modern war emerged at that point in history when ultimate and sublime values first differentiated themselves from and were deemed superior to their material form of appearance. In Chapter 3 we identified that point generally as the point when Jesus' wounds were denied entrance into heaven, when his true Body and Blood were denied a real presence in the bread and wine of the Holy Eucharist, and when the Virgin Mary's sensuous body was transformed into an angelic soul. But, as we soon discovered, these instances of disembodiment were only illustrations of a much broader and more complex set of circumstances set in motion by the harnessing of human bodies engaged in productive activity to the abstract units of time marched out by mechanical clocks. A more graphic illustration of wholesale disembodiment and disenchantment might be the increasing readiness of political and religious leaders to commit the bodies of their subjects to death in officially sanctioned mortal combat and the willingness of their subjects to offer their bodies as sacrifices to that wholly new political abstraction, the nation. Although admittedly circumstantial, the evidence is nevertheless compelling.

The most reliable compilation of statistics about officially sanctioned mass death is Matthew White's 'Historical Atlas of the Twentieth Century'.[1] There we discover that, counter to our expectations, the period from 900 to 1450 in Europe was surprisingly peaceful. During the entire period, only 435,000 soldiers died on Europe's battle-fields,[2] the majority between 1351 and 1450, during the Hundred Years War. After 1450, however, the numbers of officially sanctioned mass dead begin to climb precipitously. All told, nearly 200,000 give their lives in the fifteenth century alone. This figure then increases almost forty fold in the sixteenth century to nearly 8 million. In the seventeenth century over double this number, roughly seventeen and a quarter million, sacrifice their lives in officially sanctioned mass death. Ironically, death counts taper off in the eighteenth century – the 'Age of Enlightenment' – to just over 18 million before ballooning to a prodigious 48 million in the nineteenth and then to a grotesque 188 million in the twentieth.[3] Even when considered as a percentage of the world's population, White's data suggests that an ever larger percentage of the world's total number of potential combatants is willing to make the ultimate sacrifice, from less than one per cent (0.6%) in the eighteenth century, to just over one percent in the nineteenth century, to over 4.5 per cent in the twentieth.

Obviously, the point to such rough figures is not to show that war or death in battle is somehow unique to the modern epoch. The further we look back in time, the greater are the obstacles we face determining the number of living, much less the number of dead. Often the best we can do is carefully scrutinize the existing sources and offer our own ball-park figures. But, even if many of our figures are only rough calculations, they defy our general impression that modern social actors value and guard their bodies more jealously than did pre-moderns; or, in the alternative, that pre-moderns valued life less and therefore stood more ready to sacrifice their bodies in war than do our contemporaries. Precisely the opposite would appear to be the case. Perhaps of even greater interest, the increasing willingness of social actors to sacrifice their bodies – or, at the very least, the readiness of political and religious leaders to demand this sacrifice – coincides closely with the points when Jesus' wounds were expelled from heaven, Mary's sacred body became an angelic soul, and the Body and Blood of the crucified Jesus were withdrawn from the physical Bread and Wine of the Holy Eucharist. Could it be that social actors find a disenchanted body easier to violate and destroy than a sacred one?

To be sure, late medieval faithful were neither the first nor the only religious practitioners to differentiate between material and spiritual bodies. Nor were they the first to rank the latter higher than the former within an overall, general hierarchy of being. We need only recall the Apostle Paul's famous first century declaration that 'flesh and blood cannot inherit the kingdom of God' to recognize that pre-capitalist religious practitioners also entertained a strict, albeit minutely graduated spiritual taxonomy. Nor was this graduated taxonomy unique to the west or to so-called 'western religions'. Recent scholarship on the 'body of religion' has done much do dispel the notion – itself a product of nineteenth century 'orientalism' – that 'non-western religions' entertained views of the body more holistic and integrated than those embraced by religious practitioners in the 'west'. Where these taxonomies – whether eastern or western, Christian, Jewish, Islamic, Buddhist or Hindu – differed from their early capitalist counterparts is that prior to the emergence of capitalism, these taxonomies rarely suggested that the graduated differences in being they charted would prevent spirits from guiding, comforting and otherwise assisting the bodies they were happy to occupy and accompany in this world. After the emergence of capitalism, first in the west, but then also in the east, religious practitioners come increasingly to view these graduated differences in being in ontologically fundamental, oppositional terms so that, for example, the disembodiment entailed in death on the battlefield, far from depriving the spirit from something essential to it (i.e., the body), instead was held to infinitely enhance the value of the spirit precisely because it has been freed from the prison-house of the body. Thus, whatever the Apostle Paul may originally have meant and devout Christians originally understood by his first century declaration, twelve centuries would pass before anyone would suggest that the exclusion of 'flesh and blood' from heaven also entailed the elision of Jesus' wounds from his glorified Body or the deprivation of the Eucharistic Feast of its Real Presence.

Yet, beginning in the fourteenth century and increasingly so since then this proposition has become increasingly untenable to the point that far from being among the most straightforward dogmas entertained by the faithful, the belief that God is present in the Bread and Wine is now widely counted among the church's most inscrutable mysteries. But not universally so; in communities whose members are less thoroughly integrated into the capitalist social formation, at what is called the 'periphery' of the global economy, religious practitioners are known to still engage in rituals and practices whose efficacy depends precisely on divine presence in the material objects they manipulate. Here, however, faithful Catholics join a throng of Buddhists, Muslims, Hindus, Taoists, Shamanists and many others who have never ceased expecting or receiving divine comfort, guidance and power from the many official and unofficial 'sacraments' that endlessly replenish their worlds.

Not surprisingly, it is precisely among these 'primitive' communities, however, where the body is deemed more than simply the material elements out of which it is composed – where it is deemed a sacred vessel – that religious practitioners are least willing to offer their bodies in sacrifice to ultimate and sublime values. Here, the 'spirit of war' is largely dormant, only intermittently tormenting the bodies of the living. Clearly, therefore, the distinction that needs to be drawn here is not between Catholics and Protestants, or Christians and non-Christians, but between those communities whose members enjoy a wide variety of ways of esteeming value and those communities for whose members, value has been reduced to an immaterial, disembodied abstraction. Among the latter, the 'spirit of war' reigns and, as the statistics drawn out above indicate, this spirit reigns supreme.

But, what is this peculiarly modern and capitalist 'spirit of war'? Of what does it consist? Traditional Marxists are fond of identifying so called 'economic causes' of war. More specifically, they are fond of showing how class conflict or the drive for capital accumulation are the principle sources of interregional and international conflict. But this would suggest that the capitalist social formation touches some social actors (workers and colonial or third world subjects) while leaving others (capitalists and bourgeois social subjects) largely untouched by the forms of social subjectivity and practice that predominate in capitalist societies. Hostility to the human body, however, is not an instrument used by one class against another. Even where this hostility does take on class specific characteristics, as in the venerable and persistent practice of using the poor and minorities as 'canon fodder' in war, this does not undermine the more general observation that contemporary social actors – rich and poor – have so elevated the spirit above the body, the sublime above its material form of appearance, that all stand ready, irrespective of their class, to sacrifice their own and others' bodies for the sake of immaterial value. Here Michele Foucault was undoubtedly correct when he noted how, when the bourgeoisie was seeking to dominate, direct, and gain mastery over the body, 'it appears ... that they first tried it on themselves'.[4] According to Foucault, 'the most rigorous techniques were formed and, more particularly, applied first, with the greatest intensity, in the economically privileged and politically dominant classes'.[5] Although it was undoubtedly the most spectacular expression of bodily mortification, domination over the flesh did not express itself first or foremost in state sanctioned mass death. State sanctioned mass death is only the most extreme expression of this general hostility. Underlying and reinforcing this final liberation of spirit from flesh are countless intermediary practices that seem specifically designed either to discipline, mortify, master and otherwise bring our bodies into line, or, displaying total disregard for the body, appear designed to hasten its end. Here we therefore cannot remind ourselves enough that the obsession displayed by contemporary social actors over the body – obsessions with eating, diet, exercise, beauty, fashion, cosmetic surgery, medicine, sport and of course 'sex' – does not so much point to excessive materialism as much as to our deeply seated religious or spiritual desire to master our bodies, to bring them under control, to transcend them, punish and discipline them, push them to their limits, and to suppress or cultivate their desires. That this obsession with the body should coincide with times of ever mounting body counts in officially sanctioned mass death will only seem strange if we fail to grasp the fundamentally religious and spiritual character of our many-sided need to subject our material bodies to the domination of immaterial value. In order to grasp this uniquely modern variety of spiritually, however, we need to rethink what we think we know about religion and spirituality.

The gulf between value and body

We have already seen how Edmund Burke and Immanuel Kant first made this isolation of the sublime from its material form of appearance theoretically explicit and how south-west German neo-Kantians such as Heinrich Rickert embraced and used the isolation of the spirit from its material form of appearance to inform their interpretive categories. We also saw how Weber, first in his methodological writings and then in his *Protestant Ethic*, showed not only that ultimate and sublime values had withdrawn from the world of the senses, but that such a retreat was salutary since, without it social scientific research in Weber's sense would have been impossible. It would have been impossible because, so long as individuals imputed to physical objects sublime qualities unrelated to their material composition, it was unlikely that they would hit upon methodologically rigorous and empirically satisfying explanations for how their world worked.

Clearly, however, this was not the end of the story. For, as Guy Oakes has pointed out, Weber's early methodological essays were explicitly composed to shed light upon persistent problems within the social sciences[6] many of which still plague the social sciences over a century later. Chief among these problems, according to Fritz Ringer, was the fiercely contested terrain of methodology in the social sciences, the so called *Methodenstreit*; an argument over whether or to what extent social scientists could or should adopt the same methodology as the natural sciences.[7] Those who argued that they could and should adopt this methodology believed, in a manner similar to natural scientists, it was among the social scientists' responsibilities to discover general laws that could account for historical or social occurrences. Among these, Hegelian-leaning scholars proposed that social and historical reality fit under general laws in one manner, while positivists proposed that it fit under general laws in quite another. Those who argued that social scientists could not and should not adopt the same methodology as natural scientists claimed, first, that the objects of social scientific research differed from objects of natural scientific research and, second, that what interested social scientists in their objects differed qualitatively from what interested natural scientists about theirs. Indeed, most participants in the 'methods controversy' seriously doubted that natural scientists were interested in objects at all since they viewed these objects only as individual instances or illustrations of general, abstract laws.[8] Properly understood, in fact, only social scientists actually took an interest in the empirical object world.

Weber spent the better part of his 1902 Roscher-Knies essay refuting the positivist response to the methods controversy. In essence, Weber contested the validity of positivist methodology not only for the social, but also for the natural sciences. Since researchers always inevitably impose categories upon the objects of their research, Weber denied any validity to 'value-free' science. This was also among his chief assertions in the essay he wrote on 'Objectivity', published in the 1904 inaugural issue of his *Archiv für Sozialwissenschaft und Sozialpolitik*. Here we need only recall Weber's remarks regarding the fundamental irrationality of empirical reality. The question for Weber and for the social sciences in general was how if at all social scientists could bridge the gap between the 'ever changing finite segment of the vast chaotic stream of events'[9] they might select for their research and the concepts through which they chose to interpret this segment? Or, as Weber put it in his Roscher-Knies essay, what faced social scientists was the question of 'the "*hiatus irrationalis*" between concretely and individually given reality, on the one hand, and abstract general laws and concept, on the other'.[10] Following his fellow neo-Kantians at Heidelberg – principally Rickert and Weber's student and then colleague Emil Lask – instead of 'solving' this problem, Weber folded it into his conception of what it meant to conduct social scientific research. Unlike the natural sciences, which bracketed the question of how abstract concepts could grasp empirical objects, the social sciences were obligated because of their peculiar relationship to value to face this question directly. This is the sense in which Weber believed the social scientific approach to reality to be less irrational – because more securely grounded in the actual *irrational* character of reality – than the natural sciences.[11]

More to the point, in so far as they formed their concepts with the intention of grasping what was unique about their object and to the extent that they acknowledged the active role they played in imputing significance to the historical individuals on which they conducted their research, social scientists could legitimately claim to have adopted a method particularly well-suited to their object. But they could only make this claim to the extent that they resisted the temptation, on the one hand, of treating the objects of their research as 'emanations' of the concepts researchers applied to them and, on the other hand, of mistaking the values they imputed to the objects of their research for actual, objective, qualities they had 'intuited' from these objects.

In each particular instance, the aim of social scientific research was to this extent in fact to preserve and even exaggerate the gulf separating the concept from reality by folding it into their methodology and thereby making this gulf explicit. At the same time, social scientific research also aimed to truly grasp a 'finite segment of the vast chaotic stream of events' using concepts that by their nature were of a different order than the things they sought to explain. The aim of social scientific research, in other words, was not simply self-contemplation, but actually studying and gaining a better grasp of some finite piece of social and historical reality. To do so, in Weber's view, involved not bracketing the gulf between concept and reality, but rather folding it into the very core of the social scientific method.

Although, formally there was no logical reason why this gulf between concept and reality should translate into open social and political conflict – it was, after all, only a theoretical construct – it is clear that this gulf inspired precisely the kind of reflection that Weber found most pernicious.[12] Indeed, in so far as individuals had only become aware of this gulf over the course of the development of capitalism in the west, this fact in itself suggested to some intellectuals that political or social action might provide the necessary ingredient to bridge the gulf that theory by itself could not. It is here perhaps in Weber's early theoretical writings that we can make out the first clear outline of the cryptic remark with which Theoder Adorno introduced his *Negative Dialektik*:

> Philosophy, which once seemed obsolete, lives on because the moment to realize it was missed. The summary judgment that it had merely interpreted the world – that resignation in the face of reality had crippled it in itself – becomes a defeatism of reason after the attempt to change the world miscarried.[13]

Insofar as philosophy had disavowed any attempt to bridge the gulf separating concept from reality, insofar as it had elected instead to let this gulf stand or even to exaggerate it, therein Adorno felt that it had missed the opportunity to change the world. Not so Weber. In a manner not unlike his jealous defence of the disenchanted public sphere against any attempt to reinvent a monumental style of art or construe a new religion, Weber similarly stood guard against any attempt – whether in theory or in fact – to actually bridge the gulf fixed between concept and reality.

Weber's fears were both theoretical and practical. He distrusted scholars who under the cover of 'objectivity' imported values into their research that on their face were unsuited to their object. Such scholars not only did a disservice to their discipline, but also cultivated confusion among non-experts over precisely what scholars could and could not achieve through their research. 'Academic prophecy ... will create only fanatical sects but never a genuine community'.[14] However, Weber of course was also not blind to the political ends to which unscrupulous individuals might push their own ultimate and sublime values, not without some success. And since, in Weber's view, 'the decisive means for politics is violence',[15] his fear that a public politics of ultimate and sublime values might have catastrophic consequences must have seemed well-founded.

Was there any other alternative? Of course Weber scholars never tire of speculating over the conclusions that Weber might have drawn had he had more accurate information both about the emergence of capitalism and about the character of sixteenth century popular religion among Protestants.[16] It is not inconceivable that with more accurate or more complete information Weber might have been brought to appreciate how his neo-Kantian interpretive categories did more to frustrate than advance 'a causal explanation' for the 'course and consequences' of 'social action'. Perhaps he would have been brought to appreciate how these categories derived their interpretive adequacy in large part from the peculiar two-fold character of social action in mature capitalist societies. And perhaps then Weber might have concluded that the gulf separating concept from reality or the antagonism between the sublime and its material form of appearance were not hard-wired into human ontology, but could be overcome by a transformation in social practices commensurate to the fourteenth century transformation that introduced them in the first place.

Perhaps. And yet, at least in 1917, when the gulf between concept and reality, between the sublime and its material form of appearance, had grown so large as to demand the kind of bodily sacrifice we encounter only at Passchendaele or Auschwitz, Weber evidently felt that this sacrifice was evidence not of this gulf, but rather of the attempt to bridge it. Many of Weber's most intimate and personal friends, particularly those who had joined Max and Marianne Weber for their *Sonntagskreise*, felt differently. Otto Gross, Heidelberg's wayward disciple of Sigmund Freud and a frequent guest at the Weber's home, sought to bridge the gulf through a variety of more or less self-destructive activities including drug addiction, open relationships (which proved an endless source of legal hassles for his unofficial 'attorney', Weber), and anarchism.[17] After chaining himself to socialism in Germany, Robert Michels fled to Mussolini in Italy where he became a leader among fascism's expanding ranks.[18] Else and Frieda Richthofen, the accomplished daughters of the 'Red Baron', followed Otto Gross' lead into the pleasures of sexual liberation and political passion.[19] D.H. Lawrence, Frieda's lover, lost himself in the worlds of adventure, literature and romance.[20] Friedrich Gundolf, the literary scholar and leader of the Stephan George circle in Heidelberg, buried himself in stories of Heidelberg's and Germany's heroic mystical past.[21] All believed it possible and indeed necessary – whether through sexual or political practices, aesthetic and literary expression – to practically bridge the gulf separating concept and reality.

Among those whom Martin Green counts in the innermost of Max and Marianne's *Sonntagskreise*, Max Weber would thus appear to stand alone as the sole standard-bearer for the strict separation of concept and reality. Green's impressive list includes:

> Wilhelm Windelband and Heinrich Rickert in philosophy, Ernst Troeltsch in theology, . . . Alfred Weber [Max's brother] in sociology, Emil Kraepelin and Karl Jaspers in psychology, Friedrich Gundolf in literature. . . . At the Webers' Sunday "jours" Else Jaffé met [Georg] Simmel, Gundolf, Georg Lukács, Ernst Bloch, Mina Tobler the pianist [and Weber's lover],[22] and Kläre Schmid-Romberg the actress, along with many Russian revolutionary students.[23]

We need not search long or hard to find evidence that, contrary to Weber's *public* advice, many, perhaps most, of those who counted themselves members of his and Marianne's *Sonntagskreise* were more than ready to negotiate the gulf separating concept and reality. Indeed, albeit in an appropriately private manner, Weber himself would appear to have attempted to bridge this gulf with the affections of Mina Tobler, the Italian opera star and Else von Richthofen, D.H. Lawrence's lover. But, what is remarkable about the list of guests Max and Marianne Weber invited to share in their most intimate moments is how few of them heeded Weber's public advice to respect the boundary separating concept from reality, or ultimate and sublime values from their material form of appearance.

Weber, Lukács and Schmitt

Might Weber have been advising one thing in public and quite another in private? We may never know for sure. What we can know and do know is that many, perhaps most of Weber's students and many of his admirers were less than convinced of the salutary effects of isolating sublime values from their material form of appearance. Two figures in particular stand out: the Hungarian literary scholar Georg von Lukács whose 1922 *History and Class Consciousness* almost single-handedly created what after World War II became known as Western (as distinguished from 'Soviet') Marxism;[24] and the German political theorist and jurist Carl Schmitt whose uncompromising critique of liberalism helped frame the destruction and reconstruction of the German judicial system under National Socialism. Through his most famous disciple Leo Strauss, Schmitt's critique would also contribute to the emergence of post-democratic politics in the United States and Western Europe. We owe our interest in Lukács and Schmitt, however, not only to their indebtedness to Weber, but also to the violence that each thought necessary to bridge the gulf left open by him.

In his masterful study of Carl Schmitt, John McCormick also juxtaposed Lukács to Schmitt, but for somewhat different ends. McCormick saw Lukács' appropriation of Weber as 'the best alternative example for assessing Schmitt's confrontation with technology and politics'.[25] And, yet, as McCormick also points out, what is perhaps most remarkable are the similarities between the approaches of the Marxist theorist Lukács and the fascist jurist Schmitt.[26] These similarities arise, I would suggest, not only because both Lukács and Schmitt had in large measure adopted both Weber's interpretation of and his approach to capitalist modernity. These similarities also appear because, unlike Weber, both Lukács and Schmitt wished to see the *hiatus irrationalis* closed. As we have seen, Weber was highly suspicious of those who wished to close this chasm, seeing in their wish a desire to violate the principles of concept formation in the social sciences and indeed to violate reality itself. In their desire to bring concepts and reality into line with one another there was, he thought, 'an almost irresistible temptation to do violence to reality [*der Wirklichkeit Gewalt anzu-tun*] in order to prove the real validity of the construct'.[27] In Lukács' and Schmitt's view, however, Weber had turned the problem on its head. It was not the desire to bridge this gulf that had induced violence, but rather the gulf itself. For Lukács, who believed that this gulf reflected what he called the 'antinomies of bourgeois thought' (*Antinomien des bürgerlichen Denkens*), the only way this gulf could be bridged was through the full emancipation of the subject–object of history,[28] the industrial working class. For Schmitt, who believed that this gulf reflected the intrusion of the social and economic spheres into the sphere of the political, the only way this gulf could be bridged was through the reassertion of sovereignty of the state, the essence of what he called the 'concept of the political'.[29]

Lukács: imputed class consciousness

Here we will first consider Lukács' interpretation of the gulf that had opened up between concept and reality. We will then look at Schmitt's analysis more closely. In some respects of course Lukács' analysis of how the capitalist social formation had shaped social subjectivity was rather unremarkable. Hence, we should not be too terribly surprised to find Lukács repeating fairly orthodox lines about class interests and class antagonism. Where Lukács departed from orthodox Marxism is in the degree to which he was willing to face Marx's own mature critique of capitalism, which was itself a critique not only of capital, but also more specifically of *labour as it exists within capitalism*.[30] Practically speaking, the intimate, mutually constitutive relationship between capital and labour had always presented problems for Marxist political action since the presumptive agents of this action, workers, were themselves among capitalism's most illustrious products. Therefore, while under extreme circumstances radical political organizers could depend upon workers to defend their traditional rights and even, under some circumstances, to expand and extend those rights, it had always been something of a push to bring workers to embrace, much less understand, 'the full program'. After all, even where pride in work was difficult to come by – for example, among common labourers – an argument on behalf of the destruction of labour could strike workers as a slap in the face. To promote the victory of the working class was easy. To convince workers that labour was a large part of the problem was not so easy.

Equally important were the theoretical problems posed by workers' reluctance to seize their destiny and topple capitalism. If workers resisted their historically determined role, then in what sense could it be said that history had prepared them for this destiny? Even more problematic was the actual social class of nearly all of those who were in the leadership of revolutionary Marxist organizations. To a person, they were nearly all privileged, highly educated members of the upper or upper-middle class. Viewed from a dialectical materialist vantage point, this role reversal suggested that class might have much less to do with the gears of history than most orthodox Marxists were willing to acknowledge.

But just as Weber had embraced the gulf between concept and reality as the very essence of his sociological method, Lukács embraced this gulf as evidence of the contradictions in mature capitalist society. The fact that workers were alienated from their historically predetermined role, the fact that they had not yet achieved complete 'working class consciousness' served as an objective barometer for the revolutionary work that still lay ahead. As Lukács put it at the end of his 1920 essay on 'Class Consciousness',

> Thus we must never overlook the distance that separates the consciousness of even the most revolutionary worker from the authentic class consciousness of the proletariat. . . . *The proletariat only perfects itself by annihilating and transcending itself* [vollendet sich erst, indem es sich aufhebt], *by creating the classless society through the successful conclusion of its own class struggle.*[31]

What Lukács was contemplating is not immediately transparent. It only comes fully to light once we recognize how 'the most revolutionary worker' bears a relationship to 'authentic class consciousness' that parallels the relationship Weber drew between the 'chaos of infinitely differentiated and highly contradictory complexes of ideas and feelings' and the 'purely analytical constructs'[32] social scientists impose upon this chaos. But, whereas the 'violence to reality' that concerned Weber was primarily the violence social scientists might commit when they sought to bring reality into line with their concept, the 'annihilation and self-destruction' (*aufheben sich*) Lukács was evidently contemplating involved the practical destruction of the working class *by the working class*.

The problem of course was that the majority of workers, most of whom were nowhere near to becoming 'the most revolutionary', did not display the kind of 'authentic class consciousness' needed to bridge the gulf separating concept from reality. Had history, which should have given birth to a revolutionary self-consciousness, miscarried then?[33] Lukács thought it had not, and in support of his claim he called upon Weber's concept of 'objective possibility'.[34]

For Weber, 'objective possibility' was a purely limiting concept. It prevented social scientists from having to sort through every merely logical possibility tossed up by history. It helped answer the question, 'how in general is the attribution of a concrete effect to an individual "cause" possible and realizable in principle in view of the fact that in truth an *infinity* of causal factors have conditioned the occurrence of the individual "event"?'[35] 'Objective possibility' was Weber's answer to this question. 'In every line of every historical work', Weber noted, 'indeed in every selection of archival and source materials for publication, there are, or more correctly, must be "judgments of possibility", if the publication is to have value for knowledge'.[36] Only after the social scientist has constructed a logically consistent abstraction of social reality can it then be determined whether or not one or another historical individual logically fits within this construction. But creating this abstraction required that the social scientist both isolate specific historical individuals from their historical context and also form generalizations about this individual and its context. As Weber put it, 'the formulation of propositions about historical causal connections not only makes use of both types of abstraction', both isolation and generalization, but for this reason 'the simplest historical judgment concerning the historical "significance" of a "concrete fact" is far removed from being a simple registration of something "found" in an already finished form'.[37] Thus Weber's opposition to positivism. This was not an argument that any given historical individual actually existed, or that it existed in the form suggested by the social scientist. They did not. Weber therefore likened the category of objective possibility to tossing dice. Just as with the throw of a dice, the fact that it falls on only one of its six sides does not disprove either the existence of the other five sides, or the objective possibility that it might not have fallen on any one of them.[38] But, was 'authentic working class consciousness' an 'objective possibility' in this sense?

Lukács believed it was. But, as was the case with all historical knowledge, here too it was necessary to isolate what was significant and meaningful from the infinitely complex and ultimately irrational totality of things, events and processes. And, just as Weber felt that the 'historical 'significance' of a 'concrete fact' was 'far removed from being a simple registration of something "found" in an already finished form,' so Lukács felt no compulsion to reduce authentic working class consciousness to a simple fact. It was therefore only from the vantage point of capitalism conceived as a social scientific construct, as a 'concrete totality',[39] that authentic working class consciousness clearly displayed itself not as 'something "found," but as a valid "objective possibility"'. For, as Lukács noted:

> The relation with concrete totality and the dialectical determinants arising from it transcend pure description and yield the category of objective possibility. By relating consciousness to the whole of society it becomes possible to infer the thoughts

and feelings which men would have in a particular situation if they were *able* to assess both it and the interests arising from it in their impact on immediate action and on the whole structure of society. . . . Now class consciousness consists in the fact of the appropriate and rational reactions "imputed" [*zugerechnet*] to a particular typical position in the process of production.[40]

What this meant in effect was that the revolution would be fought on behalf of individuals whose actual thoughts and feelings might not in this instance accurately reflect their 'objective possibility' and therefore whose actual consciousness might appear far removed from their authentic working class consciousness. In this case, the violence that Weber feared the concept might impose upon reality turned out to be more than theoretical.

This proved to be so not least for Lukács himself who, once he had proved his usefulness to his party superiors, was forced to publicly renounce his youthful theoretical indiscretions and limit himself to non-political work until passing away quietly in 1971, at the age of eighty-six.[41]

Schmitt: the extreme condition

The same soviet communism that condemned Lukács to oblivion was to bring near celebrity status to his counterpart Carl Schmitt. For, were it not for his popularity among anti-communists in post-World War II America, it is doubtful that Schmitt would have been remembered for anything more than the ideological and practical assistance he provided to the National Socialist regime in Germany. As it is, largely through his disciple Leo Strauss, Schmitt has been given credit for helping build a state that is threatening to become at least as anti liberal and illiberal as the one he helped found in Germany.

If the problem for Lukács was bridging the gulf separating concept from reality, the problem for Schmitt was the reassertion of the political by a sovereign power that was ready to distinguish itself from the social and economic interests that laid claim to its allegiance. To be quite clear here, Schmitt, like Weber, believed that the modern capitalist state had become an impersonal and unresponsive machine. Thus, in language almost identical to Weber's, Schmitt in his 1923 essay on the 'Crisis of Parliamentary Democracy' described how

> the whole theory of the *Rechtsstaat* rests on the contrast between law which is general and already promulgated, universally binding without exception, and valid in principle for all times, and a personal order which varies case to case according to particular concrete circumstances. . . . This conception of law is based on a rationalistic distinction between the (no longer universal but) general and the particular, and representatives of *Rechtsstaat* thinking believe that the general has a higher value, in itself, than the particular.[42]

The entire passage recalls Weber's comments in *Economy and Society* respecting the constitutional state system (*Rechtsstaatsordnung*), which, from a religious point of view, struck him as only the most effective mimicry of brutality.[43] However, where Weber had closed the door separating the *Rechtsstaat* from the particular and personal interests of private individuals and groups, Schmitt argued passionately that it was only upon the latter, upon the personal, that politics and the state as such could legitimately be founded. Schmitt therefore felt, contrary to Weber, that the principle threat to the state came not from the reintroduction of the sublime into public life, but rather from the all encompassing, universally binding character of the *Rechtsstaat*.

But, of course, following Germany's defeat in 1918 and a revolution that lasted from 1918–21, the bureaucratic constitutional state was far from all encompassing. What could Schmitt possibly have been thinking about then? Evidently, not unlike Weber, he was thinking about the illegitimacy of the modern constitutional state's authority over matters of life and death and therefore about why it was only within the context of a personalist political order, governed by a genuine sovereign, that such authority made any sense at all. But, was he not therefore also thinking about the ways that the personalist order, instead of quietly and submissively retreating into its safe bourgeois interior, as Weber had counselled, might not rather reassert legitimate authority over the public sphere or, in the words of *Die grosse Brockhaus*, how it might 'abnormally heighten or threaten to shatter' the constitutional state's 'material form of appearance'? And while, like Weber, Schmitt believed that the proliferation of individual interests in Weimar Germany after the war might indeed prove sufficient to topple the liberal state, Schmitt believed that only a true sovereign, a 'unitary executive', a singular, personal embodiment of what he called 'the political', could re-establish authentic state legitimacy and authority. But, in order to reach this point, the state would have to come to a new understanding of the political. And this meant coming to terms with the flawed understanding of the state that had been inherited from eighteenth and nineteenth century liberal political theory.

These flaws were many and, in Schmitt, are difficult to catalogue. In one of his earliest works, *Political Romanticism*, published in 1919, the chief defect was the migration of political authority from the divinely ordained sovereign to the romantic subject. Theoretically, Schmitt traced political romanticism back to the inaccessibility of the world to abstract rationalism.[44] Political romanticism led political actors to seek to establish the state and political action on supra-rational or irrational grounds. In his 1922 work, *Political Theology*, Schmitt sought to show how concepts of sovereignty reflect theological concepts. Initially, of course, the concept of the sovereign reflected the widespread, nearly universal belief that God disposes over the world's affairs in accordance with God's own secret counsel. Not surprisingly, this theological conviction corresponded to Schmitt's decisionist and personalist concept of political sovereignty. Yet, already by the end of the eighteenth century, this theological conviction and hence the political concept based on it were no longer deemed valid.

> The general will of Rousseau became identical with the will of the sovereign; but simultaneously the concept of the general also contained a quantitative determination with regard to its subject, which means that the people became the sovereign. The decisionistic and personalistic element in the concept of the sovereign was thus lost.[45]

The problem here was thus two-fold. On the one hand, the state had lost its sovereign, the actual King. On the other hand, the sovereign it had gained, the people, came to be viewed in an increasingly impersonal, purely quantitative manner. Thus, Schmitt could conclude that since 1848, the year the last wave of bourgeois democratic revolutions began to sweep through Europe, 'the democratic notion of legitimacy has replaced the monarchical'.[46] But, since Schmitt had defined sovereignty as 'he who decides on the exception',[47] and since in the absence of a true sovereign, the ground for this decision was either arbitrary or impossible to achieve in practice, this meant that the state was paralysed. Tellingly, Schmitt devoted the final chapter of *Political Theology* to the Catholic 'counterrevolutionary Philosophy of the State', a philosophy that aimed at 'dictatorship, not legitimacy'.[48]

Which brings us back again to Schmitt's 1933 *Concept of the Political*, wherein he diagnoses the problem of the contemporary state as the inability to successfully draw an effective distinction between friend and enemy. 'The specific political distinction to which political actions and motives can be reduced', wrote Schmitt, 'is that between friend and enemy'.[49] And, this is precisely where the liberal constitutional state was either disingenuous or, due to paralysis, fell short. It was disingenuous because liberalism 'in one of its typical dilemmas . . . has attempted to transform the enemy from the viewpoint of economics into a competitor and from the intellectual point into a debating adversary'.[50] But in certain circumstances, such as those that held true for Germany from the moment it capitulated to the enemy in 1918 to the 'restoration of order' in 1932, a state might prove itself entirely incapable of distinguishing friend from enemy, in which case, practically speaking, it has ceased to exist.

> If the political power of a class or of some other group within the state is sufficiently strong to hinder the waging of wars against other states but incapable of assuming or lacking the will to assume the state's power and thereby decide on the friend-and-enemy distinction and, if necessary, make war, then the political entity is destroyed.[51]

This, of course, was the extreme case, 'the exception' as Schmitt called it. Under such circumstances, some group – whether domestic or foreign, it does not matter – invariably proved itself willing to forge a new friend–enemy relationship and therein re-establish 'the political'. 'What always matters', thought Schmitt, 'is the possibility of the extreme case taking place, the real war, and the decision whether this situation has arrived. . . . From this most extreme possibility human life derives its specifically political tension'.[52]

Schmitt acknowledged of course that many so-called 'states' existed whose leaders were reluctant or perhaps incapable of recognizing, much less defining, the friend–enemy distinction. Such states were in fact no more than federated social and economic associations cobbled together out of common interest or protection or both. If sufficiently powerful, perhaps they might even be able to dominate other nations and, when necessary, defend themselves. But, as Schmitt noted, such associations in fact were not political states in the true sense of the term.

> The pluralist theory of state is in itself pluralistic, that is, it has no center but draws its thoughts from rather different intellectual circles (religion, economics,

liberalism, socialism, etc.). It ignores the central concept of every theory of state, the political and does not even mention the possibility that the pluralism of associations could lead to a federally constructed political entity. It totally revolves in a liberal individualism. The result is nothing else than a revocable service for individuals and their free associations. In reality there exists no political society or association but only one political entity – one political community. The ever present possibility of a friend-and-enemy grouping suffices to forge a decisive entity which transcends the mere societal-associational groupings.[53]

In a sense, therefore, by its very existence 'the political', whatever or whoever it might be, restored the sovereign deposed by the Enlightenment. For just as the King proved his sovereignty by his ability to decide on the case of the exception, so whoever established the friend-and-enemy distinction, no matter what we might want to call that person or entity, is *de facto* the sovereign. And it is here that we can recognize the theoretical foundations for the notorious *Führer-Prinzip*, the 'leadership principle', that was to play so central and tragic a role in the National Socialist judicial and administrative apparatus. For it stood to reason that so long as liberal social democratic leaders during Weimar were unwilling or unable to establish the friend-enemy distinction, so long as they formed a 'mere social-associational grouping' in which a variety of other groups with potentially divergent positions were invited to play meaningful roles, the Weimar Republic lacked legitimacy. Under such circumstances, the laws of the so-called 'state' and its so-called 'leaders' must be deemed null and void until such time as a legitimate leader is able to re-establish the friend-enemy distinctiin and therein establish the legitimacy of a true state. Here 'legality' itself becomes entirely subject to the will of the leader who has successfully re-established the friend-enemy distinction. In national Socialist Germany, this meant that all officials serving in the executive branch of the *Reich*, the *Reichsregierung*, were obligated by their oath of office to support the policies and ideology of the *Führer*. In post-democratic western Europe and North America, this has meant the enforcement of what some call the 'unitary executive'.[54]

In theory, the fact that some entity did eventually establish the friend–enemy distinction might mean any number of things short of all out military conflict. Yet, as Schmitt never tired of emphasizing, although many less powerful entities might establish within their own spheres intermediate, non-lethal, friend–enemy distinctions, only the state had the power to establish that ultimate friend–enemy distinction that marked it decisively as *the political*.

> The state as the decisive political entity possesses an enormous power: the possibility of waging war and thereby publicly disposing of the lives of men. The *jus belli* contains such a disposition. It implies a double possibility: the right to demand from its own members the readiness to die and unhesitatingly to kill enemies.[55]

And while under normal circumstances this extreme case receded into the background, counting merely as the presupposition of the state's authority and power, under extraordinary conditions, the state was obligated either to reveal or to relinquish this presupposition. Here, Schmitt approvingly cited Lorenz von Stein:

In a constitutional state [*Rechtsstaat*], as Lorenz von Stein says, the constitution is "the expression of the societal order, the existence of society itself. As soon as it is attacked the battle must then be waged outside the constitution and the law, hence decided by the power of weapons."[56]

From which Schmitt drew the conclusion that 'the political', the entity or person who decides when the constitution and law are superseded, was always already 'the political', even in the absence of the exception. 'By virtue of this power over the physical life of men, the political community transcends all other associations or societies'.[57]

And, here, precisely thought Schmitt an ultimate boundary was crossed between the sacrifices the *Rechtsstaat* could reasonably demand from its citizens and the sacrifices only a true sovereign could demand. Just as Weber believed it completely senseless 'from a religious point of view' to orient politics 'to *raison d'état*, to realism, and to the autonomous end of maintaining the external and internal distribution of power',[58] so Schmitt here thought it ludicrous that these social and economic associations, these so-called states, could dispose over human life.

> Under no circumstances can anyone demand that any member of an economically determined society, whose order in the economic domain is based upon rational procedures, sacrifice his life in the interest of rational operations. To justify such a demand on the basis of economic expediency would contradict the individualist principles of a liberal economic order and could never be justified by the norms or ideals of an economy autonomously conceived.[59]

Yet, far from leading Schmitt to repudiate modern warfare, it instead brought him to demand a different kind of political entity, an entity that would itself renounce economic expediency as its highest ideal and end. 'War, the readiness of combatants to die, the physical killing of human beings who belong on the side of the enemy – all this has no normative meaning, but an existential meaning only', thought Schmitt, 'particularly in a real combat situation with a real enemy'.[60] What Schmitt needed is only what most social actors since the fourteenth century have needed: a political entity sufficiently powerful and transcendent to forcibly help them transcend the limits imposed by their bodies.

Mortifying the flesh

Are we mistaken to read Lukács, the radical founder of western Marxism, and Schmitt, the equally radical founder of contemporary anti-liberalism, together at this point? After all, some might object, beyond the brief, explosive, but ultimately benign influence Lukács exercised over the New Left during the 1960s, he cannot be said to have had anything more than a minor and passing influence on practical politics. Perhaps, his mere presence in Budapest after the close of World War II stood as proof in some people's minds that the 'evil empire' still had a human face. And perhaps were it not for Lukács and others like him, more people in the West would have actively challenged the legitimacy of soviet-style Marxism. Post-democratic theorists never tire of suggesting that any concessions to 'the social' inevitably undermine the authority of the sovereign. But, in the balance, Lukács' influence on practical politics has been negligible.

At least in the 1960s, after Schmitt returned to his home in Plettenberg, and when his most celebrated and promising student Leo Strauss was busily collecting disciples, but not much else, at the University of Chicago, it might have looked as though Schmitt too would suffer a similar fate. Schmitt passed away quietly in 1985 without much to show for his labours, beyond his profound influence upon the National Socialist legal system. And, yet, already in 1985 well-placed followers of Schmitt's most celebrated disciple, Leo Strauss, had already begun to fan out throughout the Republican Party political apparatus. Such well-known political figures as Paul Wolfowitz, Alan Keyes, Robert Bork, Clarence Thomas, William Bennet, William and Irving Kristol and Alan Bloom were destined to have a profound and lasting practical effect not only on US policy and political institutions, but also tragically on the lives of countless families throughout Africa, central and South America, Israel, Saudi Arabia, Iran, Afghanistan and Iraq, where Strauss' romantic version of post-democratic empire has been put into action.[61] Even though his death in 1973 prevented Strauss from seeing the full fruits of his labours, he might already have suspected that the empire he helped build at the University of Chicago would soon overshadow the empire his mentor had helped build.

But here we must pause to reflect on what if anything the careers and legacies of these two successors to Weber's legacy might tell us about the persistence of religion or, as Karl Jaspers called it 'spiritual situation of our age'.[62] On the one hand, there are Leo Strauss and Strauss' disciples who have maintained their intellectual father's and grandfather's campaigns to reverse the tide of political liberalism. And, on the other hand, there are Lukács and his unsought disciples, Herbert Marcuse, Theodor Adorno, Max Horkheimer, Walter Benjamin and Jürgen Habermas, who, often in opposition to the historical and philosophical Enlightenment,[63] have nevertheless fought for something like human emancipation. Indeed, Habermas' unceasing promotion of the unfinished project of Enlightenment may actually have yielded some practical political success, at least within Germany.[64] So are we to conclude from this comparison that Lukács was the father of moderation and understanding, while Strauss, to the contrary, was the father of extremism and intolerance?

Perhaps, but for our purposes this is unhelpful. After all, it is not theoretical discourse that composes political extremism under capitalism, but rather capitalism that composes theoretical and practical extremism. In practical terms, it makes some difference, perhaps even a great difference, whether we identify more with Habermas or with Strauss, with Lukács or with Schmitt.[65] Still, it was not one or the other, but both Lukács and Schmitt who found the body of contemporary social reality so unacceptably estranged from its 'objective possibility' that each was prepared to set it in opposition to a sublime force that promised to destroy its body. But the body that each was eager to destroy – the body of the actually existing working class for Lukács and the body of liberal parliamentary democracy for Schmitt – was not some abstract body. It was the empirical body, which, as Schmitt put it so eloquently, necessarily involved 'the readiness of combatants to die, the physical killing of human beings who belong to the side of the enemy'.

6   The prophetic *pneuma*

The precipitous increase in officially sanctioned mass death since the fourteenth century is, on some level, no more than circumstantial evidence of the isolation of abstract value from its material body. Still, the unanticipated spike in state sanctioned mass death, which first appeared in Western Europe and from there spread throughout the rest of the colonized world, has turned out to be statistically significant. The sadly familiar pattern it has left on the face of the globe calls into question our inclination to feel that contemporary attitudes towards the body along with the contemporary religious dispositions upon which these attitudes are often based are more healthy, wholesome and life-affirming than their traditional and ancient counterparts. Our inclination to view the pre-modern world as more violent, war-like and dangerous, on the one hand, or more spiritual, otherworldly and sheltered on the other is not borne out by the historical record. Rather, it would appear that traditional societies have by and large tended to be less violent and much more this-worldly than our own. Of course, in the absence of modern science, social actors in traditional societies interpreted their physical environments differently than we now do, searching and finding in them not only ample means for physical sustenance, but also evidence of divine guidance and comfort. Yet, in so far as they viewed the bodies that occupied their worlds, including their own bodies, as vessels filled with spiritual content and vehicles bearing divine gifts and information, traditional social actors were slow to view these bodies as mere instrumentalities whose consumption or destruction were worth the sacrifice.

Weber termed such social formations whose members entertained such views of the physical body and embodied spirits as 'traditional'. Weber set such traditional communities against a backdrop composed on the one hand of ancient religious warrior communities and, on the other hand, of the disenchanted world of capitalist modernity on the other. As it turned out Weber found that members of ancient religious warrior communities proved particularly hostile towards the emerging religious and political bureaucracies whose rational laws and systematic codes of religious conduct and ethics were diametrically opposed to the heroic codes of ethics embraced by religious warriors. But such traditional communities in turn found themselves at odds with capitalist modernity whose disembodied religion and disenchanted world struck them as contrary to everything they found meaningful.

Weber accounted for the specific position each religious formation assumed in the world in terms of its economic ethics. Here, Weber's narrative framework for the economic ethics of the world religions appears as one giant chiasm. Chiasms we might recall serve something of the same function in literary texts that mapping serves for symbolic logic. They lend a sense of symmetry to the presentation and ensure closure. If viewed from the top down, Weber's presentation begins at the top with the only historical instance when sublime religion legitimately achieved an outward, public expression: charismatically charged religious communities. This helps explain why in his address 'Science as a Vocation' Weber could compare the sublime bourgeois interior with the prophetic spirit that welded the ancient tribes of Yahweh together. Moving down the chiasm, after centuries of struggle these warrior communities were eventually defeated or pacified by the great traditional religious and social formations of India, China, Greece and Palestine. Traditional religious and social formations occupy by far the longest stretch of human history, from the emergence of human civilization in roughly 4,000 B.C.E. to the emergence of capitalism some five and a half millennia later. Within Weber's chiastic structure, the birth of capitalism signals the movement outward once again, a movement that should ultimately have ended in the re-emergence of a new sublime spirit in the public sphere.

This clearly was the trajectory of Weber's overall presentation, except that unlike its pre-historic archetype, the contemporary bourgeois sublime is in some respects even more heroic than its ancient ancestor in so far as it is denied public expression and must therefore endure the humiliation of a purely inward and private existence. For although Weber believed that the contemporary sublime displayed the same hostility to the morally desolate landscape of modern capitalism that ancient religious warriors displayed towards traditional society, he also believed that its own logic prevented it from venting this hostility in open war upon the disenchanted body of capitalist modernity. Instead, as we will see, for social actors under capitalism the appropriate object for such hostility would be the traditional body of religion, which is to say, the body of traditional religion and society. This body became an appropriate object for sublime rage in part because it confounds the sublime with its material form of appearance and therein has prevented the sublime from escaping its body. Yet, since every body suffers in some measure from this same deficiency – the defect of containing and thus frustrating the free movement of the sublime – every body is to this extent an appropriate target of sublime rage. Indeed, the chiasm that Weber created was incomplete only in theory. In fact, modernity's own religious warriors were already and have ever since been completing the chiasm Weber had purposely left undone. For insofar as the body is itself the enduring legacy of traditionalism, modernity and post-modernity routinely identify it as the object of their sublime wrath.

Here we will first examine traditionalism in general and then the traditionalism of ancient Chinese society and religion in particular. We begin here because Weber took Chinese society and religion to be the closest to the ideal-typical traditional society. After looking at Chinese society and religion, we will then explore the deficiencies this society displays from the vantage point of what Weber considered that 'great historical exception' (*die grosse historische Ausnahme*), the 'modern European West' (*der moderne europäische Okzident*).[1] These deficiencies, however, can also be viewed from the vantage point of that other even greater exception, the vantage point of the religious warrior communities, which traditional societies everywhere, including China, both pacified politically and wiped out physically. We therefore, next turn to examine Weber's descriptions of these exceptional communities as he imagined them in pre-historic China, India, Palestine and Greece. Finally, however, we turn our attention to the fate suffered by each one of these communities. The notable exception for Weber – *the exception* to the exception – is modern Judaism, which managed to preserve its exceptionalism by memorializing it in the prophetic expectation of a final battle for emancipation. Traditional China was this exception's antitype.

Confucian China and Weberian Traditionalism

Why Weber thought of China as the prototypical traditional society is not hard to guess. Historically, China had proven to be the non-western power most resistant (and most successfully resistant) to western colonization and imperialism. This resistance perhaps helps explain why Weber repeatedly turned to China when he needed to illustrate the universal validity of the social scientific method. Thus, Weber had argued in his 1904 methodological article on 'Objectivity' that 'a systematically correct scientific proof in the social sciences . . . must be acknowledged as correct even by a Chinese';[2] or, again, that 'the successful *logical* analysis of the content of an ideal and its ultimate axioms and the discovery of the consequences which arise from pursuing it, logically and practically, must also be valid for the Chinese'.[3] Whether or how far this judgment still held true for Weber fifteen years later is open to dispute. Nevertheless, as a point of departure, ancient Chinese religion and society offer insights into Weber's interpretations of religion and capitalism that his other studies do not.

It was in the 'Introduction' to his collected works on the economic ethics of the world religions, published in 1920, that Weber offered his clearest definition of 'traditionalism':

> 'Traditionalism' [*Traditionalismus*] ... shall refer to the psychic attitude-set [*seelische Eingestelltheit*] for the habitual workaday and to the belief in the everyday routine as an inviolable norm of conduct. Domination that rests upon this basis, that is upon piety for what actually, allegedly, or presumably has always existed, will be called 'traditionalist authority'.[4]

We again come across an abbreviated version of Weber's definition of domination 'on traditional grounds' in chapter three of *Economy and Society*, here in contrast to rational and charismatic grounds for legitimate domination:

> There are three pure types of legitimate domination. The validity of the claims to legitimacy may be based on: 1. Rational grounds – resting on a belief in the legality of enacted rules and the right of those elevated to authority under such rules to issue commands (legal authority). 2. Traditional grounds – resting on an established belief in the sanctity [*Heiligkeit*] of immemorial traditions and the legitimacy of those exercising authority under them (traditional authority); or, finally, 3. Charismatic grounds – resting on devotion to the exceptional sanctity [*Heiligkeit*], heroism or exemplary character [*die Heiligkeit oder die Heldenkraft oder*

die Vorbildlichkeit] of an individual person, and of the normative patterns or order revealed or ordained by him (charismatic authority).[5]

Weber traced China's traditionalism to its administrative and politico-economic institutions. These expressed China's extreme particularism, on the one hand, and its extreme centralism on the other. On account of these extremes, China never developed the variety of rationality and logic that were to characterize western European social and religious formations.

Within China's traditional authority or domination, Weber drew additional distinctions, such as those distinguishing estate varieties of traditionalism from patrimonialism and patriarchalism. China was the traditionalist religious formation *par excellence*. 'The whole of Confucianism', wrote Weber in his study of religion in China, 'became a relentless canonization of tradition'.[6] The only other religious community that could have challenged Confucianism's monopoly over the Chinese ethos was, in Weber's view, hopelessly identified with and shaped by magic. 'Taoism', he wrote, 'was essentially even more traditionalist than orthodox Confucianism. Nothing else could be expected from its magically oriented technique of salvation nor from its sorcerers'.[7] In what then did China's specific form of traditionalism consist? It consisted first and foremost for Weber in its patrimonial bureaucratic machine whose control over the countryside was secured by a complex interlocking system of taxes and prebends.

We, of course, associate prebends with the allowance the Catholic church pays to its clergy. More commonly, however, it refers to any allowance paid to officials by a governing body, usually the state. In Weber's view, the interlocking system of taxes and prebends in China constituted the objective political and economic basis for Chinese traditionalism. Beside and in some way under girding this objective basis, however, was the Chinese ethos, so that, as Weber repeatedly noted, even when the objective conditions favoured 'shattering the traditional fetters' [*die traditionellen Schranken zerbrechen*],[8] no cultural resources were at hand to allow the Chinese to take advantage of these conditions.

Weber's discussion of traditionalism in China was inextricably intertwined with his discussion of why capitalism, capitalists and modern individuals did not emerge there. Here, in order to appreciate what Weber found of interest in China *per se*, I will attempt to isolate Weber's discussion of capitalist modernity from his discussion of traditional China. What Weber found interesting was China's failure to take advantage of its resources. This may help us to understand why, at the beginning of his study, Weber explained the poor exploitation of mines in China in terms of 'the general traditionalism inherent in [its] political, economic and intellectual structure'.[9] Whenever Weber referred to the political and economic structure of China he had in mind the 'extreme administrative and politico-economic traditionalism' of the prebendal structure. To this structure Weber traced the fact that 'profit opportunities were not individually appropriated by the highest and dominant stratum of officialdom; rather, they were appropriated by the whole estate of removable officials'.[10] This might have suggested an unmanageable, top-heavy, bureaucracy of undifferentiated, homogeneous, interchangeable officials. But, while the latter certainly existed in

Weber's view, it was to another and nearly opposite feature of traditionalism that he wished to call attention here: the particularism of the provinces.

According to Weber, this particularism, 'primarily financial particularism, originated in this [Chinese] traditionalism. It arose because any administrative centralization seriously jeopardized the prebends of the provincial official and his retinue'.[11] On account of this traditionalist particularism, argued Weber, increased economic productivity and increasing supplies of money failed to yield in China the same results that they had in the West. Here, China only paralleled patterns in other traditional societies.

> Rather than weakening traditionalism, the money economy, in effect, strengthened it. . . . With every advance of the money economy in Egypt, the Islamite states, and China, we observe the concomitant and increasing prebendalization of state income. There are short intermediary periods for the appropriation of prebends to be completed, but, in general, the phenomenon presents itself which we usually evaluate as "ossification" [*Erstarrung*].[12]

Interestingly enough, *Erstarrung* or 'paralysis' was the same fate Weber feared could set-in in the West in the absence of a new and genuine prophecy.[13] In traditional China, by contrast, such a condition was 'normal'. Here taxes, prebends and provincialism reinforced and constituted China's economic paralysis. Of course, alongside this economic account and intertwined with it was Weber's equally important reflections upon the political and administrative causes for China's traditionalism. Here, however, Weber advanced what may at first sight appear nearly the opposite analysis.

If China's economic traditionalism was due to the diffuse and yet interconnected network of taxes and prebends, China's administrative and political traditionalism was due primarily to its centralization. Here, in Weber's view, Europe was 'the great historical exception' [*die große historische Ausnahme*] to which China and the rest of the world were the rule because, in Europe, 'above all, pacification of a unified empire was lacking'.[14] This, in turn, meant that, in contrast to Europe, Chinese society had never enjoyed loosely-knit civil spheres composed of a variety of interests separated from the state. Weber allowed that such spheres could have existed and, in embryonic form, had existed during the Period of the Warring States, between the fifth century and 221 B.C.E., after which the Chin unified the Empire. But, 'the impulse toward rationalization which existed while the Warring States were in competition was no longer contained in the world empire.' Moreover, reported Weber, even during 'the Period of the Warring States the scope of administrative and economic rationalization was much more limited than in the Occident'.[15] Following the Chin's unification of the Empire in 221 B.C.E. matters became much worse.

> By law, the patrimonial bureaucratic machine stood directly over the petty burgher and the small peasant. The feudal stratum which mediated during the occidental Middle Ages was non-existent *de jure* and *de facto*. Only recent times and European influence have brought about capitalist conditions in their typically occidental form. Why?[16]

The answer cannot be simply that China was not Europe. Rather, it would appear the answer lies in the fact that unlike states in Europe, China already enjoyed a degree of political, social, cultural and economic integration unknown in Europe until well after the emergence of capitalism.

This, however, begs an important question: did traditional Chinese society and religion provide Weber a model for his fears of contemporary 'paralysis' (*Erstarrung*); or might not his fears of paralysis instead have provided him a model for his interpretation of China? On many registers Weber's 'China' seems but a sounding board for identifying its alterity to the West. And, yet, on a far deeper level, China's very alterity bears remarkable similarities to the administrative and bureaucratic body of the Western State. Here, as Homi Bhabha has noted, 'the "other" is never outside or beyond us; it emerges forcefully, within cultural discourse, when we *think* we speak most intimately and indigenously "between ourselves"',[17] which certainly held true as much for Weber as it may hold true for us.

Consider, for example, how Weber contrasted the taxation and stipend system of China to the occidental social actor's clear recognition of his own and other's economic interests. To the particularism of the provinces and to their innumerable conflicting interests, he contrasted Europe's 'disinterested executive organs independent of these interest groups'. And to China's 'patrimonial bureaucratic machine' Weber contrasted Europe's 'strong and independent forces' and 'princely power' which could and did 'shatter traditional fetters'.

> These forces could use their own military power to throw off the bonds of patrimonial power. This was the case in the five great revolutions which decided the destiny of the Occident: the Italian revolution of the 12th and 13th centuries, the Netherland revolution of the 16th century, the English revolution of the 17th century, and the American and French revolutions of the 18th century. We may ask: were there no comparable forces in China?

The answer that Weber offered to this question was not so simple and straightforward as we might expect. There had once been forces, such as during the Period of the Warring States, but these had long ago been suppressed.[18]

What remained after many centuries of habituation were, therefore, not only financial and administrative traditionalism, but 'intellectual' (*geistige*) traditionalism as well. These intellectual or spiritual factors will be taken up in greater detail below. They included the absence of 'rational depersonalization of business' (*rationalen Versahlichung der Wirtschaft*),[19] the 'magical evil' (*bösen Zaubert*)[20] that common people associated with economic innovation and social change, but, more generally and consistent with his definition of traditionalism, Weber concluded that China, like India and Palestine, lacked the rational calculating outlook necessary for the development of capitalism:

> In the patrimonial state, the typical ramifications of administration and judiciary created a realm of unshakable sacred tradition alongside a realm of prerogative and favoritism. Especially sensitive to these political factors, industrial capitalism

was impeded by them in its development. Rational and calculable administration and law enforcement, necessary for industrial development, did not exist. Be it China, India, or Islam, in general, wherever rational enactment and adjudication of law had not triumphed, the dictum was: Prerogatives have precedence over common law.[21]

However, if, as Weber had suggested, Europe and European capitalism constituted 'the great historical exception [*die große historische Ausnahme*]'[22] to the above rule, then how can it make sense to conceptualize capitalism's failure to appear in China in terms of factors that were placed in the way of and thereby prevented its arrival? How can the exception prove the rule? The logic through which Weber made sense of his subjection of the rule to the exception turns out to have been a logic dictated by the value form of the commodity.

Developmental logic and religion in China

Since they were eager to avoid any association with Hegelian 'pan-logism' (*Hegelschen Panlogismus*), as Weber called it, neo-Kantians such as Weber were hard pressed when it came to explaining how history might possess a 'developmental logic'.[23] In his article on 'objectivity', for example, Weber devoted considerable attention to the topic. Yet, however much he insisted that developmental logic was always imputed to – and never discovered in – his constructs, Weber could not help but betray his implicit faith in a quasi-objective developmental logic in history. This faith rose to the surface with particular force in his discussion of Chinese religion and society. His comments on religion in China, therefore, inevitably gave the impression that here as elsewhere outside of Western Europe, religion and society had suffered from a kind of arrested historical development. 'Despite the astounding increase and the material welfare of the population', Weber noted at the beginning of his study, 'Chinese intellectual life remained completely static, and despite seemingly favourable conditions modern capitalist developments simply did not appear'.[24] Intellectual life became static in China and, as a direct consequence, 'in the European sense, "progressivism", generally speaking emerged neither in the field of technology, nor economy, nor administration'.

One problem in China was that the Chinese 'way of life could not allow man an inward aspiration toward a "unified personality", a striving which we associate with the ideal of personality. Life remained a series of occurrences. It did not become a whole placed methodically under a transcendent goal'. Another barrier to the evolution of Chinese culture resided in the Chinese language itself, to which Weber devoted a fairly lengthy section of his study. The problem was not that the Chinese language was irrational or illogical. The problem instead was what Weber termed 'the absence of speech', the absence of 'a means of attaining political and forensic effects, speech as it was first cultivated in the Hellenic *polis*'.[25] Thus, Weber noted how, 'in spite of the logical qualities of the language, Chinese thought has remained rather stuck in the pictorial and the descriptive'. According to Weber, what was lacking in the Chinese language was 'the power of *logos*, of defining and reasoning', which, in his view, 'has not been accessible to the Chinese'. As a consequence, 'the very concept of logic remained absolutely alien to Chinese philosophy, which was bound to script, was not dialectical, and remained oriented to purely practical problems as well as to the status interests of the patrimonial bureaucracy'. This practical character of Chinese thought accounted for the fact that, 'whether magical or cultic in nature, religion remained of a this-worldly turn of mind'.[26]

What is peculiar about Weber's lists of absences is how many of them come down to some kind of logical deficiency. Thus, for example, Weber found that 'a juristic, theological and philosophical "logic" failed to develop. Systematic and naturalist thought also failed to mature'. Conditions in China

> did not allow the emergence of those economic premiums which were necessary for the transition from empirical to rational technology. Thus all remained sublimated empiricism. Consequently, practical rationalism, the intrinsic attitude of bureaucracy to life, free of all competition, could work itself out fully. There was no rational science, no rational practice of art, no rational theology, jurisprudence, medicine, natural science or technology; there was neither divine nor human authority which could contest the bureaucracy.[27]

In our explanation, China would have failed to develop this peculiar variety of logic because this logic only arose out of the practices unique to commodity production and exchange. Thus, not only did the logic for which Weber was searching not exist in China, but prior to the fourteenth century, it did not exist in Europe either.[28] For Weber, however, since this logic possessed a supra-historical or trans-historical character, its failure to appear had to be explained in static categories – blockages, barriers and absences – as though, because the Chinese could no longer draw upon their primordial charismatic beginnings and had not yet encountered capitalism, traditional religion in China was incapable of producing a spirit of any sort at all.

It would have been one thing had Weber been unaware of the practical regimes that structured and shaped Chinese society. Instead, he considered the respect that villagers and religious leaders showed place, time, ancestors and nature as evidence of magical meddling. Ever since the appearance of magicians in the second century B.C.E., 'the forms of mountains, heights, rocks, plains, trees, grass, and waters have been considered geomantically significant'.[29] Today, the magic is unquestionably gone, leaving in its absence one of the most industrially toxic environments in all of Asia.[30] Not surprisingly, it was to this magic that Weber credited China's resistance to industrial exploitation of China's resources.

The magic is gone and so too is the elaborate religious formation that protected China's resources from exploitation. According to Weber, this formation 'consisted of chronometry [the science of measuring time], chronomancy [the art of manipulating time], geomancy, meteoromancy, annalistics, ethics, medicine, and classical mantically-determined [i.e., magical] statecraft'.[31]

The ultimate long-term consequences on Chinese society were profound. 'Partly as a cause and partly as an effect', wrote Weber, 'all scientific knowledge was lacking'.[32] Of equal importance, however, were the ultimate effects these arts were to have on the Chinese personality. In Weber's view, 'the preservation of this animistic magic explains the great credulity of the Chinese'.[33] More importantly, at least for Weber's purposes, it explained why capitalism encountered such fierce resistance in China. Weber's account here is worth citing in full:

> With regard to innovations, the manner of mining was always thought especially apt to incense the spirits. . . . [R]ailroad and factory installations with smoke were thought to have magically infested whole areas (anthracite coal in China was used in pre-Christian times). The magic of stereotyping of technology and economics, anchored in this belief and in the geomancers' interests in fees, completely precluded the advent of indigenous modern enterprises in communication and industry. To overcome this stupendous barrier occidental high capitalism had to sit in the saddle aided by the mandarins who invested tremendous fortunes in railroad capital. The *wu* and the *shih* [physicians and meteorologists], as well as the chronomancers and geomancers, were relegated more and more to the category of "swindlers." This could never have come about through China's own resources.[34]

And is this not then the logic that was otherwise lacking in traditional Chinese society and religion, the logic of the value form of the commodity? There was nothing in traditional Chinese society and religion – or in traditional Indian, Judean, or Greek society and religion – to emancipate the Chinese from their traditionalism. Western 'high capitalism had to sit in the saddle', which, of course, it did. Yet, we should not allow China's traditionalism to obscure the fact that China too, according to Weber, had once been ruled by charismatic religious warriors and their communities whose hostility to traditionalism of every kind was central to their very identity.

From natural to traditional religion

Although according to Weber ancient warrior religion occupied the earliest strata of the historical record, he was not unaware that even ancient warrior religions were not without their own pre-history. So long ago had it been, when religious warriors ruled the earth that when writing about them Weber often fell back upon phrases such as 'very remote in historical time'[35] (*in geschichtlicher Zeit lag das weit zurück*), 'the oldest sources'[36] or, more often, simply 'according to legend'.[37] How had this older layer itself emerged? As it turns out, ancient warrior religion emerged from what Weber called 'natural religion'. Indeed, at least initially, in Weber's view, all religious or magical action was oriented predominantly to this world. He therefore felt that it 'must not be set apart from the range of everyday purposive conduct, particularly since even the ends of religious and magical actions are predominantly economic'.[38] Originally, in fact, even the 'extraordinary powers' (*außeralltäglichen Kräfte*) derived from 'charisma' were a 'natural endowment', a 'gift', and 'not to be acquired by any means'. Perhaps even more surprising than Weber's naturalistic interpretation of primordial charisma was his conviction that 'the strongly naturalistic orientation (lately termed "pre-animistic") of the earliest religious phenomena is still a feature of folk religion'.

Nevertheless, very early on, abstraction began to remould this originally naturalistic orientation.

> A process of abstraction ... has usually already been carried out in the most primitive instances of religious behavior which we examine. Already crystallized is the notion that certain beings are concealed "behind" and responsible for the activity of the charismatically endowed natural objects, artifacts, animals, or persons. This is the belief in spirits. At the outset, "spirit" is neither soul, demon, nor god, but something indeterminate, material yet invisible, nonpersonal and yet somehow endowed with volition.[39]

Weber conceptualized a movement towards even greater abstraction in terms of practices, such as the war dance, orgy, or other ecstasy producing rituals, through which social actors became acquainted with the unseen powers that populated their world. Even if these effects and their inducement eventually became the special domain of magicians, the latter could not prevent common people from experiencing them through non-proscribed practices, especially, in Weber's opinion, the social and hence religiously general form of the orgy, whose primary significance was that out of it the concept of the soul emerged.

> Unlike the merely rational practice of wizardry, ecstasy occurs in a social form, the *orgy*, which is the primordial form of religious association. But the orgy is an occasional activity, whereas the enterprise of the magician is continuous and he is indispensable for its operation. . . . On the basis of the experience with the conditions of orgies, and in all likelihood under the influence of [the magician's] professional practice, there evolved the concept of "soul" as a separate entity present in, behind or near natural objects, even as the human body contains something that leaves it in dream, syncope [*Ohnmacht*, i.e. fainting], ecstasy, or death.[40]

Nevertheless, these practices rarely produced the highest stage of abstraction: symbolization.

This 'highest stage' in religious abstraction only appeared or, in any case, only became widespread with the emergence of warrior religions and their practice of the war dance. For, in the war dance, 'magic is transformed from a direct manipulation of forces into a *symbolic activity*'.[41] Weber went into some detail in speculating how this might take place. Why or how did the war dance differ from mere naturalistic symbolism?

> The details of the transitions from pre-animistic naturalism to symbolism are altogether variable. When the primitive tears out the heart of a slain foe, or wrenches the sexual organs from the body of his victim, or extracts the brain from the skull and then mounts the skull in his home or esteems it as the most precious of bridal presents, or eats parts of the bodies of slain foes or the bodies of especially fast and powerful animals – he really believes that he is coming into possession, in a naturalistic fashion, of the various powers attributed to these

physical organs. The war dance is in the first instance the product of a mixture of fury and fear before the battle, and it directly produces the heroic frenzy; to this extent it too is naturalistic rather than symbolic. The transition to symbolism is at hand insofar as the war dance (somewhat in the manner of our manipulations by "sympathetic" magic) mimetically anticipates victory and thereby endeavors to insure it by magical means, insofar as animals and men are slaughtered in fixed rites, insofar as the spirits and gods of the tribe are summoned to participate in the ceremonial repast, and insofar as the consumers of a sacrificial animal regard themselves as having a distinctively close kin relationship to one another because the "soul" of this animal has entered into them.[42]

From here Weber moved quickly to the relationship of symbolism to analogical thinking, from analogical thinking to syllogistic constructions of conceptions through rational subsumption, and from here to the systematization of religious and theological ideas. The entire movement from 'earliest beginnings' to 'functional gods' had taken Weber seven pages in English, six in the more economical German. But, from this point forward Weber could no longer discuss 'religion' generally. He had to move onto specific religious communities and this meant to traditional religion. For 'once systematic thinking concerning religious practice and the rationalization of life generally, with its increasing demands upon the gods, have reached a certain level . . . as a rule there is a tendency for a pantheon to evolve'.[43] Should we be surprised that it is war and the war dance that set this whole process in motion? Again, however, we must ask why war assumed such a prominent place in Weber's account and why in particular it should have assumed so central a role in Weber's explanation of how rationality may originally have been formed. Even by Weber's own account, warrior religion had been a brief phenomenon. So, why did Weber grant warrior religion so prominent a role?

Warfare and War Prophecy

Historically speaking it might appear as though warrior religions scarcely deserve the space Weber devoted to them. And, yet, in each one of the studies of religion that he wrote between 1916 and 1920, warrior religions assumed a central position. Weber's most elaborate treatment of warrior religion and war prophecy appeared in his study of ancient Judaism. 'During the old confederacy in Israel', wrote Weber, 'there was no authoritative place of justice. There was only the intermittent, varying sway of the charismatic war heroes, the prestige of proven oracle givers and of old shrines of the war god of the confederacy'.[44] Here, in Weber's view, was the point of departure at least conceptually for the great historic process whose distilled and purified spirit would eventually find its way into the twentieth century bourgeois interior.[45] When Weber spoke of the private, deeply personal, experience that corresponded to the ancient prophetic spirit, he had in mind the 'firebrand' that had swept through the communities of ancient Israel's warrior confederacy and had knit its members together.

For Weber the link between war and prophecy in Israel was central to the tribes of Yahweh. 'The *casus foederis* of the confederate war, its army leader, and the object of the war', Weber observed early in the discussion, 'were always charismatically and prophetically determined through inspirations and oracles sent by Yahwe as the war-lord.'[46] As Weber would find to be true in China and India, so in ancient Palestine as well 'the army, during holy war, had to practice the prescribed asceticism, particularly fasting and sexual abstinence'.[47] Neither did Weber find Israel unusual in the connections he drew among war, warrior ecstasy and prophecy:

> In connection with the general warrior asceticism, Israelite warfare knew the phenomena of warrior ecstasy in its two forms known elsewhere. Warrior ecstasy occurs either as collective ecstasy of the community or as individual ecstasy of the charismatic hero. The community ecstasy is produced by the war dance and the meat or alcohol orgy of the warriors. . . . The individual ecstasy of the charismatic hero is very widely diffused among the heroes of the type of Tydeus or Cuchullin or the "runner amuck," and is to be found in typical form above all in the Nordic "berserks." Their ecstasy makes them plunge themselves into the midst of the enemy in a frenzy of blood-lust and makes them half unconsciously slaughter whatever is around them.[48]

In ancient Judaism Weber found examples of these practices in Samson and in the Nazarite tradition, which provided Weber with a way to connect such practices back to the ecstatic warrior tradition and forward to the classical prophetic tradition. 'We can recognize but dimly', he wrote, 'the relation of the ancient Nazariteship to the Nebiim, another phenomenon of the time of the old peasant army'.[49]

Notwithstanding the remoteness of this tradition and its connection to the ecstatic warrior tradition, Weber grounded his analysis upon it. 'The Nazarite, the ecstatic warrior – however one may evaluate this tradition – stood near the Nabi, the magical ecstatic.' This, however, did not yet distinguish the ancient Judaic tradition from the warrior religious traditions in the other religious formations that Weber studied. 'The Nebiim are in no way phenomena peculiar to Israel or the Middle East alone', wrote Weber. 'In Israel ... as in Phoenicia and Hellas, and as in India, prophetic ecstasy in the absence of bureaucratization remained a vital force.'[50]

Nevertheless, Weber still lacked any conclusive evidence that these ancient religious warriors and their ecstatic prophets were related in any way to the classical prophetic tradition. 'There is no certain proof', he wrote, 'of the direct connection between this ecstatic war prophecy of individuals and the later schools for Nabi ecstasy. The Song of Deborah and the Book of Judges did not know the latter'.[51]

Again, notwithstanding this lack of proof, Weber was convinced that 'there certainly was a relation between them'.[52] And, indeed, once he recognized what he was looking for he was able to conclude that the 'intermediary links are to be found everywhere'.[53] Weber pointed, in particular to the stories about Saul and David.

> According to one tradition which no longer understood earlier conditions, Saul, after receiving his anointment and with it the "spirit of Yahwe," directly before his public appearance as king, found himself allegedly "by accident," in the company of Nebiim. He was seized by Nabi-ecstasy (I Sam. 10). But also later

when still engaged in his struggle against David (I Sam. 19:24) upon another, allegedly accidental, visit to Samuel's Nabi-schools he was seized by ecstasy and went around naked, spoke madly and for an entire day was in a faith. . . . His explosive fury against David is valued by the Davidian tradition as resulting from an evil but likewise Yahwe-derived spirit. He was obviously a warrior ecstatic like Mohammed. However, even as Saul, David also frequented Samuel's Nabi dwellings.[54]

And with this conflict, ancient Judaism had already reached a decisive turning point, the point at which the prophetic warrior tradition had begun to separate from the kingly and priestly traditions. 'The transformation was definitive with Solomon',[55] wrote Weber. 'Before his establishment as a city-king David was a charismatic prince in the old sense, who was by success alone legitimized as anointed by God.'[56] But according to Weber this irrevocably changed 'with the establishment of the hereditary charisma of the city-dwelling monarchy and the transformation of the military organization which followed thereupon'.[57] As will be discussed in greater detail below, this too failed to distinguish ancient Judaism's warrior religion from the warrior religions of other religious formations whose religious war clans were similarly forced from leadership by priestly and kingly elements.

In Weber's view, Israel's religious warrior formation distinguished itself from its Chinese and Indian counterparts in that, unlike them, albeit in a dramatically transformed condition, Israel's warrior religion survived into the modern epoch. This persistence was critical for Weber's interpretation because of the central importance that the prophetic spirit assumed in his description (and experience) of bourgeois interiority as a sublime and transcendent condition. In China's and India's religious formations, not only was the religious warrior tradition pushed to the periphery. It ceased to play any role at all in these formations.

However, Jewish exceptionalism may have served still another purpose for Weber. It provided him with a quasi-historical instance, stretching from pre-history to the present, of a people in whom the neo-Kantian conflict between the sublime and its material form of appearance were evident and, indeed, necessary. He could not otherwise have insisted that the disenchantment brought to a conclusion by the Protestant ethic had been the culmination of a *world-historical process extending back to the times of the prophets*. The validity of this kind of claim could not rest upon episodic appearances. It required a more continuous process. Weber found this process in the Jewish religion.

Jewish exceptionalism also provided Weber with an explanation for how it was possible for the exception to become the rule: how a phenomenon not susceptible to rational interpretive categories – the *sublime* – could provide the inner spirit for capitalist modernity. Here, it is obviously significant that Weber should have found this exception in Judaism. Nor can we simply dismiss its appearance there as incidental to Weber's interpretation of capitalism and religion. Clearly, Weber's interpretation of capitalism and religion fit into a narrative structure that singled out European Jewry and thereby may have contributed to their fate. This fate, after all, had everything to do with the role most Germans and many Europeans believed Jews had played in the emergence and persistence of capitalism. However, here it must be clearly stated that it was not simply a misinterpretation of capitalism that brought European Jewry to suffer this fate. European Jewry's citizenship, we might recall, bore a relationship to the *Rechtsstaat* that other social groups did not. By birth, Christians had been subjects of the nations in which they were born, both as political subjects, but also as members of the heavenly city. Citizenship for Jews, by contrast, rested strictly upon the political and secular character of the nation, which explains why European Jewry only enjoyed full citizenship following the birth of the modern, *secular* and *liberal* constitutional state or *Rechtsstaat*, which defined citizenship in strictly political, not religious, terms. This also helps to explain why the security of European Jewry was inevitably jeopardized whenever the legitimacy of the secular constitutional state came under fire, as it did in Europe in the 1920s and 30s, and as it is today. So, too, it helps to explain why hostility towards the state's artificiality, its constructed character, which means its liberal and secular character, invariably draws attention to European Jewry's special relationship to the secular *Rechtsstaat*. In so far as capitalism brought social subjects to dissociate sublime value from its material form of appearance, capitalism showed itself fully capable of identifying the bodies of those whom for historically specific reasons Germans and Europeans in general came to view as obstacles to their nations' spiritual destinies.[58] Did Weber then read *contemporary* Jewish exceptionalism back upon the body of its ancient antecedent?

Ancient religious warriors and the sublime

What is certain is that Weber accorded ancient Judaism a special status alongside ancient Greece as one of the historical antecedents to modern rationalism. Indeed, it is worth noting that Weber drew this connection and even inserted it into the 1920 edition of his *Protestant Ethic* only after he had concluded his research on warrior religion in Greece, India, China and ancient Palestine. In Weber's view, while the spirit of China's and India's charismatic warrior tribes was completely eradicated, leaving no trace in traditional China and India, the Greek and Jewish spirits persisted long enough to contribute to 'that great historical process in the development of religions, the elimination of magic from the world, which had begun with the old Hebrew prophets and, in conjunction with Hellenistic scientific thought' would eventually result in the repudiation of 'all magical means to salvation as superstition and sin'.[59]

Nevertheless, at least in terms of the primacy of its ancient religious warriors, neither Greece nor ancient Palestine was exceptional in Weber's view. Weber first discussed religious warriors in a 1916 study on 'Konfuzianismus', published in the *Archiv* separately from his 1920 study on religion in ancient China. Nevertheless, Weber's occasion for calling attention to China's own religious warriors was the qualitative difference he discerned between Confucian and Jewish culture. According to Weber, whereas Yahweh 'was and remained first of all a God of the extraordinary [*Außerordentlichen*], that is, of the destiny of his people in war, … the Chinese Empire, in historical times, became an increasingly pacified world empire despite its war campaigns', as it did in Europe in the 1920s and 30s, and as it is today. Thus, it was originally by way of contrast to the Israel's war god that Weber came to discuss China's pacified world empire. And this, as we already know, could only mean that, for Weber, subsequent Chinese society and religion were not extraordinary, were in fact ordinary, and therefore offered legitimate objects for sociological research. To this ordinary, traditional religion Weber devoted most of his study. But not without the following qualification:

> To be sure, Chinese culture originated under the banner of pure militarism. Originally the *shih* is the "hero," later the official. The "hall of studies" (*Pi-ung kung*) where, according to ritual, the emperor in person interpreted the classics seems originally to have been a "bachelor house" (ἀνδρείον) such as prevailed among almost all warrior and hunting peoples. There the fraternity of young warriors were garrisoned by age group away from family life. . . . Obviously the bachelor house was that of the (charismatic) warrior chieftain where diplomatic transactions (such as the surrender of enemies) were consummated, where weapons were stored, and trophies (cut-off ears) were deposited. Here the league of young warriors practiced rhythmic, that is disciplined archery, which allowed the prince to choose his followers and officials by their merits. . . . All this was very remote in historical time.

Weber called this remote historical time 'China's "homeric" age',[60] a description that may not appear remarkable at first glance or by itself. What is remarkable is that later that same year Weber would duplicate almost word for word and expand upon this description in his study on religion in India, *Hinduismus und Buddhismus*.

In this study, also originally published in the *Archiv für Sozialwissenschaft und Sozialpolitik*, we once again read:

> In the oldest sources we discern the dawn beginnings of military organization in India. We find castle-dwelling kings of the Homeric type with their sibs and followings (king's men). The universally diffused charismatic heroism in the manner of the Nordic Berserks and the Israelite Moshuahs, the charismatic "Degen" of charismatic warrior chieftains – all these belonged to the past and only traces of them survived in epic times. The ancient, universally diffused organization of warriors as a brotherhood of young men, the systematic, magical hero-asceticism of boys, the stages in the warrior novitiate, initiation of the *ephebes* into the phratry of bachelors living in collective economy with captured girls in long houses, the retirement of ex-service (militia) men into marriage and domesticity, the reservations made for elders (in Japan, *inkyo*) unable to serve – all these have vanished.[61]

The antiquity, the bachelor houses, the heroism, the charismatic and hence extraordinary foundations, the universally diffused character of religious warriors, the references to Homer and the 'homeric' – all of this India and China, and evidently Japan, Israel and northern Europe hold, or rather held, in common. In so far as they stood on charismatic and hence extraordinary foundations, these religions could not lend themselves and, in Weber's studies, did not lend themselves to sociological inquiry.

The fate of warrior religion

China, as we have already noted, also 'originated under the banner of pure militarism'. But, just as it had in India and for almost exactly the same reasons, warrior religion had vanished from China as well. Weber traced its demise to 'the dependence on river regulation and therewith the bureaucratic management by the prince'. Moreover, in China, as elsewhere, urbanization and centralization were accompanied by efforts to demilitarize and pacify the countryside. Here, according to Weber, technological innovation played an especially important role. Just as it had contributed to the demise of warrior religions in ancient Greece, the accumulation of wealth allowed the wealthy proto-technocratic military strata of society to purchase weaponry, in particular the much-vaunted chariot, that allowed them to rise above and set themselves apart from their fellow religious warriors. In China, 'the highly trained individual hero, equipped with costly arms, stepped forward.'[62]

Finally, with the notable exceptions that we will examine more closely below, Weber would find the same tragic trajectory repeated in ancient Judea. Here, Weber rejected the standard interpretation, which held that the patriarchs had been pacifist herdsmen. Instead, as he had in the cases of China and India, Weber would contend that the earliest and most reliable sources depicted the patriarchs as charismatic military heroes. So, too, Weber would again call attention to the 'warrior asceticism' of Yahweh's chosen and to 'the initiation rites of bachelor warriors'. Finally, Weber would again note the similarities between warrior religion in ancient Judea and its counterparts in China, India, 'Phoenicia and Hellas'.[63] But, we find new elaborations as well, such as Weber's discussions of the war dance, of warrior ecstasy, of the role that rhythmic music played in inducing ecstatic states, and of the simple naturalism and personalism that he found to be characteristic of all warrior religious types.

But, in ancient Judea as well, tragic processes had begun to unfold which, had Judaism not been the exceptional religion that it was, or had the Jews' covenant with their God been more typical, would presumably have led to the disappearance of its warrior religious spirit too. For, here, combined with the ascendancy of the centralized kingly bureaucracy and its priestly and scribal retainers, capital accumulation and new military technology played decisive roles in the transformation of warrior religion. 'With the increasing importance of the army of chariot fighters,' Weber noted, 'the ancient ecstatic hero charisma like the confederate army summons inevitably declined in importance.'

In ancient Judea, however, other forces were at play. For, in contrast to other civilizations, the Jews' rise to power had been much more modest and short-lived. Moreover, even had the Jews' Davidic and Solomonic empires proved more powerful and durable, prophetic activism would have prevented them from fully embracing the bureaucratic and compartmentalized example set by Egypt and other imperial formations. But, it was another feature, the peculiar relationship that had developed between Yahweh's religious warriors and their God, signified historically by an unparalleled covenant that bound both parties equally, that Weber found especially noteworthy.[64]

Under normal circumstances, a breach of the warriors' covenant would provoke an unambiguous transfer of allegiance, either from the god to another warrior clan or

from the warriors to another god. In ancient Judea, however, this conventional practice gave way to something new. For, according to Weber, there was no other god like
Yahweh who held all the nations in his hands, who governed the affairs of each and
every tribe, including the affairs of Israel's enemies. If these enemies should gain the
upper hand over Yahweh's chosen people, their defeat was held to be only temporary,
a result, it was widely believed, of Israel's momentary unfaithfulness, and not, as elsewhere, an indication that a god had transferred his allegiance.[65] Should God's chosen
people return to His ways and abide by the terms of the covenant, Yahweh would certainly utterly destroy their enemies and deliver all of creation into their hands.
Therefore, instead of driving the Jews into the hands of foreign gods, military defeat,
deportation and subjection to their enemies only drove Yahweh's people into even
stricter observance of the conditions of the covenant, which alone they believed could
guarantee their ultimate victory. And it was to this that Weber attributed the Jews'
exceptionalism, not only their historically unparalleled status as a pariah people and,
hence, their self-imposed isolation in the midst of other nations, but more importantly their simultaneous embodiment of the spirits of disenchantment and charismatic warrior religion.[66]

Indeed, so central was this exceptionalism to Weber's understanding of both ancient
and modern Judaism, that he introduced his study on *antike Judentum* by listing 'the
differences between Jewish and Indian pariah tribes':

1   Jewry was, or rather became a pariah people in a surrounding free of castes.
2   The religious promises to which the ritual segregation of Jewry was moored
    differed essentially from those of the Indian castes. Ritually correct conduct,
    i.e., conduct conforming to caste standards, carried for the Indian pariah castes
    the premium of ascent by way of rebirth into a caste-structured world thought
    to be eternal and unchangeable. . . . For the Jew the religious promise was the
    very opposite. . . . The world was conceived as neither eternal nor unchange-
    able, but rather as having been created. Its present structures were a product of
    man's activities, above all those of the Jews, and of God's creation to them.
    Hence the world was an historical product designed to give way again to the
    truly God-ordained order. The whole attitude toward life of ancient Jewry was
    determined by this conception of a future God-guided political and social
    revolution.
3   This revolution was to take a special direction. Ritual correctitude and the seg-
    regation from the social environment imposed by it was but one aspect of the
    commands upon Jewry. There existed in addition a highly rational religious
    ethic of social conduct; it was free of magic and all forms of irrational quest for
    salvation; it was inwardly worlds apart from the paths of salvation offered by
    Asiatic religions.[67]

According to Weber, these differences were to have profound world-historical
significance, a significance far surpassing the purely incidental roles Judaism would
play in providing Christianity with the earliest outlines of its religion, or in passing
on to Islam a 'warrior ethic'.

We should point out parenthetically that Weber's failure to recognize either how capitalism might command a sublime spirit all its own or how this spirit might in turn shape religious traditions beyond Christianity and Judaism had serious consequences for his interpretation of Islam. In particular, Weber's interpretation failed to appreciate how an Islamic bourgeoisie invigorated by capitalism might develop a hostility to the material body that has everywhere been among the most distinguishable traits of religion and spirituality under capitalism. In Weber's view, however, since Islam lacked 'ethical and prophetic underpinnings', he believed that it would prove powerless in the face of capitalist modernity. Thus Weber argued that Islam had lost its war-like character, and since, in contrast to Judaism and Protestantism, it had failed to promote methodical, ethical rational conduct among its members, it was no longer a decisive force in the modern capitalist world.[68]

Initially, ancient Judaism may have appeared to suffer from a similar defect. As was the case in all world religions, the warrior religion of Yahweh retreated in the face of bureaucratization and rationalization. As had been the case elsewhere, 'the definitive establishment of the hereditary charisma of the city-dwelling monarchy and the transformation of the military organization' contributed to the demise of Yahweh's warriors. So, too, did 'the changed position of the cultured strata of later kingly times', 'the bureaucratic rules and regulations', along with the 'increasing importance of the army of chariot fighters'. With these 'the ancient ecstatic hero charisma like the confederate army summons inevitably declined in importance'.[69] But, at the heart of the Jews' eschatological hopes, informing their entire salvation religion, were expectations and understandings that were missing in other cultural and religious formations.

Most important among these, in Weber's view, was the Jewish expectation that sometime in the future Yahweh would once again lead his armies into battle. Because in many other respects India's and Judea's religious warriors were so similar, Weber therefore returned to this theme at the conclusion of his study of Judaism. In what respects did Hinduism's Kshatrya differ from Judaism's religious warriors and their spirit? Why was Hinduism, at least in this respect, not Judaism? Or why was Judaism not more like Hinduism?

In his discussion of pharisaic Judaism, Weber responded to these questions by arguing that the difference between Indian and Jewish piety rested, in large measure, upon the fact that, in contrast to their Hindu counterparts, pious Jews expected, awaited and conducted themselves in light of an anticipated emancipation of all creation.

> It is clear that these expectations whenever they came to mind had to impart a tremendous pathos to the piety of the Jews. One of the basic differences from all Indian savior religion rests in the presence of such expectations of a last day. Moreover, if in view of unusual signs and revolutions, or under the influence of eschatological prophets, these expectancies seemed to come true they could and did lead to the mightiest and under certain conditions wildest enthusiasm. . . . Conduct could be influenced in practice only by the question what kind of behavior might entitle men to expect the timely advent of the redeemer and to enter personally the resurrection.[70]

Therefore, however much Israel's priestly, intellectual and kingly strata may have wished to entirely eliminate or at the very least domesticate the warrior religious elements of Yahweh's covenant, these elements retained a central position in all subsequent religious, social and political developments. As was the case nowhere else, Judaism retained both a religious warrior component, on the one hand, and an entirely disenchanted, rational emancipatory component on the other. Thus, just as it had once been a leading source and remained a sublime repository for the spirit of warrior religion, so in the modern epoch Judaism would also contribute immeasurably to this type's disenchanted antitype. In the absence of concrete political power, the rational, ritual and ethical elements of Judaism predominated. Yet, as significant as these elements would become in the development of Western civilization, it was to the peculiarities of its ancient warrior covenant and to the conviction that, at least in principle, Yahweh would deliver his people, that the Jews owed their enduring significance and continuing pariah status among the nations.[71] In this peculiar combination of secular disenchantment and warrior religion, a combination which in so many ways prefigured the tragic contradictions that would arise within capitalist modernity itself, Weber found an exemplar of his own heroic attempt to supplement an ethic of responsibility with an ethic of ultimate values.

Curiously, however, Weber did not adequately appreciate these contradictions. Having traced the 'prophetic *pneuma*' that he found pulsating in the bourgeois interior back to the heroic religious warriors that populated all civilizations at the dawn of history, it did not occur to him that the same deep-seated hostility to bureaucracy, to rationalism and institutionalization, the same antipathy to 'bourgeois' codes of ethics or formalized religious practices that he found among these ancient warriors might also display themselves among contemporary religious practitioners. Nor did it occur to him that he might have inadvertently misrecognized the present for the past. And so, it did not occur to him that the just concluded battle for Passchendaele – for this 'sacrificial ground' – where over half a million boys and men were sacrificed in less than three months, might itself illustrate the very hostility that Weber felt characteristic of religious warriors. Nevertheless, it is here I would suggest that the terrifying violence that has become so characteristic of capitalist modernity expresses the clearest aim of the value form of the commodity, the destruction of its own body.

7   The 'community unto death'

Today of course we associate the sublime with thundering waterfalls, ocean waves crashing against forbidding cliffs or a spectacular sunset, with the *adagietto* from Gustav Mahler's Fifth Symphony, or with any number of poems or paintings endorsed by Ruskin. We are therefore liable to forget that for Edmund Burke and Immanuel Kant, whose discussions of the sublime resonated with the educated British and German middle classes well into modern times, the sublime suggested not only visual or auditory violence, but actual physical brutality, terror, and pain. This was still the case in the 1930 *Grosse Brockhaus* definition of the sublime, which defined the sublime as 'an object or process whose inner excellence abnormally heightens or threatens to shatter its material form of appearance. The force it exerts must be greater than normal'.[1]

Kant as we have already seen did not hesitate to describe war as 'sublime', so long as it was 'carried on in an orderly way and with respect for the sanctity of the citizens' rights'. A people who carried on war in this way, thought Kant, were 'all the more sublime in proportion to the number of dangers in the face of which it courageously stood its ground'. By contrast, he felt that 'a prolonged peace ... tends to make prevalent a mere[ly] commercial spirit, and along with it base selfishness, cowardice, and softness, and to debase the way of thinking of that people'.[2]

So, why on 7 November 1917, a Wednesday, as the greatest war ever fought until then raged throughout Europe and North Africa, did Weber contend that the most ultimate and sublime values had retreated from public life into the bourgeois interior? Since Kant himself allowed that the sublime might achieve expression in war, our answer to this question cannot be simply or solely that it was because he was a 'neo-Kantian' that Weber deprived the Great War of this noble honour.

The answer is evidently somewhat more complex. To be sure, the foundation for Weber's theories of the world's disenchantment and secularization appear to have been laid by Kant's insistence that the sublime was not identical with its material form of appearance, that it was in fact superior and even contrary to this form. Thus, Weber appears to have concurred with Kant's definition of the sublime as that which 'by its resistance to the interest of our senses, we like directly', and as something we therefore esteem 'even against the interest of our senses'.[3] Yet, since this did not deter Kant (or, indeed, a long line of neo-Kantians)[4] from commenting on the sublime character of war, we must search elsewhere to find the impediment that prevented Weber from seeing in the Great War any evidence for the sublime in public life.

The impediment it would appear was capitalism; or, not capitalism itself but rather Weber's interpretation of it. As we have already seen, Weber's interpretation of capitalism could be taken as having both reinforced and validated his methodological isolation of value from its material form of appearance. The gulf that displayed itself in this isolation of concept from reality mirrored the increasing isolation of the bourgeois interior from the mechanistic 'technology', the *Triebwerk,* that determined the lives of 'all those born within it and not only those with direct ties to business'.[5] Thus for Weber (though apparently not for Kant or many other neo-Kantians), the prohibition against public displays of the sublime appears to have been grounded in his conviction that victorious capitalism socially and historically validated his neo-Kantian methodology. This methodology suggested that the irrational gulf separating concepts from reality, far from proving an impediment to social scientific research, in fact validated the practice of actively imputing meaning to the objects social scientists selected for their research. For, if, to the contrary, these objects suggested their own interpretive categories – if, in other words, reality already possessed a logic, which it was the researcher's responsibility to discover – then, as every Kantian knew, this jeopardized the validity of reason itself. Rather than reason imposing order on a reality which was fundamentally irrational and chaotic, reality could then be held to impose its own order on reason, a possibility no Kantian could long endure without going mad. Of course, it could be said that by failing to recognize the unique logic capitalism itself had/may have imposed upon history, Weber inadvertently formalized this logic and made it his own. Indeed, this is precisely what he did.

Nevertheless, Weber at least felt that he could have it both ways. He felt that he could both show how the variety of rationalism unique to the West had emerged historically. And he felt that the logic this process exposed could have universal significance and value. After all, even someone from China would have to acknowledge its validity. Herein, 'victorious capitalism' provided Weber with an elegant way of showing not only how a specific set of historical circumstances gave rise to a form of social subjectivity that possessed 'universal significance and value'; it also provided him with a means for showing how this universal significance and value held true *logically* even in isolation from this specific set of historical circumstances. Weber, as we have seen, was quite insistent that his logical approach to the social sciences would have to be acknowledged as valid even by members of a social formation so totally unlike his own as he believed China's to be.[6] Of course, this purely *logical* validity did not imply that Chinese would impute the same meaning that Weber had to any given constellation of historical individuals. Thus, Weber acknowledged that 'our Chinese can lack a "sense" for our ethical imperative and he can and certainly will deny the ideal itself and the concrete value-judgments derived from it'.[7] Nevertheless, in so far as the 'spirit' of capitalism had also been responsible for bringing to its conclusion that 'great historical processes in religion, the disenchantment of the world',[8] and thereby delivering to science both a method and a world adequate to that method, Weber's distinction between *logical* validity and content could seem somewhat strained. At the same time, this very strain could itself be taken to confirm Weber's point. The very best social scientists could ever offer were interpretations constructed out of the values they imputed to historical individuals or constellations of historical individuals. These individuals or constellations would of course then have to be subjected to logically rigorous interrogation to ensure that the story constructed out of them made sense. It was not Weber's aim any more than it was any other scholar's aim to construct a story so richly textured as to lose all sense of proportion or coherence. If in the end this meant that Weber had to draw a qualitative distinction between the irrationality of historical reality, on the one hand, and the logic of historical presentation, on the other, then Weber was more than willing to draw this distinction. In fact, drawing this distinction was virtually indispensable. It was, of course, indispensable for social scientific research. But, it was also indispensable for Weber's interpretation of capitalist modernity. Both required the retreat of the sublime.

In 1905, we may recall, Weber was thus ready to claim that the spirit had fled the cage. And, again, in 1917 he was still ready to affirm that the sublime had retreated from public life. The isolation of the sublime from its material form of appearance, upon which modern rationality was based, was thus preserved intact. And, of course, the public sphere had been spared the violence that would have inevitably followed from a public display of the sublime. Nevertheless, Weber was enough of a historian to realize that the story he had told about capitalism was not irreversible. This was already clear in the question within which Weber had couched the flight of the spirit of capitalism. 'Today its spirit has fled from this shell – whether for all time, who knows?'⁹ Perhaps it would return. But, if it did, this for Weber could only mean that the variety of rationality that had made his approach to social science possible would also be at risk. Like the 'Chinese', social scientists might then recognize the *logical* validity of Weber's arguments, but might find the values he imputed to his subject matter and therefore the lens through which he interpreted capitalism and religion entirely inconceivable. Or, worse still, in so far as the *social validity* of this logic was *historically* predicated upon the disenchantment of the world and the secularization of the public sphere, perhaps the validity of this logic would itself fall into doubt. In this case, perhaps ultimate and sublime values might return to public life after all, perhaps in the form of a pantheon of new gods of war.

And is this not precisely what Weber most hoped for or feared? It was always possible, Weber thought, that a new prophecy would be proclaimed and around it a new social order might be organized. Clearly, there was nothing in his neo-Kantian approach to the social sciences that categorically ruled out this possibility. But it was the other possibility that struck terror in Weber's mind.

> No one yet knows who will live in that shell in the future. Perhaps new prophets will emerge, or powerful old ideas and ideals will be reborn at the end of this monstrous development. *Or* perhaps – if neither of these occurs – "Chinese" ossification, dressed up with a new kind of desperate self-importance, will set in. Then, however, it might truly be said of the "last men" in this cultural development: "specialists without spirit, hedonists without a heart, these nonentities imagine they have attained a stage of humankind never before reached".¹⁰

Clearly in 1905 nothing ruled out any of these possibilities, at least not in theory. But spring 1905 was not the same as fall of 1917. And by November 1917 another possibility had occurred to Weber, the possibility of false prophets. But, how did one distinguish between false and genuine prophecy?

Weber was clearly aware of the problem. The monumental art he so despised continued to litter the avenues and public squares of Europe's great and lesser cities. Worst still, publishers and café-society intellectuals still fed upon the worse instincts of Europe's ever credulous reading public. Notwithstanding Weber's claims that neither intellectuals nor popular religious authors could generate a religious renaissance, it did appear, at least in November 1917, that they had produced a fairly good copy. So, in light of this preponderance of evidence, why did Weber not simply fall back to Kant's original position, namely that, particularly in the case of war, the sublime could make its public presence known? Why not?

Die Gemeinschaft bis zum Tode

On 7 November 1917, the day after the battle for Passchendaele ground to its macabre close, Georg Lukás 'stuffed his 1910–11 diary, and all of his manuscripts, drafts, notes, and correspondence into a small valise and took them to the Deutsche Bank of Heidelberg for deposit'.[11] That same day the Bolsheviks executed a successful coup d'état in Petrograd. And Max Weber delivered his famous address 'Science as a Vocation' before the Union of Free Students at Munich. The question we now need to raise is whether the story we have told up to this point – a story that may often have seemed historically and theoretically remote – might have something to do with the less historically and theoretically remote events that occurred between 31 July and 6 November 1917 along the increasingly narrow salient approaching Passchendaele. There, according to the most reliable sources, in just over three months the French lost roughly 8,500 soldiers, the Germans somewhere in the region of 200,000, and the British another 275,000.[12]

Even by today's standards, bloated by Rwanda, Cambodia, Auschwitz, Baghdad and Hiroshima, numbers such as those registered at Passchendaele are difficult to fathom. And, yet, when set alongside the ever-climbing numbers of war-dead that assault us from the fourteenth century to the present, these numbers from Passchendaele appear to fall into line with a trend that is far from abnormal. Fully four and one half per cent of all people born in the twentieth century met their end in one or another kind of officially sanctioned mass death.[13] So, how might we explain such obscene figures?

Two explanations have gained wide circulation as plausible accounts for modernity's massive officially sanctioned die-offs. On the one hand, these die-offs could be caused by the sophistication of modern weapons of mass destruction, not only atomic weapons, missiles, chemical weapons, military aircraft and land vehicles, but to a complete technological and logistical revolution in how modern combat is conceived, planned and executed. On the other hand, these die-offs could also be attributed to a primal conflict between modernity and the pre-modern itself.[14] The 'modern' here is felt to represent science, reason, rationality, technology, democracy and market capitalism, the very forces that, in the first explanation, are held liable for the massive die-offs. The 'pre-modern' or 'primitive' on the other hand are felt to be represented by nationalism, regionalism, ethnicity, race, religion and local culture. Weber would appear to have adopted a variation of the first explanation. He credited the brutality of modern war to its pure instrumentality. Yet, if Modris Eksteins is correct, then on some level modernity itself can be credited with harbouring and reinforcing a 'primitive' with which it could realize its own brutality.[15] The question is why?

At the conclusion of his 7 November 1917 address, Weber lamented the dominant role rationalism and intellectualization played in what he characterized as our now thoroughly disenchanted world. He also noted how this domination had led to the retreat of ultimate and sublime values into the bourgeois interior. Weber clearly laid responsibility for the massive state sanctioned die-offs squarely at the feet of the forces of rationalization and intellectualization, products both of capitalist modernity, and not at the feet of those ultimate and sublime values that had retreated inward. And, yet, strangely enough, when Weber came to describe the spirit that had retreated from the public sphere into the bourgeois interior, what he described was the spirit of an ancient war god, Yahweh, and the community this spirit had welded together like a firebrand; or, perhaps, more generally, it may not have been Yahweh that Weber had in mind, but rather an ideal-typical religious war god.

Do we need to remind ourselves of Weber's own response to depersonalization of political authority in the modern constitutional state (*Rechtsstaat*)? The impersonalism of the constitutional state had struck Weber as 'comparable to the impersonal retribution of *karma*, in contrast to Yahweh's fervent quest for vengeance'. Yet, when he came to describe the spirit pulsating in the bourgeois interior he had not described this spirit in Indic terms, but rather in terms comparable to Yahweh's fervent quest for vengeance. Of perhaps even greater importance, Weber had described the spirit of the legitimate violence exercised by and on behalf of constitutional state 'from the religious point of view' as 'the most effective mimicry of brutality' and 'completely senseless'.[16] In other words, here Weber was clearly associating Yahweh's vengeance and the religious point of view with open, militant hostility to the modern constitutional state. Is it possible then that Weber was entirely unaware that it was precisely this sense of divine vengeance against the sclerotic constitutional state that drove many young men to their deaths between 1914 and 1919?

No, Weber was not unaware. And in 1915, in a study titled 'Zwischenbetrachtung', or interim observations, published in his *Archiv für Sozialwissenchaft und Sozialpolitik*, Weber wrote presciently of what he then called the modern state's 'community unto death' (*Gemeinschaft bis zum Tode*). Here in fact in his 1915 article we find the earliest evidence of Weber's rhetorical 'religious point of view' that he would then continue to deploy on many occasions. In 1915 Weber began his discussion of the 'community unto death' by noting how 'in contrast to naïve, primitive heroism, it is typical of the rational state systems [*rationalen Staat*] for groups or rulers to line up for violent conflict, all quite sincerely believing themselves to be "in the right"'.[17] He then deployed the now familiar phrase, noting how 'to any consistent religious rationalization, this must seem only an aping of ethics'.[18] And again, 'the more matter-of-fact and calculating politics is, and the freer of passionate feelings, of wrath, and of love it becomes, the more it must appear to an ethic of brotherliness to be estranged from brotherliness'.[19] And then we read the following:

> The mutual strangeness of religion and politics, when they are both completely rationalized, is all the more the case because, in contrast to economics, politics may come into direct competition with religious ethics at decisive points. As the consummated threat of violence among modern polities, war creates a pathos and a sentiment of community. War thereby makes for an unconditionally devoted and sacrificial community among the combatants and releases an active mass compassion and love for those who are in need.[20]

Obviously what Weber meant to suggest here was that, in so far as both war and religion produce and draw upon the same or similar emotions, they could easily find themselves in competition with one another. But, who is to say that the emotions that war draws upon or that it creates are not themselves authentic religious emotions? Who is to say that the practicing Lutheran, Baptist or Catholic, the devout Presbyterian, Jew, Muslim or Hindu who finds himself drawn to the battlefield to sacrifice his body for sublime values is not, at the moment of sacrifice, engaging in a supremely religious act, an act no less religious and spiritual than prayer, meditation, or giving alms? Indeed, as Weber himself must have known, this question could not be avoided, particularly in light of the fact that so many of those who most eagerly supported military action in August 1914 were also deeply and profoundly religious. Thus, Weber had to acknowledge that 'as a mass phenomenon, these feelings break down all naturally given barriers of association. In general, religions can show comparable achievements only in heroic communities professing an ethic of brotherliness'.[21] But then why not also in heroic communities professing an ethic of war?

In social formations that place a high premium on bodily integrity, upon the intimate relationship between the sacred body and the embodied spirit, social actors spend a great deal of energy avoiding officially sanctioned mass death, making it necessary for authorities to press them into service. In mature capitalist social formations, where social actors have grown accustomed to radically distinguishing immaterial value from its material form of appearance, war and death in combat can strike social actors as the height of spiritual service. Indeed, this seems consistent with Weber's interpretation of the 'community unto death', which he described as follows:

> Moreover, war does something to the warrior which, in its concrete meaning, is unique: it makes him experience a consecrated meaning of death which is characteristic only of death in war. The community of the army standing in the field today feels itself – *as in the times of the war lords "following"* – to be a community unto death [*eine Gemeinschaft bis zum Tode*], and the greatest of its kind.[22]

The problem Weber faced here was clear. The community he saw forming in the shadow of the state sanctioned mass death of 1914 and 1915 appeared to him to reflect in almost every respect the same community that he was then studying in ancient Greece, China, India and Palestine all the way down to 'the war lord's following'. It is possible, of course, that the modern 'community unto death' provided the model and archetype upon which he then based the ancient community. Yet, in either case, Weber was faced with the same dilemma. Methodologically as early as 1902 he had already written religion and spirituality out of the public sphere. And, yet, here in 1915 Weber saw indisputable evidence of 'something pulsating' that looked very similar to the warrior communities 'as in the times of the war lords "following"' in ancient China, India, Greece and Palestine. Even more telling, since he realized that traditional religion no longer dominated religious subjectivity and practice under capitalism, Weber had to acknowledge the possibility that war itself might provide the ultimate meaning that traditional religion no longer could, particularly at the moment of death.

> Death on the field of battle differs from death that is only man's common lot. Since death is a fate that comes to everyone, nobody can say why it comes precisely to him and why it comes just when it does. As the values of culture increasingly unfold and are sublimated to immeasurable heights, such ordinary death marks an end where only a beginning seems to make sense. Death on the field of battle differs from this merely unavoidable dying in that in war, and in this massiveness *only* in war, the individual can *believe* that he knows he is dying "for" something. . . . This location of death within a series of meaningful and consecrated events ultimately lies at the base of all endeavors to support the autonomous dignity of the polity resting on force.[23]

What Weber was watching unfold before him, which he took to be the formation of a new religious community, so confounded his sense of the emptiness of capitalist modernity and so threatened his methodologically rigorous understanding of how religion and capitalism must be related to one another that he was forced to draw a line between authentic, sublime (which is to say *private*) religion, on the one hand, and inauthentic, merely outward (which is to say *public* religion) on the other.

And, yet, notwithstanding this distinction, which Weber clung to through the end of the war, the Great War clearly pushed him to the limit both methodologically and theoretically, as this final quote from his *Zwischenbetrachtung* indicates:

> The very extraordinary quality of brotherliness of war, and of death in war, is shared with sacred charisma and the experience of the communion with God, and this fact raises the competition between the brotherliness of religion and of the warrior community to its extreme height.[24]

To be sure, some, perhaps many or even most of those who were *genuinely* religious or spiritual might in principle have opposed war. Still, even today our most sensitive survey instruments confirm that those among us who count themselves most religious are also those who are most ready to make the ultimate sacrifice and most likely to support political leaders who ask them to do so.[25] Death and religion, mortality and spirituality would thus appear to be tightly intertwined, at least under capitalist modernity. Why?

Death and the value form of the commodity

In his mature social theory, Marx identified a social form, the value form of the commodity, which reproduced itself by retreating behind and annihilating its own material form of appearance. Might it be that this description also accurately captures the character of contemporary religion and spirituality? Marx it seems clear, was a remarkably good social theorist. Long before anyone else, he saw that capitalism was not principally a means to produce material wealth, but a vehicle for producing and enhancing immaterial value. Moreover, Marx saw how a society whose social relations were governed by the production of abstract value might have to endure certain social pathologies that differed from those encountered by other social formations. Yet, because Marx was a poor student of religion and spirituality, he almost always drew the wrong theological or religious conclusions from his economic and social analysis. This, as we saw, was notably the case when he mistook the theological parallel of commodity fetishism to be some variety of spiritualism. It is not the products of human brains that become autonomous figures in contemporary religion or spirituality, but the dynamic, vibrant value form itself. Similarly, when Marx drew upon Hegel's description of the *Weltgeist* or World Spirit to reinforce his own analysis of the value form of the commodity, the appropriate spiritual analogy would not have been the Son's differentiation from the Father in Trinitarian Christianity, but the near universal isolation of the immaterial spirit from its own material forms of appearance.

But, perhaps the most egregious oversight both by Marx and by Marxist interpreters of religion is to view contemporary religion solely or predominantly as an 'opiate of the masses', a drug designed to deaden the pain, but also to mask the true causes for the violence to which they are subject. What makes this oversight so particularly egregious is that it entirely misses the way that the value form of the commodity actually bears society forward, effectively structuring social relations and guiding social subjectivity and action towards the kind of officially sanctioned mass death that has become characteristic of our age. The value form is therefore not an illusory force. Nor is it an opiate. It has created and it guides the world in which we live and move and have our being. But, since its own movement, the movement of the value form of the commodity, is directed towards the annihilation of its own body, and towards the creation of its body only so that it can be annihilated, this world in which we live and move and have our being is already always a 'community unto death'. This is because the only procedure through which the value form can successfully make its way back to itself is by shedding its material body and returning to its pure immaterial form. We may be inclined to view this language as metaphorical. But, as we have seen, it may also be viewed as the way the value form negotiates its way through the world of the senses. Like the Kantian sublime it makes its way through the world by bringing social actors to love it in spite of the violence it commits against them – or perhaps because of this violence.

Passchendaele: the sacrificial ground

But here we are again thrown back upon the real experience of war. Paul Fussell has noted how war almost invariably displays a certain doubled quality. In fact, Fussell reports how one soldier 'bogged down in the [Ypres] Salient in September 1917, devoted many passages in his diary to considering the anomaly: '"I often think how strange it is that quiet home life is going on at Weybridge, and everywhere else in England, all the time that these terrific things are happening here"'.[26] Another participant in the war, Fussell tells us, recalled a similar doubling and recorded his recollections in a novel: 'Hard to believe. Impossible to believe. That other life, so near in time and distance, was something led by different men. Two lives that bore no relation to each other. That was what they all felt, the bloody lot of them'.[27] However, this doubling, while perhaps exaggerated in war, is not unique to war. Indeed, what I have suggested is that our very readiness for war in the modern epoch is a feature of our doubledness, of the experience all of us have of existing both as an immaterial self and as a body that is not only not identical with that self, but which we are everywhere encouraged to master, transcend and leave behind.

Finally, Fussell also mentions another feature of modern war, its interminableness. As proof that this impression, widespread during the Great War, might actually have legs, Fussell noted the headline of a 1 September 1972 *New York Times* article, which read: 'U.S. AIDES IN VIETNAM SEE AN UNENDING WAR.' But, thirty years on, what is most interesting about Fussell's remarks regarding the interminableness of war is that this could have been said at almost any moment during the past five centuries. Ours is a social formation that lives off of death, that consumes itself and that lives off of consuming itself. As Joseph Schumpeter noted over a half century ago, capitalism is a system that depends upon a process of 'creative destruction'.[28] What Schumpeter did not note and indeed what most social scientists have overlooked is that this creative destruction exists side-by-side in a social formation that is also deeply, actively and publicly religious.

The question we have sought to address is how these two facts might be related to one another. What if this 'creatively destructive' isolation of the sublime from its material form of appearance is what ultimately distinguishes religious subjectivity and practices in the capitalist social formation from their counterparts elsewhere? This predisposition emerged half way through the fourteenth century when the value of productive human activity was first subjected to the abstract equal units of time marched out by city clocks. Herein, abstract value became increasingly isolated from the material bodies whose values it measured. But herein also, social actors were predisposed to experiencing and explaining value, including religious and spiritual value, in terms that were increasingly isolated from their material forms of appearance. The fact that from this point forward social actors have proven themselves increasingly ready to sacrifice their bodies on behalf of sublime values would strongly suggest that the isolation of the sublime from its material forms of appearance is a socially generalized phenomenon. It identifies what is unique about religion and spirituality under capitalism.

8 The body of religion

The story we have told is grim. If we are correct, the intimate relationship that has developed between contemporary spirituality and the value form of the commodity has formed a substance more toxic than any other in history. It may therefore be valuable for us to bear in mind, first, that social formations are never as uniform, nor as totalizing in practice as they may appear in theory; and, second, that the 'community unto death', while real, forms only the most extreme experience of contemporary religious subjectivity and practice. Short of death on the battlefield, contemporary religious practitioners have rediscovered and have themselves created a wide variety of ways in which the sublime can set itself over against its own material form of appearance. For example, sociologist Donald E. Miller has conducted a comprehensive study of the two most powerful and influential brand-name Protestant mega-churches to emerge over the past three decades: the Vineyard and Calvary. Miller restricts the bulk of his analysis to communities in the United States. Still, some might be surprised to learn how many mega-churches Vineyard and Calvary organizers have 'planted' elsewhere in the world: over 270, including twenty in Australia, fifty-two in Canada, twenty-nine in England, thirteen in New Zealand, and eighteen in South Africa.[1] Obviously, however, even these numbers pale when set over against the more than 1,020 Vineyard (406) and Calvary (614) fellowships in the United States.[2]

Miller calls these new fellowships 'new paradigm churches'. According to him, new paradigm churches 'are contributing to what has been called a new era of post-denominational Christianity in America, reflecting a general disillusionment with bureaucratic hierarchies and organizational oversight'.[3] This hostility towards hierarchies and organizational structures is, of course, a signature trait of the sublime. 'Sublime', after all, 'is what, by its resistance to the interest of the senses, we like directly'.[4] Indeed, although most new paradigm Christians would certainly disavow any connection, this resistance to the interest of the senses was a central feature of the teachings of early nineteenth century theologian Friedrich Schleiermacher, widely considered the founder of liberal Christianity. In his most famous work, titled simply *Über die Religion: Reden an die Gebildeten unter ihren Verächtern (On Religion: Speeches to Its Cultured Despisers)*, written in 1799, Schleiermacher invited Christians to qualitatively differentiate between an institutional, historical religion, and its sublime supra-historical reality, which, following Kant, he felt was superior to any standard of sense.[5] To this extent, new paradigm churches may indicate a far less radical turn in contemporary religion than Miller suggests, signalling not so much a departure from mainline Protestant Christianity as much as an intensification of the same.

In fact, it is worth noting how new paradigm churches reinforce and play into the near universal hostility towards and fear of secularization and disenchantment. In what is by almost all measures a decidedly non-secular, anti-secular and profoundly religious social formation, Miller states explicitly that the new paradigm 'churches are a counterpoint to secular society'.[6] This, of course, reinforces our claim that hostility against secularity has less to do with whether in fact institutions or laws are in some objective sense secular than with a much deeper and pervasive hostility against the body – including the institutional body – as such. But, perhaps even more telling, Miller shows how new paradigm churches fit an organizational model specially suited to what business management guru Peter Drucker uncharacteristically misrecognized as the 'post-capitalist society'.[7] Drucker, whose intellectual capital has declined significantly in the post-dot-com slump,[8] was in 1997 still 'one of the twentieth century's most influential business theorists'.[9] Drucker correctly noted how the successful institution needs 'to build in organized abandonment of everything it does. It has to learn to ask every few years of every process, every product, every procedure, every policy: "If we did not do this already, would we go into it now, knowing what we now know?"'[10] Miller believes that new paradigm churches are inadvertently confirming Drucker's analysis. He is right, of course. They are. But, this is no more evidence of a post-capitalist society than was the 'creative destruction'[11] that Schumpeter noted over a half century ago or, for that matter, the 'melting of all that is solid into air' noted by Marx over a century and a half ago.[12]

Rather than indicating a radical countercultural paradigm shift in contemporary religion, new paradigm fellowships epitomize the variety of disembodied religion and spirituality that since the mid-fourteenth century has shown increasing hostility towards the body of religion. This was already evident early on in what was not yet the Protestant Reformation. For what was most distinctive about the early Reformation's transformation in religious subjectivity was the profound discomfort and embarrassment reformers displayed over the body of religion in all of its specific manifestations: the unflattering history of the institutional church, with its unending political intrigue, deceit, greed, lasciviousness, lewdness and crime; Canon Law, with its hubris to state in human words what only God had the power to state in Holy Writ; Holy Sacrament, with its embarrassing belief that God could be physically present to the Church in something so common as Bread and Wine; the whole cult of relics and saints, with its magical expectation that the spirits of the departed might convey divine power through bones, hair, teeth, clothing or common household items. It is not as though Christians were unaware of these things prior to the fourteenth century. Nor is it that Christians were not disturbed by them. But in so far as social actors implicitly understood that divine embodiment was a necessary and good, albeit messy and risky, affair, these attributes of embodiment were not only tolerated, but, as Bakhtin has convincingly shown, even celebrated.[13]

The embarrassment, distrust and hostility that new paradigm (Miller also calls them 'post-modern') Christians display towards the body of religion – its institutionally, economically, socially, historically, creedally embodied character – is one of contemporary religion's most distinguishing characteristics. We, therefore, need to bear in mind that when new paradigm religious practitioners file out of mainline churches, synagogues, mosques and ashrams and into new paradigm religious bodies, they are only filing out of some of capitalism's most illustrious creations and into their successors.

On the more humorous side, what Miller calls new paradigm fellowships, Charles Trueheart calls the 'Next Church'.[14] In his 1996 *Atlantic Monthly* cover story, Trueheart tells us how the next church appears to satisfy contemporary social actors' loss of a sense of belonging to a community.

> Social institutions that once held civic life together – schools, families, govern-ments, companies, neighborhoods, and even old-style churches – are not what they used to be (if ever they were what we imagined). The new congregations are reorganizing religious life to fill that void. The Next Church in its fully realized state can be the clearest approximation of community, and perhaps the most important civic structure, that a whole generation is likely to have known or likely to find anywhere in an impersonal, transient nation.[15]

Yet, the deeper we probe into this community the more it begins to morph into what might be called an infinitely transportable sense of community, the very opposite of an embodied community; more like a transfigured religious suburb than 'our town'.[16] Not surprisingly, like Miller, Trueheart also finds a place for business consultant Drucker in the next church. Only it is Drucker's three questions that come to mind for Trueheart: 'What is our business? Who is our customer? What does the customer consider value?'

These are questions that investors ask, that money managers ask, that chief exec-utive or operating officers ask? Are they also the questions that neighbours ask one another, that school principles ask teachers, that husbands or wives or children ask one another? Is this what we mean by community? What is remarkable about new paradigm and next church religious communities, however, is that their members view their unabashed business outlook and style as not only truly radical, but also authentically biblical and religious. It is taken as authentically biblical and religious, however, not because new paradigm religious practitioners actually have any famil-iarity with the institutions, practices, thought forms or structures that helped com-pose first century Christianity. Rather, as Miller puts it, the 'truth to which new paradigm Christians commit their lives is based on the original gospel, rather than emphasizing twenty centuries of interpretation and rationalization'.[17]

> For them, the appeal of the simple worship of the first-century church is that it was not conditioned by professional clergy, by specialists in managing access to the sacred. Those early Christian radicals worshiped in house churches, where very little doctrine had evolved and a complex liturgy, artfully constructed by professional priests, had not yet been born. New paradigm pastors identify with these first-century Jesus followers, who were seeking a more direct relationship with God.[18]

Here, what is remarkable is that new paradigm religious practitioners evidently actually believe this story to be accurate. Without interest in the scholarly research documenting the practices, thought forms, institutional constraints and social forces that shaped first century Christianity, new paradigm leaders and believers are perfectly happy to drift into what Frederic Jameson has called the 'new nostalgia', a longing for a 'past' which is entirely devoid of a 'historical referent'.[19] What early Christians were like, apparently, is savvy Peter Drucker-style business consultants.

Radical orthodoxy[20]

In light of this dramatic departure from anything remotely connected to traditional religion or spirituality, indeed from history itself, some scholars within the Roman Catholic Church have advocated a return to what they are calling 'radical orthodoxy'. In a manner not entirely dissimilar from the approach we took at the outset of our study, scholars such as Catherine Pickstock and John Milbank have sought to show that sometime in the thirteenth or fourteenth centuries religion and spirituality went off track. In Pickstock's view, this derailment occurred sometime in the late thirteenth century when John duns Scotus advanced 'doctrines – univocity of being and the "formal distinction"' which in Pickstock's view were 'deliberately and consciously opposed to those of Aquinas'.[21] We, too, suggested that there was an affinity between nominalism as a theoretical system and the new forms of practice and practical knowledge that arose in conjunction with the measurement of productive human activity in abstract equal units of time. Yet, whereas Pickstock invites her readers to celebrate the Eucharist and allow its divine powers to emancipate them, we suggest a different although not necessarily hostile approach. If the isolation of the sublime from its material form of appearance can be held in some sense responsible for 'the destruction from within of the liturgical city', then the liturgical city cannot be achieved without simultaneously challenging the practical isolation of the sublime from its material form of appearance as this has unfolded within the capitalist social formation.

Here too we might also offer a friendly correction to John Milbank's misinterpretation of Marxian social theory. In a chapter titled 'Policing the Sublime', Milbank argues that 'the sociology of religion ought to come to an end' since, 'from a deconstructive angle, the priority of society over religion can always be inverted, and every secular positivism is revealed to be also a positivist theology'.[22] Of course, this had been Carl Schmitt's claim as well.[23] Milbank's principle objection would appear to be that social scientists wrongly situate religion within the Kantian sublime.

> Normative value, including religion, is consequently relocated by sociology "at the margins" – either at the point where the individual is supposed to stand outside and over-against the social, meaning the realm of verifiable facts (Weber) or else as the mysterious ether which mediates between one ineffable individual and the other and yet goes up to make the social substance of practical reason (Durkheim and Simmel). Thus religion is regarded by sociology as belonging to the Kantian sublime: a realm of ineffable majesty beyond the bounds of the

possibility of theoretical knowledge, a domain which cannot be imaginatively represented, and yet whose overwhelming presence can be acknowledged by our frustrated imaginative powers.[24]

Here too, Milbank offers an argument not altogether dissimilar from the one I have offered above. Where it differs is that whereas Milbank appears to credit social theory with having invented the sublime into which it then relocates religion, in our view the sublime is in fact the soul and substance of contemporary religion and spirituality. Because we have interpreted the Kantian sublime not solely as a transcendental category or fundamentally ontological reality, but, also as a social form generated by a dramatic transformation in practice – the emergence of capitalism – we are under no obligation to accord the sublime a supra- or trans-historical character. Marx, we have noted, completely misrecognized how contemporary religion and spirituality are composed. Nevertheless, it was Marx's immanent social critique that allowed us to attribute social and historical validity to the sublime without having then either to grant it 'ineffable majesty' or to simply limit our research to 'verifiable facts' (which is not quite what Weber did either). Indeed, once we recognize that the sublime value form of the commodity sets itself over against its own material form of appearance – which is to say, the commodity's own brute objectivity – the transhistorical validity of this sublime value and this phantom objectivity are both equally called into question.

Finally, however, we must also disagree with Milbank's insistence that the sociology of religion come to an end. Rather, what might come to an end is its reluctance to come to terms with the social and historical embeddedness of its own interpretive categories, a reluctance it shares with the advocates of 'radical orthodoxy'. Here, one of the outcomes of the present study could be that social theorists and researchers come to a deeper understanding of how Weber's interpretive categories were decisively shaped by the very phenomenon, capitalism, he was seeking to explain. Heaven knows how often it has been said that Weber was a neo-Kantian. Yet, of far greater importance it strikes me is the fact that both Kant and Weber reflected upon their worlds from within a social formation – capitalism – that lent social validity to Kant's interpretive categories. It is to Weber's credit that, in his *Protestant Ethic*, he went some distance towards identifying the historical and social forces that lent relative validity to his categories. Sadly, however, he did not seem to recognize that the overarching distinction that hovered over his entire project, the distinction that Kant had drawn between the sublime and its material form of appearance, was the decisive point. As a consequence, when at the end of his study he had the spirit of capitalism escape from the iron cage, Weber was unaware that, precisely at that moment, he was most guilty of misrecognizing the true movement of the sublime value form of the commodity.

Embodied religion – spiritual bodies

This also helps to explain why, although we share radical orthodoxy's critique of capitalist ontology, we depart from its pursuit of a liturgical future. For while Pickstock and Milbank already know in advance and are ready to enforce for all time the liturgical practices which they are certain will transform the world and restore it to its rightful place, we are forced to face the embeddedness of our own thought and practice and therefore also to face the embeddedness of our interpretive categories. These categories, no less than Weber's or Marx's categories, are themselves products of the capitalist social formation. Indeed, in so far as thought itself is never as free from its body as it fears and/or wishes, this embeddedness might turn out to be what is good and wholesome, even emancipatory, about thought itself. This I take was the point Theodor Adorno hoped to make when, in the concluding aphorism to his *Minima Moralia*, he identified 'the only philosophy which can be responsibly practiced in face of despair' with

> the attempt to contemplate all things as they would present themselves from the standpoint of redemption [*vom Standpunkt der Erlösung*]. Knowledge has no light but that shed on the world by redemption: all else is reconstruction, mere technique. Perspectives must be fashioned that displace [*ähnlich sich versetzt*] and estrange [*verfremdet*] the world, reveal it to be, with its rifts and crevices, as indigent and distorted [*bedürftig und entstellt*] as it will appear one day in the messianic light.[25]

Yet, here even Adorno revealed himself to be too much of a Kantian to see that reconstruction and mere technique, so long as they are not granted transcendental status, are not in and of themselves lacking in redemption. Indeed, it was on some level precisely Weber's misidentification of the mechanical foundations of capitalism with Kant's world of the senses (in opposition to the sublime) that misled him to mistake the flight of the spirit from capitalism for proof of its disenchantment and secularization. Had he instead recognized that the *Triebwerk* of capitalism, its 'engine', was neither its cold, hard shell, nor its storehouse of commodities, but rather its hot, dynamic interior, Weber might then have concluded that modern capitalism, far from reinforcing disenchantment, is among the most spiritually and religiously dynamic social formations in history.

Post-capitalism religion

This, however, brings us in closing to the perplexing question of what might become of religion and spirituality once capitalism, like every social formation, runs its course and gives way to something new. Here, too, we are forced to depart not only from Pickstock and Milbank, but from Marx and Weber as well. As for Weber, even though he confessed that 'no one yet knows who will live in that shell in the future', he appears himself to have known enough to offer two divergent alternatives:

> Perhaps new prophets will emerge, or powerful old ideas and ideals will be reborn at the end of this monstrous development. *Or* perhaps – if neither of these occurs – "Chinese" ossification, dressed up with a kind of desperate self-importance, will set in. Then, however, it might truly be said of the "last men" in this cultural

development: "specialists without spirit, hedonists without a heart", these nonentities imagine they have attained a stage of humankind never before reached.[26]

Can there be any doubt but that of these two alternatives Weber favoured the former over the latter? And, yet, tragically, it is clear that these new prophets have already arrived. Weber himself was already familiar with them. They were his students. To the extent that Weber's own interpretation of the prophetic spirit was modelled after the sublime value form of the commodity, these prophets could not help but emerge bearing both powerful old ideas as well as new. And, yet, as Weber himself appears to have realized, even these thoughts went too far. 'Here ... we are getting into the area of judgments of value and belief, with which', he felt, 'this purely historical study should not be encumbered'.[27] Yet, like all intellectual work, Weber's study was inevitably so encumbered.

But, then, what of Marx's post-religious future? Here, again, Marx proved his own worst enemy. Like a bad comic who is least comical when he is most self-conscious of his humour, Marx was most theologically tone-deaf at those points where he self-consciously addressed the topic of religion. Here his comments on the future of religion are no exception. Marx's clearest and most succinct remarks appear at the beginning of his *Contribution to the Critique of Hegel's Philosophy of Right: Introduction*, where he asserted that:

> For German, the *criticism of religion* has been essentially completed, and the crit-
> icism of religion is the prerequisite of all criticism. The *profane* existence of error
> is compromised as soon as its *heavenly oratio pro aris et focis* [plea on behalf of
> hearth and home] has been refuted. Man, who has found only the *reflection* of
> himself in the fantastic reality of heaven, where he sought a superman, will no
> longer feel disposed to find the mere *appearance* of himself, the non-man, where
> he seeks and must seek his true identity.[28]

The tragedy for Marx, particularly with respect to religion, was that he only had eyes for religious and spiritual formations constituted *within* the capitalist social forma-tion. Such religious and spiritual formations, it is true, appear to transcendentalize and ontologize a feature of human social subjectivity – the sublime – which is in fact the objective agent of contemporary humanity's greatest suffering. But, prior to and perhaps after the passing of the value form of the commodity, it is not inconceivable that social actors will rediscover (and, indeed, help constitute) spiritual realities that are not easily reducible to the value form of the commodity. Here, it is clear that it never occurred to Marx that among the forces that might shape human identity (and shape it for the better) were those in the natural world around him. The re-enchantment of this world, its repopulation by 'spirits' able to sound out warnings of impending danger and the cultivation of ears attuned to hearing such warnings might not be an unreasonable expectation for religious practitioners in a truly post-capitalist world.

Here, as we might have anticipated, it was where Marx was least aware of the religious implications of his reflections that he turns out to have offered his most penetrating insight into the religious constitution of a post-capitalist world. At the end of the final volume of *Capital*, in a passage that has troubled orthodox and traditional Marxists ever since its implicit Aristotelian assumptions[29] were first explicitly exposed, Marx commented rather freely on the conditions that he felt were required for the realization of true freedom.

> The realm of freedom really begins only where labour determined by necessity and external expediency ends; it lies by its very nature beyond the sphere of material production proper. Just as the savage must wrestle with nature to satisfy his needs, to maintain and reproduce his life, so must civilized man, and he must do so in all forms of society and under all possible modes of production. This realm of natural necessity expands with his development, because his needs do too; but the productive forces to satisfy these expand at the same time. Freedom, in this sphere, can consist only in this, that socialized man, the associated producers, govern the human metabolism with nature in a rational way, bringing it under their collective control instead of being dominated by it as a blind power; accomplishing it with the least expenditure of energy and in conditions most worthy and appropriate for their human nature. But this always remains a realm of necessity. The true realm of freedom, the development of human powers as an end in itself, begins beyond it, though it can only flourish with this realm of necessity as its basis.[30]

Obviously we cannot agree with everything – perhaps not even with most – that Marx wrote here. For us, Marx's remarks still display too much of what Jean Baudrillard called a 'productivist' mentality.[31] Likewise, though we get his point, we would just as soon that Marx had not used the derogatory *der Wilde* (the savage) in his reference to social actors in face-to-face communities.[32] Yet, Marx's point is not altogether at odds with the position Hannah Arendt articulated in the diatribe she once launched against him,[33] namely that it is those who act and not those who labour who are truly free. Also like Arendt, Marx contemplated a world not unlike our own in which productivity had been so enhanced as to allow human beings, those who formerly laboured, to become those who act.[34] Yet, in contrast to Arendt, who would not allow herself to believe that labourers could ever meaningfully take advantage of such a realm of freedom, Marx felt that human dignity demanded nothing less. So, against Arendt, who believed that 'we are confronted with … the prospect of a society of laborers without labour, that is, without the only activity left to them. Surely, nothing could be worse',[35] Marx contemplated a significant, practically induced transformation in human ontology. He contemplated human beings who no longer identified themselves with labour. Sadly, Arendt held that labourers were labourers not because of the social formation in which they were born, but, as Aristotle had once put it, because they were 'natural slaves'.[36]

Yet it is something else that strikes me as peculiar about Marx's discussion of freedom. In a manner that is not true (or not as true) for, let us say, the first three chapters of *Capital*, Marx here appears entirely at home contemplating a non-antagonistic relationship between human beings, their actions, and the realms both of necessity and of freedom.

Few people have thought more carefully about this passage in Marx than the French sociologist André Gorz, whose *Farewell to the Working Class*[37] and *Critique of Economic Reason*[38] have now become classics of post-fordist scholarship. In the latter work, Gorz notes how the free time released by ever increasing productivity is immediately recolonized by our own compulsion to sell our free time for even more commodities and services. Gorz catalogues the seemingly endless list of tasks we once performed without care for the time they consumed, precisely because, as Marx once observed, they lacked (abstract) value.[39] Gorz' rallying cry is that we should claim the time delivered to us through our ever mounting advancements in productivity. 'An expansion in the sphere of autonomous activities', writes Gorz, 'cannot, by definition, *come about as a result of* a policy which reduces state provision and state services, thus leaving those social strata least able to do so to fend for themselves.'

> The expansion of a sphere of autonomy always presupposes that, time no longer being counted, individuals have chosen to repatriate into the domestic or microsocial sphere of voluntary co-operation activities which, for want of time, they had abandoned to external services.

Here, however, Alberto Alesina, Edward Glaeser and Bruce Sacerdote, of the Harvard Institute of Economic Research, have a slightly different take. They note that it was only under collective mutual coercion that Europe's labour unions and governing bodies succeeded in shortening the work day, thereby freeing up time for all workers across the board. For so long as any significant body of workers is left out of the mix, suspicions will linger among those who are not working that they are being cheated out of potential income.[40] This also was Marx's point. The form of domination under which we labour is only *socially* related to labour time. 'The real wealth of society and the possibility of a constant expansion of its reproduction process,' wrote Marx just before the passage above, 'does not depend on the length of surplus labour but rather on its productivity and on the more or less plentiful conditions of production in which it is performed. The realm of freedom really begins only where labour . . . ends'.[41] Yet, Gorz' counsel should not be dismissed lightly. For what is to prevent social actors, once granted more time, from simply reproducing the only domination they know, wage labour, privately? According to Alesina's, Glaeser's and Sacerdote's research, the only thing to prevent them from doing so is that, once a four day week or a six hour day acquire the patina of 'normality', workers so habituated come to think of the foreshortened workday as normal. Repatriation of the private sphere must therefore be accompanied by rigorously enacted and enforced public policy. But, is this enough?

The problem is, capitalism aims not to produce material wealth, but immaterial value. For this reason alone, its appetite is insatiable. For while it is always possible for individuals to know when they have eaten or drunk too much, when they have purchased too many pairs of shoes, or when they own more books than they can possibly read, at what point would we know that we had accumulated too much abstract value? The sublime value form of the commodity is such that it cannot help but expand. Time freed up by ever greater productivity is time made available for ever new rounds of production and consumption – not, it should be noted, because we lack material wealth, but because immaterial value knows no limit.

Most of those trained in the social sciences are inclined to attack this problem from the side of production. We hand out tax credits and incentives to enterprises whose investors are willing to adopt responsible business practices. And, yet, since the abstract domination under which we labour is constituted by the connection we have drawn socially between productive human activity and abstract time, the only way to truly break this cycle of domination would be to dissociate value from productive activity – i.e. to shorten the working day. Indeed, in 1988, when Gorz' critique of economic reason was first published in France, it looked very much as though labour was prepared to further weaken this tie between abstract value and productive human activity. The dissociation of the two could have dealt a serious blow to capital accumulation were it not for the late twentieth century's post-democratic adjustment.

Michigan sociologist George Steinmetz has suggested that this threat to capital accumulation may even help account for the rise of political authoritarianism and economic imperialism in post-fordist America.[42] If so, then this may also help to explain why the authoritarian turn in the United States has been accompanied by a ramping up of religious support for American military adventurism abroad and political authoritarianism at home.[43] For what is at stake is not simply a specific political agenda or economic policies that promise to enhance returns on investment for investors. What is at stake is the vitality of the sublime value form of the commodity, the very heart and soul of contemporary religion and spirituality. Or, more precisely, what is at stake is a specific experience and understanding of the religious sublime that is inextricably bound to the value form of the commodity.

If we are correct, however, and it is only within the last six centuries that religion and spirituality have tied themselves to the value form of the commodity, then this would suggest that there is nothing intrinsic to religion that requires that it maintain its relationship with capital. To the contrary, this relationship has greatly distorted religion and spirituality, depriving them not only of what for centuries was widely deemed most indispensable to them – their very body – but also tragically bringing them to embrace a disembodied, de-historicized, anti-historical and largely empty notion of freedom. In principle, neither religion nor spirituality is under any compulsion to abandon their bodies in their pursuit of freedom. The more pressing question may therefore be how religion and spirituality can retain their body while pursuing freedom.

In the final volume of *Capital*, Marx clearly identified the precondition for freedom; not revolution, not overthrowing the bourgeois state, not taking over the means of production, but precisely the shortening of the work day.

> The true realm of freedom, the development of human powers as an end in itself, begins beyond [the realm of labour], ... it can only flourish with this realm of necessity as its basis. . . . The reduction of the working day is the basic prerequisite.[44]

If we are correct and the form of social domination under which we live has also completely transformed religious subjectivity and practice, then perhaps Marx's solution may also help religious practitioners rediscover the body of religion, not by removing the mystical veil that 'conceals' the actual material basis of social life from them. To the contrary, once the social basis for sublime value has been exposed, once value has been freed from its dependence on abstract time, the material world may itself also be restored and transformed into the complex, many-sided, and profoundly sacred place most religious practitioners throughout history have believed it to be. Here, they might not only rediscover the body of religion. Here, the body of religion might also rediscover its own embodied spirit.

Perhaps such discoveries or rediscoveries are already on the horizon. Perhaps they still lie several decades or centuries in the future. At this point, since capitalism appears prepared to destroy every last living body, including the body of religion, for the sake of the sublime value form of the commodity, it is far from clear that religious practitioners will have an opportunity to re-embody their own spirits, much less those found in the world about them. In any event, our aim here was not so much to predict what may become of either religion or capitalism, but to identify the intimate, mutually constitutive, and ultimately morbid relationship that binds the two together in our society. If this characterization of contemporary religion holds true, as I believe it does, then it would appear to be of the greatest importance not least for religious practitioners themselves to reexamine how religious disciplines and spiritual practices may have been perverted by capitalism and to explore ways of engaging capitalism less as a partner than as a competitor in the struggle over values in our increasingly post-democratic world.

Notes

Preface

1 Max Weber, 'Wissenschaft als Beruf,' *Gesammelte Aufsätze zur Wissenschaftslehre*, ed. Johannes Winckelmann, 6th edition (Tübingen: J. C. B. Mohr (Paul Siebeck), 1985), p. 612; Max Weber, 'Science as a Vocation,' *From Max Weber: Essays in Sociology*, trans. H.H. Gerth and C. Wright Mills (New York: Oxford University Press, 1958), p. 155.

2 Ibid.

3 Ibid.

4 Theodor W. Adorno and Max Horkheimer, *Dialectic of enlightenment*, trans. John Cumming (New York: Continuum, 1993); Jürgen Habermas, *The theory of communicative action*, vol. 2, trans. Thomas McCarthy (Boston: Beacon Press, 1989), pp. 113–197; Herbert Marcuse, *One-dimensional man: studies in the ideology of advanced industrial society* (Boston: Beacon Press, 1966); Jean-François Lyotard, *The postmodern condition: a report on knowledge*, trans. Geoff Bennington and Brian Massumi (Minneapolis: University of Minnesota Press, 1989), pp. 18–27; Jacques Derrida, 'Structure, sign and play in the discourse of the human sciences,' *Writing and difference*, trans. Alan Bass (Chicago: University of Chicago Press, 1978), pp. 278–293.

5 World Values Study Group, *World Values Survey*, 1981–1984 and 1990–1993. 2nd ICPSR version (Ann Arbor, MI: Institute for Social Research, 1999).

6 Stephen L. Carter, *The culture of disbelief: how American law and politics trivialize Religious devotion* (New York: Anchor Books, 1994).

7 Regis A. Factor, *Guide to the Archiv für Sozialwissenschaft und Sozialpolitik Group, 1904–1933: A History and Comprehensive Bibliography*. Bibliographies and Indexes in Law and Political Science 9 (New York: Greenwood Press, 1988).

8 Richard Benz, *Heidelberg: Schicksal und Geist* (Konstanz: J. Thorbecke, 1961); Helene Tompert, *Lebensformen und Denkwisen der akademischen Welt Heidelbergs im Wilhelminischen Zeitalter: Vornehmlich im Spiegel Zeitgenossischer Selbstzeugnisse* (Hamburg: Matthiesen, 1969); Martin Burgess Green, *The von Richthofen sisters; the triumphant and the tragic modes of love: Else and Frieda von Richthofen, Otto Gross, Max Weber and D.H. Lawrence in the years 1870–1970* (New York: Basic Books, 1974).

9 Guy Oakes, *Weber and Rickert: concept formation in the cultural sciences* (Cambridge, MA: The MIT Press, 1988); Guy Oakes, 'Introductory Essay,' *Roscher and Knies: The logical problems of historical economics*, trans. Guy Oakes (New York: Free Press, 1975).

10 Wolfgang Schluchter, *Rationalism, religion, and domination: a Weberian perspective*, trans. Neil Solomon (Berkeley: University of California Press, 1989); Dirk Käsler, *Max Weber: an introduction to his life and work*, trans. Philippa Hurd (Chicago: University of Chicago Press, 1988).

11 Moishe Postone, *Time, labor, and social domination: a reinterpretation of Marx's critical theory* (New York: Cambridge University Press, 1993); David S. Landes, *Revolution in time: clocks and the making of the modern world* (Cambridge, MA: Harvard University Press, 1983); Jacques le Goff, *Time, Work, and Culture in the Middle Ages*, trans. Arthur Goldhammer (Chicago: University of Chicago Press, 1982); E.P. Thompson, *Customs in Common: studies in traditional popular culture* (New York: The New Press, 1993).

1   Introduction: Contemporary religion

1 Theodor Adorno and Max Horkheimer, *Dialectic of Enlightenment*, trans., John Cumming (New York: Continuum, 1993), p. 3.

2 Georg Steinmetz, 'The State of Emergency and the Revival of American Imperialism: Toward an Authoritarian Post-Fordism,' *Public Culture* 15:2 (2003), pp. 323–345.

3 Stephen L. Carter, *The culture of disbelief: how American law and politics trivialize religious devotion* (New York: Anchor Books, 1994).

4 A.J. Taylor, 'Stanley Baldwin, heresthetics and the realignment of British politics,' *British Journal of Political Science* 35:3 (July 2005), pp. 429–463; C. Collet, 'Bloc voting, polarization and the panethnic hypothesis: the case of Little Saigon,' *Journal of Politics* 67:3 (August 2005), pp. 907–933; M.D. Brewer, 'The rise of partisanship and the expansion of partisan conflict within the American electorate,' *Political Research Quarterly* 58:2 (June 2005), pp. 219–229; J.P. Hoffmann and S.M. Johnson, 'Attitudes toward abortion among religious traditions in the United States: Change or continuity?' *Sociology of Religion* 66:2 (Summer 2005), pp. 161–182; H. Schoen, 'Candidate orientations in election campaigns: an analysis of the German federal election campaigns, 1980–1998,' *Politische Vierteljahresschrift* 45:3 (September 2004), pp. 321+; R. Johnston, K. Jones, R. Sarker, S. Burgess and A. Bolster, 'Party support and the neighbourhood effect: spatial polarization of the British electorate, 1991–2001,' *Political Geography* 23:4 (May 2004), pp. 367–402.

5 Jürgen Habermas, *Theory of communicative action*, vol. 1, trans. Thomas McCarthy (Boston: Beacon Press, 1984), p. xxxix.

6 Karl Marx, 'Critique of Hegel's Philosophy of Right. Introduction,' *Early Writings*, trans. Rodney Livingstone and Gregor Benton (New York: Vintage Books, 1975), p. 244; Karl Marx, 'Zur Kritik der Hegelschen Rechtsphilosophie. Einleitung,' *Werke* (Berlin: Dietz-Verlag, 1956), p. 378.

7 Karl Marx, *Capital: a critique of political economy*, vol. 1, trans. Ben Fowkes (New York: Penguin Books, 1990), p. 149; Karl Marx, *Das Kapital: Kritik der politischen Ökonomie*, vol. 1, in *Marx/Engels Werke*, vol. 23, (Berlin: Dietz-Verlag, 1956), pp. 52–53, 71–72.

8 Marx, *Capital*, vol. 1, p. 165; Marx, *Kapital*, vol. 1, p. 86–87

9 Adam Smith, *An inquiry into the nature and causes of the wealth of nations*, ed. Edwin Cannan (Chicago, IL: University of Chicago Press, 1976), p. 34.

10 Robert Bellah et al., Habits of the Heart: *Individualism and Commitment in American Life* (Berkeley: University of California Press, 1996).

11 Karl Marx, *Capital*, vol. 1, pp. 255–256.

12 Ibid., p. 256.

13 G.F.W. Hegel, *Phenomenology of Spirit*, trans. A.V. Miller (New York: Oxford University Press, 1977), p. 10.

14 European Values Study Group and World Values Survey Association, *European and World Values Surveys Integrated Data File, 1999–2002. Release I*, 2nd ICPSR version (Ann Arbor, MI: Interuniversity Consortium for Political and Social Research, 2004).

15 Jean-François Lyotard, *The postmodern condition: a report on knowledge*, trans. Geoff Bennington and Brian Massumi (Minneapolis: MN: University of Minnesota Press, 1989), 26.

16 Immanuel Kant, 'Analytic of the Sublime,' *Critique of Judgment*, trans. Werner S. Pluhar (Indianapolis: Hackett Publishing Company), p. 106. [*emphasis* in original.]

17 Harry Garuba, 'Explorations in Animist Materialism: Notes on Reading/Writing African Literature, Culture, and Society', *Public Culture* 15(2): 261–285.

18 Thomas Luckmann, *The invisible religion: the problem of religion in modern society* (New York: Macmillan, 1967).

19 Karl Jaspers, *Die geistige Situation der Zeit* (Berlin: W. de Gruyter, 1933).

20 Pierre Bourdieu, *Outline of a theory of practice*, trans. Richard Nice (New York: Cambridge University Press, 1990), pp. 18–19.

21 Joseph Schumpeter, *Capitalism, Socialism and Democracy*, 3rd ed. (New York: Harper & Row, 1962), pp. 81–86.

2 The retreat of ultimate and sublime values

1 Max Weber, 'Science as a Vocation,' in *From Max Weber: Essays in Sociology*, trans. and ed. H.H. Gerth and C. Wright Mills (New York: Oxford University Press, 1958), p. 155.
2 Ibid.
3 Ibid.
4 Dirk Käsler, *Max Weber: an introduction to his life and work*, trans. Philippa Hurd (Chicago: University of Chicago Press, 1988), p. 210.
5 Max Weber, *Die protestantische Ethik, und der Geist des Kapitalismus*, vol. 1, *Gesammelte Aufsätze zur Religionssoziologie*, 8th ed. (Tübingen: J. C. B. Mohr (Paul Siebeck), 1986), p. 204.
6 Weber, 'Science as a Vocation,' p. 155; Max Weber, 'Wissenschaft als Beruf,' in *Gesammelte Aufsätze zur Wissenschaftslehre*, ed. Johannes Winckelmann, 6th rev. ed. (Tübingen: J. C. B. Mohr (Paul Siebeck), 1985), p. 612.
7 Max Weber, *The Protestant Ethic and the 'Spirit' of Capitalism and other writings*, ed. and trans. Peter Baehr and Gordon C. Wells (New York: Penguin Books, 2002), p. 121.
8 Weber, 'Wissenschaft als Beruf,' p. 612.
9 Ibid.
10 M. Rainer Lepsius, 'Mina Tobler and Max Weber: Passion Confined,' trans. Sam Whimster, *Max Weber Studies* (2004).
11 Käsler, *Max Weber*, p. 16.
12 Joseph Lough, 'The Extraordinary Science of Ernst Troeltsch,' *Papers of the Nineteenth Century Working Group of the American Academy of Religion*, ed. Sandra Yocum Mize and Walter E. Wyman, Jr. (Colorado Springs, CO: The Colorado College, 1991), pp. 98–108.
13 Marianne Weber, *Max Weber: A Bibliography*, trans. Harry Zohn (New Brunswick: Transaction Books, 1988), pp. 466–468; Martin Green, *The von Richthofen Sisters: The Triumphant and the Tragic Modes of Love* (New York: Basic Books, Inc., 1974), pp. 140–147, 189–191.
14 Weber, 'Wissenschaft als Beruf,' p. 612.
15 Max Weber, *Wirtschaft und Gesellschaft: Grundriß der verstehenden Soziologie*, 5th ed., (Tübingen: J. C. B. Mohr (Paul Siebeck), 1980), p. 683.
16 Max Weber, *Das Antike Judentum*, vol. 3, *Gesammelte Aufsätze zur Religionssoziologie*, 8th ed (Tübingen: J. C. B. Mohr (Paul Siebeck), 1986), p. 138; Max Weber, *Ancient Judaism*, trans. Hans H. Gerth and Don Martindale (New York: The Free Press, 1967), p. 128.
17 Weber, 'Science as a Vocation,' p. 155.
18 Ronald Inglehart, et al. *World Values Surveys and European Values Surveys, 1981–1984, 1990–1993, and 1995–1997*. ICPSR version (Ann Arbor, MI: Institute for Social Research, 2000).
19 Max Weber, 'Intellectualism and Salvation Religion,' *Economy and Society*, vol. 1, trans. E. Fischoff, H. Gerth, et al. (Berkeley: University of California Press, 1978), p. 517.
20 Thomas Luckmann, *The invisible religion: the problem of religion in modern society* (New York: Macmillan, 1967), p. 106.
21 Max Weber, 'Religious Ethics and the World: Politics,' *Economy and Society*, vol. 1, trans. E. Fischoff, Hans Gerth, et al. (Berkeley, CA: University of California Press, 1978), pp. 600–601.

3 Disembodiment and the sublime: The birth of modern religion

1 Matthew White, 'Historical Atlas of the Twentieth Century,' online, available HTTP: <http://users.erols.com/mwhite28/warstat0.htm#European> (accessed 31 August 2005).
2 Modris Eksteins, *Rites of spring: the Great War and the birth of the modern age* (New York: Anchor Books, 1989), p. xvi.
3 Donna Spivey Ellington, *From sacred body to angelic soul: Understanding Mary in late medieval and early modern Europe* (Washington, DC: Catholic University of America Press, 2001), p. 60.
4 Ibid., pp. viii, 263, 201, 235.

5 Peter Widdicombe, 'The wounds of the ascended body: the marks of crucifixion in the glorified Christ from Justin Martyr to John Calvin,' *Laval théologique et philosophique* 59:1 (*février 2003*).

6 Ibid., p. 138.

7 Ibid., pp. 139–140, citing E. Goodspeed, ed., *Die ältesten Apologeten* (Göttingen: Vandenhoeck & Ruprecht, 1914), p. 132–133.

8 Ibid.

9 Ibid., p. 141.

10 Ibid., p. 147.

11 Ibid.

12 Ibid., p. 149.

13 Ibid., p. 150.

14 Ibid.

15 Ibid., p. 154.

16 Ibid.

17 Ellington, *From Sacred Body*, p. vii.

18 St Thomas Aquinas, *Summa Theologica*, III.75.1, trans. Fathers of the English Dominican Province (New York: Benziger Brothers, 1947–48), p. 3262. Online, available HTTP: <http://www.ccel.org/ccel/aquinas/summa.html> (accessed 28 September 2004)

19 Ibid., III.60.1–8, pp. 3121–3131.

20 André Lapidus, 'Metal, Money, and the Prince: John Buridan and Nicholas Oresme after Thomas Aquinas,' *History of Political Economy* 29:1 (1997), p. 25.

21 Ibid., p. 29.

22 Ibid., p. 32.

23 Moishe Postone, *Time, labor, and social domination: a reinterpretation of Marx's critical theory* (New York: Cambridge University Press, 1993), pp. 202–203.

24 Ibid., p. 209.

25 Ibid., p. 208.

26 Ibid., pp. 209–210.

27 Ibid., p. 210.

28 Ibid.; see also, Jacques le Goff, *Time, Work, and Culture in the Middle Ages*, trans. Arthur Goldhammer (Chicago: University of Chicago Press, 1982), pp. 45–46.

29 Postone, *Time, Labor, and Social* Domination, p. 210.

30 Ibid., p. 211.

31 E.P. Thompson, 'Time, Work-Discipline and Industrial Capitalism,' *Customs in Common: studies in traditional popular culture* (New York: The New Press, 1993), p. 357.

32 Ibid.

33 Ibid., pp. 357–358.

34 Postone, *Time, Labor, and, Social Domination*, p. 209.

35 Ibid., p. 214.

36 Ibid., p. 214.

37 E.P. Thompson, 'Time and Work-Discipline,' pp. 370–382.

38 Simon Schama, *The embarrassment of riches: an interpretation of Dutch culture in the Golden Age* (New York: Knopf, 1987).

39 Adam Smith, 'Of the Real and Nominal Price of Commodities, or of their Price in Labour, and their Price in Money,' *Wealth of Nations* (Chicago: University of Chicago Press, 1976), p. 34.

40 Karl Marx, 'The Value-Form or Exchange Value,' *Capital: a critique of political economy*, vol. 1, trans. Ben Fowkes (New York: Penguin Books, 1990), pp. 138–153.

41 Pierre Bourdieu, *Outline of a theory of practice*, trans. Richard Nice (New York: Cambridge University Press, 1990).

42 Mikhail Bakhtin, *Rabelais and his world*, trans. Helene Iswolsky (Bloomington, IN: Indiana University Press, 1984).

43 Ibid., p. 22.

44 Edmund Burke, *A Philosophical Enquiry into the Origin of our ideas of the Sublime and Beautiful* (Notre Dame, IN: University of Notre Dame Press, 1968), p. 73.

45 Ibid., p. 64.
46 Ibid., p. 39.
47 Luke Gibbons, *Edmund Burke and Ireland: Aesthetics, politics and the colonial sublime* (New York: Cambridge University Press, 2003); Peter J. McCormick, *The Negative Sublime: Ethics, warfare and the dark borders of reason* (Heidelberg: Winter, 2003); Pierre V. Zima, *La negation esthetique: le sujet, le beau et le sublime de Mallarme et Valery 'a Adorno et Lyotard* (Paris: Harmattan, 2002).
48 Burke, *The Sublime and Beautiful*, pp. 39, 57, 64, 71.
49 Ibid., p. 57.
50 Immanuel Kant, 'Analytic of the Sublime,' *Critique of Judgment*, trans. Werner S. Pluhar (Indianapolis: Hackett Publishing Company), p. 106. [*emphasis* in original.]
51 Ibid.
52 Vanessa L. Ryan, 'The Physiological Sublime: Burke's Critique of Reason,' *Journal of the History of Ideas* 62:2 (2001), pp. 265–279.
53 Ibid., p. 109.
54 Ibid.
55 Ibid., p. 103.
56 Immanuel Kant, 'Analytik des Erhabenen,' *Kritik der Ästhetischen Urteilskraft*, ed. Wilhelm Weischedel (Frankfurt aM: Suhrkamp Verlag, 1974), p. 181; Kant, 'Analytic of the Sublime,' p. 115.
57 Georg Lukács, *History and class consciousness: studies in Marxist dialectics*, trans. Rodney Livingstone (Cambridge, MA: The MIT Press, 1971), pp. 89–90.
58 Kant, 'Analytic of the Sublime,' p. 116.
59 Ibid., p. 106.
60 Ibid., p. 117.
61 Kant, 'Analytik des Erhabenen,' p. 193; Kant, 'Analytic of the Sublime,' p. 127.
62 G.F.W. Hegel, *Aesthetics: Lectures on Fine Art: Volume I*, trans. T.M. Knox (New York: Oxford University Press, 1998), pp. 362–363.
63 Ibid., p. 363.
64 Ibid.
65 Hegel, *Aesthetics*, p. 363.
66 Max Weber, 'Science as a Vocation,' *From Max Weber: Essays in Sociology*, trans. H.H. Gerth and C. Wright Mills (New York: Oxford University Press, 1958), p. 155.
67 *Der Grosse Brockhaus*, 15th ed., vol. 5 (Leipzig: F.U. Brockhaus, 1930), p. 633.

4   The 'spirit' of capitalism

1 Max Weber, 'Roscher und Knies und die logischen Probleme der historischen Nationalökonomie,' *Gesammelte Aufsätze zur Wissenschaftslehre*, 6th ed., ed. Johannes Winckelmann. (Tübingen: J. C. B. Mohr (Paul Siebeck), 1985) p. 22; Max Weber, 'Roscher and Knies: The Logical Problems of Historical Economics,' trans. Guy Oakes (New York: The Free Press, 1975), p. 73.
2 Max Weber, '"Objectivity" in social science and social policy,' *The methods of the Social Sciences*, trans. Edward A. Shils (New York: The Free Press, 1949), p. 76.
3 Ibid., p. 72.
4 Ibid., p. 110.
5 Max Weber, '"Vorbemerkung," zu den "Gesammelten Aufsätzen zur Religionssoziologie,"' *Gesammelte Aufsätze zur Religionssoziologie*, vol. 1, 8th ed. (Tübingen: J. C. B. Mohr (Paul Siebeck), 1986), p. 1; Max Weber, 'Author's Introduction,' *Protestant Ethic and the Spirit of Capitalism*, trans. Talcott Parsons (Boston: Unwin Hyman, 1989), p. 13.
6 Weber, 'Objectivity,' p. 112.
7 Ibid.
8 Max Weber, *The Protestant Ethic and the 'Spirit' of Capitalism and other writings*, ed. and trans. Peter Baehr and Gordon C. Wells (New York: Penguin Books, 2002), p. 4; Max Weber, *Die protestantische Ethik, und der Geist des Kapitalismus*, vol. 1, *Gesammelte Aufsätze zur Religionssoziologie*, 8th ed. (Tübingen: J. C. B. Mohr (Paul Siebeck), 1986), p. 22.

9 Ibid.
10 Weber, *Protestant Ethic*, p. 4; Weber, *Protestantische Ethik*, p. 23.
11 Weber, *Protestant Ethic*, pp. 4–5.
12 Ibid., pp. 5, 6, 12, 7–8.
13 Ibid., p. 8.
14 Ibid.
15 Weber, *Protestantische Ethik*, p. 30.
16 Ibid.
17 Weber, *Protestant Ethic*, pp. 13, 83; Weber, *Protestantische Ethik*, p. 119.
18 Ibid., p. 17; Weber, *Protestantische Ethik*, p. 46.
19 Ibid., p. 24.
20 Ibid., p. 33.
21 Ibid., pp. 70–71.
22 Ibid., pp. 73–74.
23 Ibid., p. 74.
24 Ibid., p. 78.
25 Ibid., p. 104.
26 Ibid., p. 105.
27 Ibid., p. 8.
28 Ibid., p. 116.
29 Ibid., pp. 116–117.
30 Weber, *Protestant Ethic*, p. 121; Weber, *Protestantische Ethik*, p. 203.
31 Weber, *Protestant Ethic*, p. 120.
32 Weber, *Protestant Ethic*, pp. 120–121; Weber, *Protestantische Ethik*, p. 203.
33 Weber, *Protestant Ethic*, p. 121.
34 Ibid., p. 74.
35 Ibid., p. 88.
36 Heinrich Rickert, *The limits of concept formation in natural science*, trans. Guy Oakes (New York: Cambridge University Press, 1986).
37 Guy Oakes, 'Introductory Essay,' *Roscher and Knies: The logical problems of historical economics*, trans. Guy Oakes (New York: Free Press, 1975), p. 4.
38 Marianne Weber, *Max Weber: A Bibliography*, trans. Harry Zohn (New Brunswick: Transaction Books, 1988), p. 260.
39 Ibid., p. 100.
40 Ibid.
41 Jürgen Habermas, *The theory of communicative action*, vol. 2, trans. Thomas McCarthy (Boston: Beacon Press, 1989), pp. 153–197.
42 Weber, 'Objectivity,' p. 77.
43 Ibid., p. 72.
44 Ibid.
45 Ibid., p. 73.
46 Ibid., pp. 78–79.
47 Max Weber, *Wirtschaft und Gesellschaft: Grundriß der verstehenden Soziologie*, 5th ed., (Tübingen: J. C. B. Mohr (Paul Siebeck), 1980), p. 1402.
48 Weber, 'Objectivity,' pp. 78–79; Max Weber, 'Die 'Objektivität' sozialwissenschaftlicher und sozialpolitischer Erkenntnis,' *Gesammelte Aufsätze zur Wissenschaftslehre*, 6th ed., ed. Johannes Winckelmann. (Tübingen: J. C. B. Mohr (Paul Siebeck), 1985), p. 178.
49 Ibid.
50 Weber, *Protestantische Ethik*, p. 204.
51 Weber, 'Objectivity,' p. 79.
52 Weber, *Protestantische Ethik*, pp. 35, 54, 55, 62.
53 Weber, 'Author's Introduction,' p. 13.
54 Karl Mannheim, *Ideology and utopia: an introduction to the sociology of knowledge*, trans. Louis Wirth and Edward Shils (New York: Harcourt Brace Jovanovich, 1936), p. 155.
55 Weber, *Protestantische Ethik*, p. 205.

56   Max Weber, 'Science as a Vocation,' *From Max Weber: Essays in Sociology*, trans. H.H. Gerth and C. Wright Mills (New York: Oxford University Press, 1958), p. 155.
57   Ibid.
58   Weber, 'Objectivity,' p. 111; 'Objektivität,' p. 213. [*emphasis added*]
59   Ibid.
60   Kant, 'Analytic of the Sublime,' p. 106.
61   Ibid., p. 127.
62   Ibid.
63   Weber, 'Science as a Vocation,' p. 155.
64   Kant, 'Analytic of the Sublime,' pp. 121–122.
65   Weber, 'Science as a Vocation,' p. 155.
66   Weber, *Protestant Ethic*, p. 74.
67   Peter Gay, *The cultivation of hatred: the bourgeois experience, Victoria to Freud* (New York: WW Norton, 1993).

5   The hiatus irrationalis

1   Matthew White, 'Historical Atlas of the Twentieth Century,' online available HTTP: <http://users.erols.com/mwhite28/20centry.htm> (accessed 13 August 2005).
2   Ibid.
3   Ibid.
4   Michele Foucault, *The History of Sexuality. Volume I: an introduction*, trans. Robert Hurley (New York: Vintage, 1980), p. 122.
5   Ibid., p. 120.
6   Guy Oakes, 'Introductory Essay,' *Roscher and Knies: The logical problems of historical economics*, trans. Guy Oakes (New York: Free Press, 1975), pp. 24–25.
7   Fritz K. Ringer, *Decline of the German mandarins: the German academic community, 1890–1933* (Cambridge, MA: Harvard University Press, 1969), pp. 301–302.
8   Guy Oakes, *Weber and Rickert: concept formation in the cultural sciences* (Cambridge, MA: The MIT Press, 1988), pp. 21–22.
9   Max Weber, '"Objectivity" in social science and social policy,' *The methods of the Social Sciences*, trans. Edward A. Shils (New York: The Free Press, 1949), p. 111.
10   Max Weber, 'Roscher and Knies: The Logical Problems of Historical Economics,' trans. Guy Oakes (New York: The Free Press, 1975), p. 85.
11   Weber, 'Roscher and Knies,' p. 67.
12   Ringer, *Decline*, pp. 353–366.
13   Theodor W. Adorno, *Negative Dialectics*, trans. E.B. Ashton (New York: Continuum, 1983), p. 3.
14   Max Weber, 'Science as a Vocation,' *From Max Weber: Essays in Sociology*, trans. H.H. Gerth and C. Wright Mills (New York: Oxford University Press, 1958), p. 155.
15   Max Weber, 'Politics as a Vocation,' *From Max Weber: Essays in Sociology*, trans. H.H. Gerth and C. Wright Mills (New York: Oxford University Press, 1946), p. 121.
16   See *Weber's Protestant Ethic: Origins, Evidence, Contexts*, ed. Hartmut Lehmann and Guenther Roth (New York: University of Cambridge Press, 1993).
17   Martin Green, *The von Richthofen Sisters: The Triumphant and the Tragic Modes of Love* (New York: Basic Books, Inc., 1974), pp. 10, 31–33, 40–41, 43, 46, 52–53.
18   David Beetham, 'From socialism to fascism: the relation between theory and practice in the work of Robert Michels,' *Political Studies* 25:1–2 (1977), pp. 3–24, 161–181.
19   Green, *von Richthofen Sisters*, pp. 31–33, 40, 41, 44, 47–59, 71, 170, 366.
20   Ibid., *passim*.
21   Ibid., p. 22, 30, 187, 221.
22   M. Rainer Lepsius, 'Mina Tobler and Max Weber: Passion Confined,' trans. Sam Whimster, *Max Weber Studies* (2004), pp. 9–21.
23   Green, *von Richthofen Sisters*, p. 30.

24 Andrew Arato and Paul Breines, *The young Lukács and the origins of western Marxism* (New York: The Seabury Press, 1979).

25 John McCormick, *Carl Schmitt's Critique of Liberalism: Against Politics as Technology* (New York: University of Cambridge Press, 1999), p. 33.

26 Ibid., pp. 35–36.

27 Weber, 'Objectivity,' 103; Weber, 'Objektivität,' p. 204.

28 Georg Lukács, *History and class consciousness: studies in Marxist dialectics*, trans. Rodney Livingstone (Cambridge, MA: The MIT Press, 1971), p. 149.

29 Carl Schmitt, *Concept of the Political*, trans. George Schwab (New Brunswick, NJ: Rutgers University Press, 1976), p. 47.

30 Moishe Postone, *Time, labor, and social domination: a reinterpretation of Marx's critical theory* (New York: Cambridge University Press, 1993), pp. 138–166.

31 Lukács, *History and Class Consciousness*, p. 80; Georg Lukács, 'Klassenbewusstsein,' *Geschichte und Klassenbewusstsein*, Kleine Revolutionäre Bibliothek, vol. 9 (Berlin: Der Malik Verlag, 1923), p. 93.

32 Weber, 'Objectivity,' p. 96.

33 Theodor W. Adorno, *Negative Dialectics*, trans. E.B. Ashton (New York: Continuum, 1983), p. 3.

34 Max Weber, 'Objective possibility and adequate causation in historical explanation, II,' in 'Critical Studies in the Logic of the Cultural Sciences,' *The Methodology of the Social Sciences*, trans., Edward A. Shils and Henry A. Finch (New York: The Free Press, 1949), pp. 164–188.

35 Ibid., p. 169.

36 Ibid., p. 173.

37 Ibid., p. 175.

38 Ibid., pp. 182–183.

39 See Martin Jay, *Marxism and totality: the adventures of a concept from Lukács to Habermas* (Berkeley: University of California Press, 1984).

40 Lukács, *History and Class Consciousness*, p. 51; Lukács, *Geschichte und Klassenbewusstsein*, p. 62.

41 Arato and Breines, *The young Lukács*, pp. 217–218.

42 Carl Schmitt, *The crisis of Parliamentary Democracy*, trans. Ellen Kennedy (Cambridge, MA: The MIT Press, 1988), p. 42.

43 Max Weber, *Wirtschaft und Gesellschaft: Grundriß der verstehenden Soziologie*, 5th ed., (Tübingen: J. C. B. Mohr (Paul Siebeck), 1980), p. 361.

44 Carl Schmitt, *Political Romanticism*, trans. Guy Oakes (Cambridge, MA: The MIT Press, 1986), p. 54.

45 Carl Schmitt, *Political Theology: four chapters on the concept of sovereignty*, trans. George Schwab (Cambridge, MA: The MIT Press, 1988), p. 48.

46 Ibid., p. 51.

47 Ibid., p. 5.

48 Ibid., 66.

49 Schmitt, *Concept of the Political*, p. 26.

50 Ibid., 29.

51 Ibid., p. 38.

52 Ibid., p. 35.

53 Ibid., pp. 44–45.

54 With the recent appointment and confirmation of Samuel Alito to the US Supreme Court, the doctrine of the unitary executive, defended by Carl Schmitt and instituted by the National Socialists, has now become law in the United States. For a contemporary defence of the unitary executive, see Steven G. Calabresi and Christopher S. Yoo, "The Unitary Executive During the First Half-Century," Case Western Reserve Law Revew, Vol. 47, p. 1451, 1997; Christopher S. Yoo, Steven G. Calabresi, and Anthony J. Colangelo, "The Unitary Executive in the Modern Era, 1945–2004", Iowa Law Review, Vol. 90, No. 2, p. 601, 2005; Christopher S. Yoo, Steven G. Calabresi and Laurence Nee, "The Unitary Executive During the Third Half-Century, 1889–1945," Notre Dame Law Review, Vol. 80, November 2004; Christopher S. Yoo, Steven G. Calabresi, "The Unitary Executive

During the Second-Half Century," Harvard Journal of Law and Public Policy, Vol. 26, p. 667, 2003. See also Sidney Blumenthal, "The career of the latest supreme court nominee has been marked by his hatred of liberalism," The London Guardian Online, 2006 January 12 <http://www.guardian.co.uk/usa/story/0.12271.1684464.00.html> (accessed 1 March 2006).

55 Ibid., p. 46

56 Ibid., p. 47.

57 Ibid.

58 Max Weber, 'Religious Ethics and the World: Politics,' *Economy and Society,* vol. 1, trans. E. Fischoff, Hans Gerth, et al. (Berkeley, CA: University of California Press, 1978), p. 601.

59 Schmitt, *Concept of the Political*, p. 48.

60 Ibid., pp. 48–49.

61 Shadia B. Drury, *Leo Strauss and the American right* (New York: St. Martin's Press, 1999); 'Philosophers and kings: a strange waltz involving George Bush, ancient Greece and a dead German thinker,' *The Economist* 19 June 2003, Online Lexis-Nexis® Academic. (accessed 31 August 2005); Anne Norton, *Leo Strauss and the politics of American empire* (New Haven, CT: Yale University Press, 2004); Brian Danoff, 'Leo Strauss, George W. Bush, and the problem of regime change,' *Social Policy* 34:2/3 (Winter-Spring 2004), pp. 35–41; Matthew Sharpe, 'Leo Strauss and the "New American Century."' *Quadrant* 48:9 (September 2004), pp. 34–38; Earl Shorris, 'Ignoble liars: Leo Strauss, George Bush, and the philosophy of mass deception,' *Harper's Magazine* 308:1849 (June 2004), pp. 65–72; Alan Wolfe, 'A facist philosopher helps us understand contemporary politics,' *The Chronicle of Higher Education* 50:30 (2 April 2004), pp. B16–B17.

62 Jürgen Habermas, ed., *Observations on 'the spiritual situation of the age': contemporary German perspectives*, trans. Andrew Buchwalter (Cambridge, MA: The MIT Press, 1984).

63 Theodor Adorno and Max Horkheimer, *Dialectic of Enlightenment*, trans., John Cumming (New York: Continuum, 1993).

64 Jürgen Habermas, The Philosophical Discourse of Modernity, trans. Frederick G. Lawrence (Cambridge, MA: The MIT Press, 1984), pp. 34–36; Andrew Moravcsik, Larry Siedentop, Gisela Stuart, John Kay, Sunder Katwala, Charles Grant, 'Europe without illusions,' *Prospect* (23 June 2005) Online Lexis-Nexis® Academic (accessed 31 August 2005); 'German intellectuals in French vote appeal,' *EUObserver.com* (4 May 2005) Online Lexis-Nexis® Academic. (accessed 31 August 2005); Honor Mahony, 'Power: The Time's List Of The World's Most Influential People In Full,' *Independent on Sunday (London)* (18 April 2004), p. 3; 'Habermas seeks release of Korean-German held in South Korea, Seoul,' *Deutsche Presse-Agentur* (24 December 2003) Online Lexis-Nexis® Academic. (accessed 31 August 2005); 'PROFILE: Habermas - Germany's champion of Western democracy, Frankfurt,' *Deutsche Presse-Agentur* (14 October 2001) Online Lexis-Nexis® Academic. (accessed 31 August 2005); 'German philosopher Habermas calls for European constitution,' *Agence France Presse* (English) (28 June 2001) Online Lexis-Nexis® Academic. (accessed 31 August 2005).

65 Unfortunately, Habermas resists the full implications of his immanent critique of capitalism and therefore unintentionally ontologizes and trans-historicizes distinctions that he otherwise attributes to capitalist modernity (Jürgen Habermas, *The theory of communicative action*, vol. 2, trans. Thomas McCarthy (Boston: Beacon Press, 1989), pp. 156–160).

6 The prophetic pneuma

1 Max Weber, *The Religion of China*, trans. Hans H. Gerth (New York: The Free Press, 1968), p. 61; Max Weber, *Konfuzianismus und Taoismus*, in *Gesammelte Aufsätze zur Religionssoziologie*, vol. 1, 8th ed. (Tübingen: J. C. B. Mohr (Paul Siebeck), 1986), p. 348.

2 Max Weber, '"Objectivity" in social science and social policy,' *The methods of the Social Sciences*, trans. Edward A. Shils (New York: The Free Press, 1949), p. 58.

3 Ibid.

4 Max Weber, 'The Social Psychology of the World Religions,' *From Max Weber: essays in sociology*, ed. H.H. Gerth and C. Wright Mills (New York: Oxford University Press, 1958),

p. 296; Max Weber, 'Einleitung,' *Die Wirtschaftsethik der Weltreligionen*, vol. 1, *Gesammelte Aufsätze zur Religionssoziologie*, vol. 3, 8th ed. (Tübingen: J. C. B. Mohr (Paul Siebeck), 1986), p. 269.

5 Max Weber, *Economy and Society: an outline of interpretive sociology*, vol. 1, trans. Ephraim Fischoff, Hans Gerth, et al. (Berkeley: University of California Press, 1978), p. 215; Max Weber, *Wirtschaft und Gesellschaft: Grundriss der Verstehenden Soziologie*, 5th ed., ed. Johannes Winckelmann (Tübingen: J.C.B. Mohr (Paul Siebeck), 1980), p. 124.

6 Weber, *Konfuzianismus und Taoismus*, p. 452; Weber, *Religion of China*, p. 164.

7 Weber, *Religion of China*, p. 205; Weber, *Konfuzianismus und Taoismus*, p. 489.

8 Weber, *Konfuzianismus und Taoismus*, p. 349.

9 Weber, *Konfuzianismus und Taoismus*, pp. 281–282; Weber, *Religion of China*, p. 6. [*translation altered*]

10 Weber, *Konfuzianismus und Taoismus*, p. 347; Weber, *Religion of China*, p. 61.

11 Weber, *Religion of China*, p. 60; Weber, *Konfuzianismus und Taoismus*, p. 347.

12 Weber, *Religion of China*, p. 60; Weber, *Konfuzianismus und Taoismus*, p. 348.

13 Max Weber, *Die protestantische Ethik, und der Geist des Kapitalismus*, vol. 1, *Gesammelte Aufsätze zur Religionssoziologie*, 8th ed. (Tübingen: J. C. B. Mohr (Paul Siebeck), 1986), p. 121.

14 Weber, *Religion of China*, p. 61; Weber, *Konfuzianismus und Taoismus*, p. 348.

15 Weber, *Religion of China*, p. 62; Weber, *Konfuzianismus und Taoismus*, p. 349.

16 Weber, *Religion of China*, p. 83; Weber, *Konfuzianismus und Taoismus*, p. 372.

17 Homi K. Bhabha, 'Introduction,' *Nation and narration*, ed., Homi K. Bhabha (New York: Routledge, 1990), p. 4.

18 Weber, *Religion of China*, pp. 60, 62; Weber, *Konfuzianismus und Taoismus*, pp. 347, 349.

19 Weber, *Religion of China*, p. 83; Weber, *Konfuzianismus und Taoismus*, p. 372.

20 Weber, *Religion of China*, p. 96; Weber, *Konfuzianismus und Taoismus*, p. 386.

21 Weber, *Religion of China*, p. 11; Weber, *Konfuzianismus und Taoismus*, pp. 390–391.

22 Weber, *Religion of China*, p. 61; Weber, *Konfuzianismus und Taoismus*, p. 348.

23 Max Weber, 'Die "Objektivität" sozialwissenschaftlicher und sozialpolitischer Erkenntnis,' *Gesammelte Aufsätze zur Wissenschaftslehre*, 6th ed., ed. Johannes Winckelmann. (Tübingen: J. C. B. Mohr (Paul Siebeck), 1985), p. 187.

24 Weber, *Religion of China*, p. 55.

25 Ibid., p. 127.

26 Ibid., pp. 55, 125, 127, 144, 150, 151, 235.

27 Ibid., pp. 150, 151.

28 David S. Landes, *Revolution in time: clocks and the making of the modern world* (Cambridge, MA: Harvard University Press, 1983), pp. 72–73; Moishe Postone, *Time, labor, and social domination: a reinterpretation of Marx's critical theory* (New York: Cambridge University Press, 1993), pp. 186–260.

29 Weber, *Religion of China*, p. 198.

30 Judith M. Dean, Mary E. Lovely, and Hua Wang, *Foreign direct investment and pollution havens: evaluating the evidence from China* (Washington, D.C.: Office of Economics, US International Trad Commission, 2004); Hua Wang, and Wenhua Di, *The determinants of government environmental performance: an empirical analysis of Chinese townships* (Washington, D.C.: World Bank, Develpment Research Group, Infrastructure and Environment, 2002); Hua Wang, et al., *Incomplete enforcement of pollution regulation: bargaining power of Chinese factories* (Washington, D.C.: world Bank, Development Research Group, Infrastructure and Environment, 2002); Hua Wang, *Pollution charges, community pressure, and abatement cost of industrial pollution in China* (Washington, D.C.: World Bank, Development Research Group, Infrastructure and Environment, 2002); Vaclav Smil, *Environmental problems in China: estimates of economic costs* (Honolulu: East-West Center, 1996).

31 Weber, *Religion of China*, p. 199.

32 Ibid., p. 227.

33 Ibid., p. 233.

34 Ibid., p. 199.

35 Weber, *Konfuzianismus und Taoismus*, 302; Weber, *Religion of China*, p. 24.

36 Max Weber, *Hinduismus und Buddhismus*, in *Gesammelte Aufsätze zur Religionssoziologie*, vol. 3, 8th ed. (Tübingen: J. C. B. Mohr (Paul Siebeck), 1986), p. 64; Max Weber, *The Religion of India: the sociology of Hinduism and Buddhism*, trans. Hans H. Gerth and Don Martindale (Glencoe, IL: The Free Press, 1958), p. 63.

37 Weber, *Hinduismus und Buddhismus*, p. 66; Weber, *Religion of India*, p. 65.

38 Weber, 'Religious Groups (the sociology of religion),' in *Economy and Society*, p. 400; Weber, 'Religionssoziologie (Typen Religiöser Vergemeinschaftung),' *Wirtschaft und Gesellschaft*, p. 245.

39 Weber, 'Religious Groups,' p. 401; Weber, *Religionssoziologie*, p. 246.

40 Weber, 'Religious Groups,' pp. 401–402; Weber, *Religionssoziologie*, p. 246.

41 Weber, 'Religious Groups,' p. 403; Weber, *Religionssoziologie*, p. 248.

42 Weber, 'Religious Groups,' pp. 406–407; Weber, *Religionssoziologie*, pp. 249–250.

43 Weber, 'Religious Groups,' p. 407; Weber, *Religionssoziologie*, p. 250.

44 Max Weber, *Ancient Judaism*, trans. Hans H. Gerth and Don Martindale (New York: The Free Press, 1967), p. 90; Max Weber, *Das Antike Judentum*, vol. 3, *Gesammelte Aufsätze zur Religionssoziologie*, 8th ed (Tübingen: J. C. B. Mohr (Paul Siebeck), 1986), p. 98.

45 Weber, *Protestantische Ethik*, 94–95.

46 Weber, *Ancient Judaism*, pp. 90–91; Weber, *Das antike Judentum*, p. 99.

47 Weber, *Ancient Judaism*, p. 94; Weber, *Das antike Judentum*, pp. 102–103.

48 Ibid.

49 Weber, *Ancient Judaism*, p. 96; Weber, *Das antike Judentum*, p. 105.

50 Weber, *Ancient Judaism*, pp. 96–97; Weber, *Das antike Judentum*, pp. 105–106.

51 Ibid.

52 Weber, *Ancient Judaism*, p. 97; Weber, *Das antike Judentum*, p. 106.

53 Weber, *Ancient Judaism*, p. 98; Weber, *Das antike Judentum*, p. 107.

54 Weber, *Ancient Judaism*, p. 99; Weber, *Das antike Judentum*, p. 108.

55 Weber, *Ancient Judaism*, p. 97; Weber, *Das antike Judentum*, p. 107.

56 Weber, *Ancient Judaism*, p. 99; Weber, *Das antike Judentum*, p. 108.

57 Weber, *Ancient Judaism*, pp. 97–99; Weber, *Das antike Judentum*, pp. 106–108.

58 Moishe Postone, 'Anti-Semitism and National Socialism: Notes on the German Reaction to "Holocaust",' *New German Critique* 19:1 (Winter 1980), pp. 97–115.

59 Max Weber, *Protestant Ethic and the Spirit of Capitalism*, trans. Talcott Parsons (Boston: Unwin Hyman, 1989), p. 105.

60 Weber, *Konfuzianismus und Taoismus*, p. 301–303; Weber, *Religion of China*, p. 23–24

61 Weber, *Hinduismus und Buddhismus*, pp. 64–65; Weber, *Religion of India*, p. 63.

62 Weber, *Religion of China*, pp. 24, 25, 52.

63 Weber, *Ancient Judaism*, pp. 25, 93, 96.

64 Weber, *Ancient Judaism*, p. 94, 97, 99, 100, 126, 119.

65 Weber, *Ancient Judaism*, pp. 303, 311, 321, 334–335.

66 Weber, *Ancient Judaism*, pp. 336–355.

67 Weber, *Ancient Judaism*, pp. 3–4.

68 Weber, 'Religious Groups,' p. 574.

69 Ibid., pp. 96, 98–100.

70 Weber, *Ancient Judaism*, p. 399.

71 Ibid., p. 320.

7   The community unto death

1 'Erhaben,'*Der Grosse Brockhaus* 15th ed., vol. 5 (Leipzig: F.U. Brockhaus, 1930), p. 633.

2 Immanuel Kant, 'Analytic of the Sublime,' *Critique of Judgment*, trans. Werner S. Pluhar (Indianapolis: Hackett Publishing Company), p. 122.

3 Immanuel Kant, 'Analytik des Erhabenen,' *Kritik der Ästhetischen Urteilskraft*, ed. Wilhelm Weischedel (Frankfurt aM: Suhrkamp Verlag, 1974), p. 193.

4 Here are just some of the more recent articles whose authors address Kantian and neo-Kantian perspectives on war and peace: M. Schattenmann, 'War and international justice: a Kantian

perspective, ' *Kant-Studien* 95:3 (2004), pp. 383–385; G Geismann, 'Peace and war in Kant's writings,' *Kant-Studien* 95:1 (2004), pp. 128–129; K. Stoppenbrunk, 'The war against a villain state? (Kant, Rawls)' *Merkur-Deutsche Zeitschrift fur europaisches Denken* 58:1 (January 2004), pp. 81–84; P. James, 'Civil-military relations in a neo-Kantian world, 1886–1992,' *Armed Forces & Society* 30:2 (Winter 2004), pp. 227+; V. Gerhardt, 'Kant and the war in Iraq, a rejoinder,' *Merkur-Deutsche Zeitschrift fur europaisches Denken* 57:12 (December 2003), pp. 1174–1176; M. Bierwisch, 'Kant and the war in Iraq, a reply,' *Merkur-Deutsche Zeitschrift fur europaisches Denken* 75:11 (November 2003), pp. 1075–1079; SW Choi and P James, 'No professional soldiers, no militarized interstate disputes? A new question for neo-Kantianism,' *Journal of Conflict Resolution* 47:6 (December 2003), pp. 796–816; B. Buchan, 'Explaining war and peace: Kant and liberal IR theory,' *Alternatives* 27:4 (Oct–Dec 2002), pp. 407–428; S.M. Mitchell, 'A Kantian system? Democracy and third-party conflict resolution,' *American Journal of Political Science* 46:4 (October 2002), pp. 749–759.

5   Max Weber, *Die protestantische Ethik, und der Geist des Kapitalismus*, vol. 1, *Gesammelte Aufsätze zur Religionssoziologie*, 8th ed. (Tübingen: J. C. B. Mohr (Paul Siebeck), 1986), p. 203.

6   Max Weber, '"Objectivity" in social science and social policy,' *The methods of the Social Sciences*, trans. Edward A. Shils (New York: The Free Press, 1949), p. 58.

7   Ibid., p. 58–59.

8   Weber, *Protestantische Ethik*, p. 94–95.

9   Ibid., p. 204.

10 Max Weber, *The Protestant Ethic and the 'Spirit' of Capitalism and other writings*, ed. and trans. Peter Baehr and Gordon C. Wells (New York: Penguin Books, 2002), p. 121.

11 Levee Blanc, 'Georg Lukács: The Antinomies of Melancholy,' *Other Voices* 1:1 (March 1977), online, available HTTP: <http://www.othervoices.org/blevee/lukacs.html> (accessed 18 August 2005).

12 Nigel Steel and Peter Hart, *Passchendaele: the Sacrificial Ground*. Cassell Military Paperbacks (London: Cassell & Co, 2001), p. 303; Robin Prior and Trevor Wilson, *Passchendaele: The Untold Story* (New Haven: Yale University Press, 2002), p. 195.

13 Matthew White, 'Deaths by Mass Unpleasantness: Estimated Totals for the Entire 20th Century,' online, available HTTP: <http://users.erols.com/mwhite28/warstat8.htm> (accessed 20 August 2005).

14 Jeffrey Herf, *Reactionary Modernism: Technology, culture, and politics in Weimar and the Third Reich* (New York: Cambridge University Press, 1984).

15 Modris Eksteins, *Rites of spring: the Great War and the birth of the modern age* (New York: Anchor Books, 1989), p. xvi.

16 Max Weber, 'Religious Ethics and the World: Politics,' *Economy and Society*, vol. 1, trans. E. Fischoff, Hans Gerth, et al. (Berkeley, CA: University of California Press, 1978), pp. 600–601.

17 Max Weber, 'Religious rejections of the world and their directions,' *From Max Weber: Essays in Sociology*, trans. H.H. Gerth and C. Wright Mills (New York: Oxford University Press, 1958), p. 334.

18 Ibid.

19 Ibid., pp. 334–335.

20 Ibid., p. 335.

21 Ibid.

22 Ibid.; Max Weber, 'Zwischenbetrachtung: Theorie der Stufen und Richtungen religiöser Weltablehnung,' *Die Wirtschaftsethik der Weltreligionen*, in *Gesammelte Aufsätze zur Religionssoziologie*. 8th ed., vol. 1 (Tübingen: J. C. B. Mohr (Paul Siebeck), 1986), p. 548.

23 Ibid.

24 Weber, 'Religious rejections,' p. 336; Weber, 'Zwischenbetrachtung,' p. 549.

25 Of all those surveyed in a recent World Values Survey, fully eighty-eight percent of those who said they were willing to fight for their country said that they believe in God, whereas only twelve percent said they did not believe in God. In the same survey, of those

who said they were willing to fight, forty-seven percent said that religion was very important to them, twenty-eight percent said that it was rather important, and only thirty percent said that religion was less or not important to them (European Values Study Group and World Values Survey Association, *European and World Values Surveys Integrated Data File, 1999–2002, Release I*, 2nd ICPSR version (Ann Arbor, MI: Interuniversity Consortium for Political and Social Research, 2004)).

26 Paul Fussell, *The Great War and Modern Memory* (New York: Oxford University Press, 1977), p. 64.

27 Ibid.

28 Joseph Schumpeter, *Capitalism, Socialism and Democracy*, 3rd ed. (New York: Harper & Row, 1962), pp. 81–86.

8   The body of religion

1 Donald E. Miller, *Reinventing American Protestantism: Christianity in the new millennium* (Berkeley: University of California Press, 1997), pp. 193–194.

2 Ibid., pp. 191–192.

3 Ibid., p. 1.

4 Immanuel Kant, 'Analytic of the Sublime,' *Critique of Judgment*, trans. Werner S. Pluhar (Indianapolis: Hackett Publishing Company), p. 127.

5 Gunter Meckenstock, *Deterministische Ethik und kritische Theologie: die Auseinandersetzung des fruhen Schleiermacher mit Kant und Spinoza, 1789–1794* (Berlin: W. de Gruyter, 1988); Hermann Baum, 'Zum funktionalen Interesse philosophischer Reflexionen über das Phänomen Religion bei Descartes, Kant und Schleiermacher,' *Neue Zeitschrift für systematische Theologie und Religionsphilosophie* 28 (1986), pp. 14–28; Immanuel Kant, *Religion within the limits of reason alone*, trans. Theodore M. Greene and Hoyt H. Hudson (New York: Harper & Row, 1960).

6 Miller, *Reinventing American Protestantism*, p. 16.

7 Peter Drucker, *The post-capitalist society* (New York: HarperBusiness, 1993).

8 Sumathi Bala, 'Dogged survivor of the dotcom bubble keeps its head above water,' *The Financial Times Limited* (21 March 2005), p. 7.

9 Ibid., p. 155.

10 Drucker, *The post-capitalist society*, p. 59.

11 Schumpeter, *Capitalism, Socialism and Democracy*, pp. 81–86.

12 'All that is solid melts into air.' (Karl Marx and Friedrich Engels, *Manifest der kommunistischen Partei*, Werke, vol. 4 (Berlin: Dietz-Verlag, 1956ff.), p. 465.)

13 Mikhail Bakhtin, *Rabelais and his world*, trans. Hélène Iswolsky (Bloomington, IN: Indiana University Press, 1984).

14 Charles Trueheart, 'Welcome to the Next Church,' *Atlantic Monthly* 278:2 (August 1996), pp. 37–53; *Expanded Academic ASAP*. Gale Group Databases. University of California, Berkeley, Library, online, available HTTP: <http://www.infotrac.galegroup.com>. (accessed 27 August 2005)

15 Ibid., p. 1

16 Thornton Wilder, *Our town: a play in three acts* (Avon, CT: Limited Editions Club, 1974).

17 Miller, *Reinventing American Protestantism*, pp. 145–146.

18 Ibid., p. 146.

19 Frederic Jameson, *Postmodernism, or, the cultural logic of late capitalism* (Durham: Duke University Press, 1992), pp. 21–25.

20 R.K. Bradt, 'The radical Christian orthodoxy of John Milbank: The historical contextuality of its development,' *Soundings* 86:3–4 (Fall-Winter 2003), pp. 315–349; C.E. Michalson, 'Re-reading the post-Kantian tradition with Milbank,' *Journal of Religious Ethics* 32:2 (Summer 2004), pp. 357–383; A. Pabst, 'From Christendom to modernity? A critical re-reading of radical Orthodoxy's theses on Scotist and Ockhamist divisions and

the retrieval of the theology of Saint Thomas Aquinas,' *Revue des Sciences Philosophiques et Theologiques* 86:4 (October-December 2002) 561–599; K.H, Ruhstorfer, 'Radical Orthodoxy? A Catholic enquiry,' *Philosophisches Jahrbuch* 109:1 (2002), pp. 237–241; D.F. Ford, 'Radical Orthodoxy. A new theology,' *Scottish Journal of Theology* 54:3 (2001), pp. 385–404.

21 Catherine Pickstock, *After Writing: on the liturgical consummation of philosophy* (Malden, MA: Blackwell Publishers, Inc., 1998), p. 122.

22 John Milbank, *Theology and Social Theory: Beyond Secular Reason* (Cambridge, MA: Blackwell Publishers, 1990), p. 139.

23 Carl Schmitt, *Political Theology: Four Chapters on the Concept of Sovereignty*, trans. George Schwab (Cambridge, MA: The MIT Press, 1988).

24 Milbank, *Theology and Social Theory*, p. 104.

25 Theodor W. Adorno, *Minima Moralia: Reflections from Damaged Life*, trans. E.F.N. Jephcott (New York: Verso Press, 1987), p. 247; Theodor W. Adorno, *Minima Moralia: Reflexionen aus dem beschaedigten Leben* (Berlin: Suhrkamp Verlag, 2001), p. 480–481.

26 Weber, *The Protestant Ethic and the 'Spirit' of Capitalism and other writings*, ed. and trans. Peter Baehr and Gordon C. Wells (New York: Penguin Books, 2002), p. 121.

27 Ibid.

28 Karl Marx, 'Critique of Hegel's Philosophy of Right. Introduction,' *Early Writings*, trans. Rodney Livingstone and Gregor Benton (New York: Vintage Books, 1975), pp. 243–244.

29 Patricia Springborg, 'Arendt, Republicanism and Patriarchalism,' *History of Political Thought* 10:3 (1989), pp. 499–523.

30 Karl Marx, *Capital: A Critique of Political Economy*, vol. 3, trans. David Fernbach (New York: Penguin Books, 1991), p. 958–959.

31 Jean Baudrillard, *The Mirror of Production*, trans. Mark Poster (St. Louis, MO: Telos Press, 1975).

32 Karl Marx, *Das Kapital*, vol. 3, in *Marx/Engels Werke*, vol. 25 (Berlin: Berlin: Dietz-Verlag, 1956 ff.), p. 828.

33 Hannah Arendt, *The Human Condition* (Chicago: University of Chicago Press, 1958).

34 Ibid., p. 5.

35 Ibid., *Human Condition*, p. 5.

36 Darrell Dobbs, 'Natural Right and the Problem of Aristotle's Defense of Slavery,' *The Journal of Politics* 56:1 (February 1994), pp. 69–94; Patricia Springborg, 'Arendt, Republicanism and Patriarchalism,' *History of Political Thought* 10:3 (1989), pp. 499–523.

37 André Gorz, *Farewell to the working class: an essay on post-industrial socialism*, trans. Michael Sonenscher (London : Pluto Press, 1982).

38 André Gorz, *Critique of economic reason*, trans. Gillian Handyside and Chris Turner (New York: Verso Press, 1989).

39 Ibid., p. 153; Marx: 'A thing can be useful, and a product of human labour, without being a commodity. He who satisfies his own need with the product of his own labour admittedly creates use-values, but not commodities' (Karl Marx, *Capital: a critique of political economy*, vol. 1, trans. Ben Fowkes (New York: Penguin Books, 1990), p. 131).

40 Alberto Alesina, Edward Glaeser, and Bruce Sacerdote, 'Work and Leisure in the U.S. and Europe: Why so Different?' *Harvard Institute of Economic Research Discussion Paper Number 2068* (April 2005), online, available HTTP: <http://post.economics.harvard.edu/hier/2005papers/2005list.html> (accessed 31 August 2005).

41 Marx, *Capital*, vol. 3, pp. 958–949.

42 George Steinmetz, 'The State of Emergency and the Revival of American Imperialism: Toward an Authoritarian Post-Fordism,' *Public Culture* 15:2 (2003), pp. 323–345.

43 Guy Dinmore, 'Role of religion in US politics under question,' *The Financial Times Limited Financial Times* (8 April 2005), p. 12; Scott Heiser, 'Republican students on the march for Bush's "just war" in Iraq,' *The Financial Times Limited* (12 July 2005), p. 6.

44 Marx, *Capital*, vol. 3, p. 959.

Bibliography

Max Weber in German

Das Antike Judentum. In *Gesammelte Aufsätze zur Religionssoziologie.* Volume 3. 8th Edition. Tübingen: J. C. B. Mohr (Paul Siebeck), 1986.

Die protestantische Ethik und der Geist des Kapitalismus. In *Gesammelte Aufsätze zur Religionssoziologie.* Volume 1. 8th Edition. Tübingen: J. C. B. Mohr (Paul Siebeck), 1986.

Die Wirtschaftsethik der Weltreligionen. Gesammelte Aufsätze zur Religionssoziologie. 8th edition. Tübingen: J. C. B. Mohr (Paul Siebeck), 1986.

Gesammelte Aufsätze zur Religionssoziologie. 8th Photographically produced Edition, Tübingen: J. C. B. Mohr (Paul Siebeck), 1986.

Gesammelte Aufsätze zur Wissenschaftslehre. 6th Revised Edition. Edited by Johannes Winckelmann. Tübingen: J. C. B. Mohr (Paul Siebeck), 1985.

Hinduismus und Buddhismus. In *Gesammelte Aufsätze zur Religionssoziologie.* Volume 2, 8th Edition. Tübingen: J. C. B. Mohr (Paul Siebeck), 1986.

Konfuzianismus und Taoismus. In *Gesammelte Aufsätze zur Religionssoziologie.* Volume 1. 8th Edition. Tübingen: J. C. B. Mohr (Paul Siebeck), 1986.

Roscher und Knies und die logischen Probleme der historischen Nationalökonomie. Gesammelte Aufsätze zur Wissenschaftslehre. 6th Edition. Edited by Johannes Winckelmann. Tübingen: J. C. B. Mohr (Paul Siebeck), 1985.

Wirtschaft und Gesellschaft. Grundriss der verstehenden Soziologie. Based on the 4th German edition. Edited by Johannes Winkelmann. Tübingen: J.C.B. Mohr (Paul Siebeck), 1956, 1–550, 559–822, as revised in the 1964 paperback edition (Köln–Berlin: Kiepenheuer & Witsch), with appendices from Max Weber, *Gesammelte Aufsätze zur Wissenschaftslehre*, 2nd rev. edition, Johannes Winckelmann, ed. Tübingen: J.C.B. Mohr (Paul Siebeck), 1951, 441–467 (selected passages), and Max Weber, *Gesammelte politische Schriften*, 2nd expanded edition, Johannes Winckelmann, ed. Tübingen: J.C.B. Mohr (Paul Siebeck), 1958, 294–394.

Max Weber in Translation

'Author's Introduction'. In *Protestant Ethic and the Spirit of Capitalism.* Translated by Talcott Parsons. Boston: Unwin Hyman, 1989, pp. 13–31.

Ancient Judaism. Translated and Edited by Hans. H. Gerth and Don Martindale. New York: The Free Press, 1967.

Economy and society: an outline of interpretive sociology. 2 volumes. Edited by Guenther Roth and Claus Wittich. Translated by Ephraim Fischoff, Hans Gerth, A.M. Henderson, Ferdinand Kolegar, C. Wright Mills, Talcott Parsons, Max Rheinstein, Guenther Roth, Edward Shils, and Claus Wittich. Berkeley: University of California Press, 1978.

From Max Weber: Essays in Sociology. Translated and edited by H.H. Gerth and C. Wright Mills. New York: Oxford University Press, 1958.

Roscher and Knies: the logical problems of historical economics. Translated with an Introduction by Guy Oakes. New York: The Free Press, 1975.

The Methodology of the Social Sciences. Translated and Edited by Edward A. Shils and Henry A. Finch with a Foreword by Edward A. Shils. New York: Free Press, 1949.

The Protestant Ethic and the Spirit of Capitalism. Translated by Talcott Parson with an Introduction by Anthony Giddens. Boston: Unwin Hyman, 1989.

The Religion of China: Confucianism and Taoism. Translated and Edited by Hans. H. Gerth with an Introduction by C.K. Yang. New York: The Free Press, 1964.

The Religion of India: the Sociology of Hinduism and Buddhism. Translated and Edited by Hans H. Gerth and Don Martindale. Glencoe, IL: The Free Press, 1958.

Other Books

Adorno Theodor W. and Max Horkheimer. *Dialectic of Enlightenment.* Translated by John Cumming. New York: Continuum, 1993.

Adorno Theodor W. *Minima Moralia: Reflections from Damaged Life.* Translated by E.F.N. Jephcott. New York: Verso Press, 1987.

————. *Minima Moralia: Reflexionen aus dem beschaedigten Leben.* Berlin: Suhrkamp Verlag, 2001.

Arato, Andrew and Paul Breines. *The young Lukács and the origins of western Marxism.* New York: The Seabury Press, 1979.

Bakhtin, Mikhail. *Rabelais and his world.* Translated by Helene Iswolsky. Bloomington, IN: Indiana University Press, 1984.

Bellah, Robert, et al. *Habits of the heart: individualism and commitment in American life.* Berkeley: University of California Press, 1996.

Benz, Richard. *Heidelberg: Schicksal und Geist.* Konstanz: J. Thorbecke, 1961.

Biller, Peter and A.J. Minnis, editors. *Medieval Theology and the Natural Body.* Rochester, NY: York Medieval Press, 1997.

Blumenthal, Sidney. 'The career of the latest supreme court nominee has been marked by his hatred of liberalism', *The London Guardian Online,* 2006 January 12 <http://www.guardian. co.uk./usa/story/0.12271.1684464.00.html> (accessed 1 March 2006).

Boitani, Piero and Anna Torti, editors. *The Body and the Soul in Medieval Literature.* The J. A. W. Bennett Memorial Lectures. 10th Series. Cambridge: Brewer. 1999.

Bordo, Susan. *Unbearable Weight: Feminism, Western Culture, and the Body.* Berkeley: University of California Press, 1993.

Bourdieu, Pierre. *Outline of a Theory of Practice.* Cambridge Studies in Social Anthropology 16, ed. Jack Goody. Translated by Richard Nice. New York: Cambridge University Press, 1990.

Burke, Edmund. *A Philosophical Enquiry into the Origin of our Ideas of the Sublime and Beautiful.* Edited with an Introduction and Notes by James T. Boulton. Notre Dame, IN: University of Notre Dame Press, 1968.

Butler, Judith. *Bodies that matter: on the discursive limits of "sex."* New York: Routledge, 1993.

Carter, Stephen L. *The Culture of Disbelief: How American Law and Politics Trivialize Religious Devotion.* Updated with a Foreword by the Author. New York: Anchor Books, 1994.

Coakley, Sarah, ed. *Religion and the Body.* Cambridge Studies in Religious Traditions 8. New York: Cambridge University Press, 1997.

Dean, Judith M., Mary E. Lovely, and Hua Wang. *Foreign direct investment and pollution havens: evaluating the evidence from China.* Washington, D.C.: Office of Economics, US International Trade Commission, 2004.

Drucker, Peter. *The post-capitalist society.* New York: HarperBusiness, 1993.

Drury, Shadia B. *Leo Strauss and the American right*. New York: St. Martin's Press, 1999.

Eksteins, Modris. *Rites of Spring: the Great War and the Birth of the Modern Age*. New York: Anchor Books, 1989.

Ellington, Donna Spivey. *From sacred body to angelic soul: understanding Mary in late medieval and early modern Europe*. Washington, D.C.: Catholic University of America Press, 2001.

Factor, Regis A. *Guide to the "Archiv für Sozialwissenschaft und Sozialpolitik" Group, 1904–1933: A History and Comprehensive Bibliography*. Bibliographies and Indexes in Law and Political Science 9. New York: Greenwood Press, 1988.

Falk, Pasi. *The consuming body*. London: Sage Publications, 1994.

Featherstone, M., M. Hepworth, and B.S. Turner, editors. *The body: social process and cultural theory*. London: Sage Publications, 1991.

Foucault, Michel. *An Introduction*. Volume One. *The History of Sexuality*. Translated by Robert Hurley. New York: Vintage Books, 1980.

Fussell, Paul. *The Great War and Modern Memory*. New York: Oxford University Press, 1977.

Garuba, Harry. 'Exploration in animist materialism: notes on reading/writing African literature, culture, and society', *Public Culture* 15:2 (2003): 261–285.

Gay, Peter. *The Cultivation of Hatred*. Volume 3, *The Bourgeois Experience, Victoria to Freud*. New York: W.W. Norton & Company, 1993.

Gibbons, Luke. *Edmund Burke and Ireland: Aesthetics, politics and the colonial sublime*. New York: Cambridge University Press, 2003.

Gorz, André. *Critique of economic reason*. Translated by Gillian Handyside and Chris Turner. New York: Verso, 1989.

———. *Farewell to the working class: an essay on post-industrial socialism*. Translated by Michael Sonenscher. London: Pluto Press, 1982.

Green, Martin. *The von Richthofen Sisters: the triumphant and the tragic modes of love. Else and Frieda von Richthofen, Otto Gross, Max Weber, and D.H. Lawrence, in the Years 1870–1970*. New York: Basic Books, 1974.

Habermas, Jürgen, editor. *Observations on "the spiritual situation of the age": contemporary German perspectives*. Translated by Andrew Buchwalter. Cambridge, MA: The MIT Press, 1984.

———. *The Philosophical Discourse of Modernity*. Translated by Frederick G. Lawrence. Cambridge, MA: The MIT Press, 1984.

———. *The theory of communicative action*. 2 volumes. Translated by Thomas McCarthy. Boston: Beacon Press, 1987/1989.

Harvey, David. *The Condition of Postmodernity: an Enquiry into the Origins of Cultural Change*. Cambridge, MA: Basil Blackwell, 1990.

Hegel, Georg Friedrich Wilhelm. *Aesthetics: Lectures on Fine Art: Volume I*. Translated by T.M. Knox. New York: Oxford University Press, 1998.

———. G.F.W. *Phenomenology of Spirit*. Translated by A.V. Miller with Analysis of the text and Foreword by J.N. Findlay. New York: Oxford University Press, 1977.

———. *Philosophy of Right*. Translated with Notes by T.M. Knox. New York: Oxford University Press, 1967.

Heppe, Heinrich. *Reformed Dogmatics: a Compendium of Reformed Theology*. Revised and Edited by Ernst Bizer. Translated by G.T. Thomson. New York: London: Allen & Unwin, 1950. Reprint: London: Wakeman Great Reprints, 2004.

Herf, Jeffrey. *Reactionary Modernism: Technology, culture, and politics in Weimar and the Third Reich*. New York: Cambridge University Press, 1984.

Jaggar, Alison M. and Susan R. Bordo, editors. *Gender/Body/Knowledge: Feminist Reconstructions of Being and Knowing*. New Brunswick: Rutgers University Press, 1989.

Jameson Frederic. *Postmodernism, or, the cultural logic of late capitalism*. Durham: Duke University Press, 1992.

Jaspers, Karl. *Die Geistige Situation der Zeit*. Berlin: W. de Gruyter, 1933.

Jelen, Ted Gerard and Clyde Wilcox, editors. *Religion and Politics in Comparative Perspective: The One, the Few, and the Many*. New York: Cambridge University Press, 2002.

Kandinsky, Wassily and Franz Marc. *The Blaue Reiter Almanac*. New Documentary Edition. Edited with an Introduction by Klaus Lankheit. New York: Da Capo Press, 1974.

Kandinsky, Wassily. *Concerning the spiritual in art*. Translated with an Introduction by M.T.H. Sadler. New York: Dover Publications, 1977.

Kant, Immanuel. *Critique of Judgment*. Translated with an Introduction by Werner S. Pluhar, with a Foreword by Mary J. Gregor. Indianapolis: Hackett Publishing Company, 1987.

———. *Kritik der Urteilskraft*. Werkausgabe Volume 10. Edited by Wilhelm Weischedel. Suhrkamp Taschenbuch Wissenschaft 57. Frankfurt am Main: Suhrkamp Taschenbuch Verlag, 1974.

———. *Religion within the limits of reason alone*. Translated by Theodore M. Greene and Hoyt H. Hudson. New York: Harper & Row, 1960.

Käsler, Dirk. *Max Weber: An Introduction to his Life and Work*. Translated by Philippa Hurd. Chicago: University of Chicago Press, 1988.

Landes, David S. *Revolution in time: clocks and the making of the modern world*. Cambridge, MA: Harvard University Press, 1983.

Law, Jane Marie, editor. *Religious Reflections on the Human Body*. Bloomington and Indianapolis: Indiana University Press, 1995.

Le Goff, Jacques. *Time, Work, and Culture in the Middle Ages*. Translated by Arthur Goldhammer. Chicago: University of Chicago Press, 1982.

Lehmann, Hartmut and Guenther Roth, editors. *Weber's "Protestant Ethic": Origins, Evidence, Contexts*. Publications of the German Historical Institute, Washington, D.C. Edited by Hartmut Lehmann. New York: Cambridge University Press, 1993.

Lough, Joseph W.H. *The Persistence of the Sublime: Capitalism and Max Weber's Sociology of Religion*. Ph.D. diss., University of Chicago, 1999. Ann Arbor, MI: UMI, 1999.

Luckmann, Thomas. *The Invisible Religion: the problem of religion in modern society*. New York: The MacMillan Company, 1967.

Lukács, Georg. *Geschichte und Klassenbewußtsein: Studien über Marxistische Dialektik*. Kleine Revolutionäre Bibliothek. Volume 9. Berlin: Der Malik Verlag, 1923.

———. *History and Class Consciousness: Studies in Marxist Dialectics*. Translated by Rodney Livingstone. Cambridge, MA: The MIT Press, 1971.

Lyotard, Jean-François. *The Postmodern Condition: a Report on Knowledge*. Theory and History of Literature 10. Translated by Geoff Bennington and Brian Massumi with a Foreword by Fredric Jameson. Minneapolis, MN: University of Minnesota Press, 1989.

Makela, Maria. *The Munich Secession: art and artists in turn-of-the-century Munich*. Princeton: Princeton University Press, 1990.

Mannheim, Karl. *Ideology and utopia: an introduction to the sociology of knowledge*. Translated by Louis Wirth and Edward Shils. New York: Harcourt Brace Jovanovich, 1936.

Marcuse, Herbert. *One-dimensional man: studies in the ideology of advanced industrial society*. Boston: Beacon Press, 1966.

Marx, Karl and Friedrich Engels. *Manifest der kommunistischen Partei*. In *Marx/Engels Werke*. Volume 4. Edited for the Institut für Marxismus-Leninismus by the Central Committee of the Sozialistschen Einheitspartei Deutschlands [SED]. Berlin: Dietz-Verlag, 1956.

Marx, Karl. *Capital: A Critique of Political Economy*. Volume 3. Translated by David Fernbach. New York: Penguin Books, 1991.

———. *Capital: A Critique of Political Economy*. Volume 1. Translated by Ben Fowkes. Introduced by Ernest Mandel. New York: Penguin Books, 1976.

———. *Das Kapital: Kritik der politischen Ökonomie*, Volumes 1 and 3. In *Marx/Engels Werke*. Volumes 23 and 25. Edited for the Institut für Marxismus-Leninismus by the

Central Committee of the Sozialistschen Einheitspartei Deutschlands [SED]. Berlin: Dietz-Verlag, 1956.

———. *Early Writings*. The Marx Library. Translated by Rodney Livingstone and Gregor Benton with an Introduction by Lucio Colletti. New York: Vintage Books, 1975.

McCormick, John P. *Carl Schmitt's critique of liberalism: against politics as technology*. Modern European Philosophy Series, ed. Robert B. Pippin. New York: Cambridge University Press, 1999.

McCormick, Peter J. *The Negative Sublime: Ethics, warfare and the dark borders of reason*. Heidelberg: Winter, 2003.

Meckenstock, Gunter. *Deterministische Ethik und kritische Theologie: die Auseinandersetzung des fruhen Schleiermacher mit Kant und Spinoza, 1789–1794*. Berlin: W. de Gruyter, 1988.

Milbank, John. *Theology and Social Theory: Beyond Secular Reason*. Cambridge, MA: Blackwell Publishers, 1993.

Miller, Donald E. *Reinventing American Protestantism: Christianity in the new millennium*. Berkeley: University of California Press, 1997.

Norton Anne. *Leo Strauss and the politics of American empire*. New Haven, CT: Yale University Press, 2004.

Oakes, Guy. *Weber and Rickert: Concept Formation in the Cultural Sciences*. Cambridge, MA: The MIT Press, 1988.

Pickstock, Catherine. *After Writing: on the liturgical consummation of philosophy*. Malden, MA: Blackwell Publishers, Inc., 1998.

Pior, Robin and Trevor Wilson. *Passchendaele: the untold story*. 2nd Edition. New Haven: Yale University Press, 2002.

Postone, Moishe. *Time, Labor, and Social Domination: a reinterpretation of Marx's critical theory*. New York: Cambridge University Press, 1993.

Rickert, Heinrich. *The limits of concept formation in natural science*. Translated by Guy Oakes. New York: Cambridge University Press, 1986.

Ringer, Fritz K. *The decline of the German Mandarins: the German Academic Community, 1890–1933*. Cambridge, MA: Harvard University Press, 1969.

Schama, Simon. *The embarrassment of riches: an interpretation of Dutch culture in the Golden Age*. New York: Knopf, 1987.

Schluchter, Wolfgang. *Rationalism, Religion and Domination: a Weberian Perspective*. Translated by Neil Solomon. Berkeley: University of California Press, 1989.

Schmitt, Carl. *Political Romanticism*. Translated with an Introductory Essay by Guy Oakes. Cambridge, MA: The MIT Press, 1986.

———. *Political Theology: four chapters on the concept of sovereignty*. Translated by George Schwab. Cambridge, MA: The MIT Press, 1988.

———. *The Concept of the Political*. Translated with an Introduction and Notes by George Schwab and Comments on Schmitt's Essay by Leo Strauss. New Brunswick, NJ: Rutgers University Press, 1976.

———. *The crisis of Parliamentary Democracy*. Translated with an Introductory Essay by Ellen Kennedy. Cambridge, MA: The MIT Press, 1988.

Schumpeter, Joseph. *Capitalism, Socialism and Democracy*. 3rd Edition. New York: Harper & Row, 1962.

Smil, Vaclav. *Environmental problems in China: estimates of economic costs*. Honolulu: East–West Center, 1996.

Smith, Adam. *An Inquiry into the Nature and Causes of the Wealth of Nations*. Edited by Edwin Cannan. Chicago: University of Chicago Press, 1976.

Smith, Christian, editor. *The secular revolution: power, interests, and conflict in the secularization of American public life*. Berkeley: University of California Press, 2003.

Steel, Nigel and Peter Hart. *Passchendaele: the Sacrificial Ground.* Cassell Military Paperbacks. London: Cassell & Co., 2001.

Thompson, E.P. *Customs in Common: studies in traditional popular culture.* New York: The New Press, 1993.

Tompert, Helene. *Lebensformen und Denkwisen der akademischen Welt Heidelbergs im Wilhelminischen Zeitalter: Vornehmlich im Spiegel Zeitgenossischer Selbstzeugnisse.* Hamburg: Matthiesen, 1969.

Wang, Hua and Wenhua Di. *The determinants of government environmental performance: an empirical analysis of Chinese townships.* Washington, D.C.: World Bank, Develpment Research Group, Infrastructure and Environment, 2002.

Wang, Hua et al. *Incomplete enforcement of pollution regulation: bargaining power of Chinese factories.* Washington, D.C.: World Bank, Development Research Group, Infrastructure and Environment, 2002

Wang, Hua. *Pollution charges, community pressure, and abatement cost of industrial pollution in China.* Washington, D.C.: World Bank, Development Research Group, Infrastructure and Environment, 2002.

Weber, Marianne. *Max Weber: a Bibliography.* Translated and Edited by Harry Zohn with a new Introduction by Guenther Roth. New Brunswick, NJ: Transaction Books, 1988.

Westerlund, David, editor. *Questioning the Secular State: The Worldwide Resurgence of Religion in Politics.* London: Hurst & Co., 1996.

Zima, PierreV. *La negation esthetique: le sujet, le beau et le sublime de Mallarme et Valery à Adorno et Lyotard.* Paris: Harmattan, 2002.

Zimmerman, Jonathan. *Whose America? Culture Wars in the Public Schools.* Cambridge, MA: Harvard University Press, 2002.

Data Sets

European Values Study Group and World Values Survey Association, *European and World Values Surveys Integrated Data File, 1999–2002, Release I,* 2nd ICPSR version. Ann Arbor, MI: Interuniversity Consortium for Political and Social Research, 2004.

European Values Study Group and World Values Survey Association. *European and World Values Surveys Integrated Data File, 1999–2002, Release I.* Ann Arbor, MI: Interuniversity Consortium for Political and Social Research, 2004.

Inglehart Ronald, et al. *World Values Surveys and European Values Surveys,* 1981–1984, 1990–1993, and 1995–1997. ICPSR version. Ann Arbor, MI: Institute for Social Research, 2000.

World Values Study Group, World Values Survey, 1981–1984 and 1990–1993. 2nd ICPSR version. Ann Arbor, MI: Institute for Social Research, 1999.

Articles

"German intellectuals in French vote appeal," *EUObserver.com* (4 May 2005) Online Lexis-Nexis® Academic (accessed 31 August 2005).

"German philosopher Habermas calls for European constitution," *Agence France Presse* (English) (28 June 2001) Online Lexis-Nexis® Academic (accessed 31 August 2005).

"Habermas seeks release of Korean–German held in South Korea, Seoul," *Deutsche Presse-Agentur* (24 December 2003) Online Lexis-Nexis® Academic (accessed 31 August 2005).

"Philosophers and kings: a strange waltz involving George Bush, ancient Greece and a dead German thinker," *The Economist* 19 June 2003, Online Lexis-Nexis® Academic (accessed 31 August 2005).

"PROFILE: Habermas – Germany's champion of Western democracy, Frankfurt," *Deutsche Presse-Agentur* (14 October 2001) Online Lexis-Nexis® Academic (accessed 31 August 2005).

Alesina, Alberto, Edward Glaeser, and Bruce Sacerdote. "Work and Leisure in the U.S. and Europe: Why so Different?" *Harvard Institute of Economic Research Discussion Paper Number 2068* (April 2005) Online. Available HTTP: <http://post.economics.harvard.edu/hier/2005papers/2005list.html> (accessed 31 August 2005).

Asad, Talal. "Remarks on the anthropology of the body," in *Religion and the body*, edited by Sarah Coakley, New York: Cambridge University Press, 1997 pp. 42–52. .

Bailey, Michael E. "The wisdom of serpents: Why religious groups use secular language (Examining widespread religious infestation into public political discourse)." *Journal of Church and State* 44:2 (Spring 2002), pp. 249–269.

Bala, Sumathi. "Dogged survivor of the dotcom bubble keeps its head above water." *The Financial Times Limited* (21 March 2005), p. 7.

Barash, Jeffrey Andrew. "The sense of history: on the political implications of Karl Löwith's concept of secularization." *History and Theory* 37:1 (February 1998), pp. 69–82.

Baum, Hermann, "Zum funktionalen Interesse philosophischer Reflexionen über das Phänomen Religion bei Descartes, Kant und Schleiermacher." *Neue Zeitschrift für systematische Theologie und Religionsphilosophie* 28 (1986), pp. 14–28.

Beetham, David. "From socialism to fascism: the relation between theory and practice in the work of Robert Michels." *Political Studies* 25:1–2 (1977), pp. 3–24, 161–181.

Bhabha, Homi K. "Introduction," in *Nation and narration*, edited by Homi K. Bhabha. New York: Routledge, 1990, p. 4.

Bierwisch, M. "Kant and the war in Iraq, a reply." *Merkur-Deutsche Zeitschrift fur europaisches Denken* 75:11 (November 2003), pp. 1075–1079.

Blanc, Levee. "Georg Lukács: The Antinomies of Melancholy." *Other Voices* 1:1 (March 1977). Online. Available HTTP: <http://www.othervoices.org/blevee/lukacs.html> (accessed 18 August 2005).

Bordo, Susan. "'Material Girl': The Effacements of postmodern culture," in *The Madonna Connection*, edited by C. Swichtenberg. Boulder, CO: Western Press, pp. 265–290.

Bradt, R.K. "The radical Christian orthodoxy of John Milbank: The historical contextuality of its development." *Soundings* 86:3–4 (Fall–Winter 2003), pp. 315–349.

Brewer, M.D. "The rise of partisanship and the expansion of partisan conflict within the American electorate." *Political Research Quarterly* 58:2 (June 2005), pp. 219–229.

Buchan, B. "Explaining war and peace: Kant and liberal IR theory." *Alternatives* 27:4 (Oct.–Dec. 2002), pp. 407–428.

Charles, Trueheart. "Welcome to the Next Church." *Atlantic Monthly* 278:2 (August 1996), pp. 37–53; *Expanded Academic ASAP*. Gale Group Databases. University of California, Berkeley, Library. Online. Available HTTP: <http://www.infotrac.galegroup.com> (accessed 27 August 2005).

Choi, S.W. and P. James. "No professional soldiers, no militarized interstate disputes? A new question for neo-Kantianism." *Journal of Conflict Resolution* 47:6 (December 2003), pp. 796–816.

Coakley, Sarah. "Introduction: religion and the body," *Religion and the body*, edited by Sarah Coakley, New York: Cambridge University Press, 1997 pp. 1–14.

Collet, C. "Bloc voting, polarization and the panethnic hypothesis: the case of Little Saigon," *Journal of Politics* 67:3 (August 2005), pp. 907–933.

Danoff, Brian. "Leo Strauss, George W. Bush, and the problem of regime change." *Social Policy* 34:2/3 (Winter–Spring 2004), pp. 35–41.

Derrida, Jacques. *Writing and difference*. Translated by Alan Bass. Chicago: University of Chicago Press, 1978.

Dinmore, Guy. "Role of religion in US politics under question." *Financial Times* (8 April 2005), p. 12.

Djupe, Paul A. and J. Tobin Grant. "Religious Institutions and Political Participation in America." *Journal for the Scientific Study of Religion* 40:2 (2001), pp. 303–314.

Dobbs, Darrell. "Natural Right and the Problem of Aristotle's Defense of Slavery." *The Journal of Politics* 56:1 (February 1994), pp. 69–94.

Epstein, Steven A. "The theory and practice of the just price." *Journal of Medieval History* 17 (1991), pp. 53–69.

Ferguson, R. Brian. "The Birth of War." *Natural History*. (July/August 2003), pp. 28–35.

Ford, D.F. "Radical Orthodoxy. A new theology." *Scottish Journal of Theology* 54:3 (2001), pp. 385–404.

Geismann, G. "Peace and war in Kant's writings." *Kant-Studien* 95:1 (2004), pp. 128–129.

Gerhardt, V. "Kant and the war in Iraq, a rejoinder." *Merkur-Deutsche Zeitschrift fur europaisches Denken*. 57:12 (December 2003), pp. 1174–1176.

Gilliat-Ray, Sophie. "The trouble with 'inclusion': a case study of the faith zone at the Millennium Dome." *The Sociological Review* 52:4 (2004), 459–477.

Glassner. B. "Fitness and the postmodern self." *Journal of Health and Social Behavior* 30, pp. 180–191.

Green, John C., Mark J. Rozell and Clyde Wilcox. "Social Movements and Party Politics: The case of the Religious Right." *Journal for the Scientific Study of Religion* 40:3 (2001), 413–426.

Hanegraaff, Wouter J. "New Age Spiritualities as Secular Religion: a Historian's Perspective." *Social Compass* 46:2 (1999), 145–160.

Heiser, Scott, "Republican students on the march for Bush's 'just war' in Iraq." *The Financial Times Limited* (12 July 2005), p. 6.

Hervieu-Léger, Danièle. "Pour une sociologie des 'modernités religieuses multiples': une autre approche de la 'religion invisible' des sociétes européennes." *Social Compass* 5:3 (2003), pp. 287–295.

Hoffmann, J.P. and S.M. Johnson. "Attitudes toward abortion among religious traditions in the United States: Change or continuity?" *Sociology of Religion* 66:2 (Summer 2005), pp. 161–182.

Holmqvist, Kenneth and Jaroslaw Pluciennik. "A short guide to the theory of the sublime." *Style* 36:4 (2002), 718–737.

Hood, III, M.V. and Mark Caleb Smith. "On the prospect of linking Religious-Right Identification with Political Behavior: Panacea or Snipe Hunt?" *Journal for the Scientific Study of Religion* 41:4 (2002), 697–710.

Hopson, Ronald E. and Donald R. Smith. "Changing Fortunes: An Analysis of Christian Right Ascendance within American Political Discourse." *Journal of the Scientific Study of Religion* 38:1 (March 1999), 1–13.

James, P. "Civil-military relations in a neo-Kantian world, 1886–1992." *Armed Forces & Society* 30:2 (Winter 2004), pp. 227.

Johnston R., K. Jones, R. Sarker, S. Burgess and A. Bolster. "Party support and the neighbourhood effect: spatial polarization of the British electorate, 1991–2001." *Political Geography* 23:4 (May 2004), pp. 367–402.

Knoblauch, Hubert. "Europe and Invisible Religion." *Social Compass* 50:3 (2003), pp. 267–274.

Lapidus, André. "Metal, Money, and the Prince: John Buridan and Nicholas Oresme after Thomas Aquinas." *History of Political Economy* 29:1 (1997), pp. 21–54.

Lepsius, M. Rainer. "Mina Tobler and Max Weber: Passion Confined." Translated by Sam Whimster. *Max Weber Studies* 4:1 (2004), pp. 9–21.

Luckmann, Thomas. "Transformations of religion and morality in Europe." *Social Compass* 5:3 (2003), pp. 275–285.

Maddox, Graham. "The 'Crusade' against Evil: Bush's Fundamentalism." *Australian Journal of Politics and History* 49:3 (2003), pp. 398–411.

Mahony, Honor. "Power: The Times List Of The World's Most Influential People In Full." *Independent on Sunday (London)* (18 April 2004), p. 3.

Marler, Penny Long and C. Kirk Hadaway. "'Being Religious' or 'Being Spiritual' in America: A Zero-Sum Proposition?" *Journal for the Scientific Study of Religion* 41:2 (2002), pp. 289–300.

McGuire, M. "Religion and the Body: Rematerializing the Human Body in the social sciences of religion." *Journal of the Scientific Study of Religion* 29, pp. 283–296.

McKenzie, Brian D. "Self-selection, Church Attendance, and Local Civic Participation." *Journal for the Scientific Study of Religion* 40:3 (2001), pp. 479–488.

Michalson, C.E. "Re-reading the post-Kantian tradition with Milbank." *Journal of Religious Ethics* 32:2 (Summer 2004), pp. 357–383.

Midgley, Mary. "The soul's successors: philosophy and the 'body'." in *Religion and the body*, edited by Sarah Coakley, New York: Cambridge University Press, 1997 pp. 53–69.

Mitchell, S.M. "A Kantian system? Democracy and third-party conflict resolution." *American Journal of Political Science* 46:4 (October 2002), pp. 749–759.

Moravcsik, Andrew, Larry Siedentop, Gisela Stuart, John Kay, Sunder Katwala, Charles Grant. "Europe without illusions." *Prospect* (23 June 2005) Online Lexis-Nexis® Academic (accessed 31 August 2005).

O'Neill, Daniel I. "Burke on Democracy as the Death of Western Civilization." *Polity* 36:2 (2004), pp. 201–225.

Oakes, Guy. "Introductory Essay." In *Roscher and Knies: the logical problems of historical economics,* translated by Guy Oakes. New York: The Free Press, 1975, pp. 1–49.

Pabst, A. "From Christendom to modernity? A critical re-reading of radical Orthodoxy's theses on Scotist and Ockhamist divisions and the retrieval of the theology of Saint Thomas Aquinas." *Revue des Sciences Philosophiques et Theologiques* 86:4 (October–December 2002), pp. 561–599.

Postone, Moishe. "Anti-Semitism and National Socialism: Notes on the German Reaction to 'Holocaust'." *New German Critique* 19:1 (Winter 1980), pp. 97–115.

Ruhstorfer, K.H. "Radical Orthodoxy? A Catholic enquiry." *Philosophisches Jahrbuch* 109:1 (2002), pp. 237–241.

Ryan, Vanessa L. "The Physiological Sublime: Burke's Critique of Reason." *Journal of the History of Ideas* 62:2 (2001), pp. 265–279.

Schattenmann, M. "War and international justice: a Kantian perspective." *Kant-Studien* 95:3 (2004), pp. 383–385.

Schoen, H. "Candidate orientations in election campaigns: an analysis of the German federal election campaigns, 1980–1998." *Politische Vierteljahresshchrift* 45:3 (September 2004), pp. 321.

Sharpe, Matthew. "Leo Strauss and the 'New American Century.'" *Quadrant* 48:9 (September 2004), pp. 34–38.

Shorris, Earl. "Ignoble liars: Leo Strauss, George Bush, and the philosophy of mass deception." *Harper's Magazine* 308:1849 (June 2004), pp. 65–72.

Simpson, J.H. "Religion and the Body: Sociological Themes and Prospects." *A Future for Religion? New Paradigms for Social Analysis,* edited by W.H. Swatos, Jr. London: Sage Publications, 1993, pp. 149–164.

Springborg, Patricia. "Arendt, Republicanism and Patriarchalism." *History of Political Thought* 10:3 (1989), pp. 499–523.

Steinmetz, George. "The State of Emergency and the Revival of American Imperialism: Toward an Authoritarian Post-Fordism." *Public Culture* 15:2 (2003), pp. 323–345

Stoppenbrunk, K. "The war against a villain state? (Kant, Rawls)" *Merkur-Deutsche Zeitschrift fur europaisches Denken* 58:1 (January 2004), pp. 81–84.

Sullivan, L.E. "Body Works: Knowledge of the Body in the Study of Religion." *History of Religions* 30, pp. 86–99.

Taylor, A.J. "Stanley Baldwin, heresthetics and the realignment of British politics." *British Journal of Political Science* 35:3 (July 2005), pp. 429–463.

Turner, Bryan S. "The body in Western society: social theory and its perspectives." *Religion and the body*, edited by Sarah Coakley, New York: Cambridge University Press, 1997 pp. 15–41.

Uslaner, Eric M. "Religion and Civic Engagement in Canada and the United States." *Journal for the Scientific Study of Religion* 41:2 (2002), pp. 239–254.

White Matthew, "Historical Atlas of the Twentieth Century." Online. Available HTTP: <http://users.erols.com/mwhite28/warstat0.htm#European> (accessed 31 August 2005).

Wilcox, Clyde and Rachel Goldberg. "Public Opinion on Church–State Issues in a Changing Environment." *Journal for the Scientific Study of Religion* 41:2 (2002), pp. 369–376.

Wilder, Thornton. *Our town: a play in three acts.* With an Introduction by Brooks Atkinson and Illustrations by Rober J. Lee. Avon, CT: Limited Editions Club, 1974.

Wolfe Alan, "A facist philosopher helps us understand contemporary politics," *The Chronicle of Higher Education* 50:30 (2 April 2004), pp. B16–B17.

Yamane, D. "Naked public square or crumbling wall of separation? Evidence from legislative hearings in Wisconsin," *Review of religious research* 42:2 (2000): pp. 175–192.

Yoo, Christopher S. and Steven G. Calabresi. 'The Unitary Executive During the First Half-Century. *Case Western Reserve Law Review* 47 (1997), p. 1451.

Yoo, Christopher S., Steven G. Calabresi, and Anthony J. Colangelo. 'The Unitary Executive in the Modern Era, 1945–2004'. *Iowa Law Review* 90(2) 2005, p. 601.

Yoo, Christopher S., Steven G. Calabresi and Laurence Nee. 'The Unitary Executive During the Third Half-Century, 1889–1945'. *Notre Dame Law Review* 80 (November 2004).

Yoo, Christopher S., Steven G. Calabresi. 'The Unitary Executive During the Second-Half Century'. *Harvard Journal of Law and Public Policy* 26 (2003), p. 667.

Reference Works

"Erhaben," *Der Grosse Brockhaus* 15th edn, vol. 5 (Leipzig: F.U. Brockhaus, 1930), p. 633.

Index

Printed in the United States
by Baker & Taylor Publisher Services